T0195588

HONORING
Anna

HONORING Anna

DOUGLAS HOFF

Visit our website at http://www.honoringanna.net

HONORING ANNA

iUniverse books may be ordered through booksellers or by contacting:

iUniverse
1663 Liberty Drive
Bloomington, IN 47403
www.iuniverse.com
844-349-9409

ISBN: 978-1-5320-4195-2 (sc)
ISBN: 978-1-5320-4197-6 (hc)
ISBN: 978-1-5320-4196-9 (e)

Library of Congress Control Number: 2018903222

Print information available on the last page.

iUniverse rev. date: 10/19/2020

Contents

1

Anna Ingevich

Even sitting here in her tiny two-room home made primarily of South Dakota sod, sandstone and granite rocks, Anna could close her eyes and dream, and pray. There were no windows, but she often would move her creaky oak rocking chair outside (when the weather permitted) and take in the windswept prairie landscape, scouting for rattlesnakes and wolves. Her thoughts sometimes took her back to her childhood in Norway and her voyage to America. And often to Rasmus. No matter how hard she tried to block him out he seemed to find a way to intrude, silently stealing her thoughts and replacing them with his.

Sometimes the memories took her to the worst day of her life, back in 1899, when her mother Karin died at the age of 30 bringing Anna's brother Ole into the world. Anna knew, even at the age of 9, that her life would never be the same. Her mom had been her best friend, her teacher, her protector, her idol. She had taught Anna to always do her best and that girls could do as much as the boys could if they put their minds to it. She had taken Anna with her to church and had taught Anna that there were two sides of Jesus. He wasn't all law and authority, as the church had often preached with fire and brimstone. He was also love, and Anna could put her faith and trust in Him. Anna's future would require a lot of this trust, an abundance of this faith.

Anna fondly remembered Karin's cooking. She could still smell and taste the fresh pies, stews, and those special Norwegian pastries. If her Mom had fresh eggs, cream, and butter she could bring to life the most tasteless of vegetables and soups. Anna usually liked working outdoors better than in the house, but she was always happy to help Karin with her kitchen work.

Karin also taught Anna how to take care of a house and how to keep it organized and clean. She often said, "A clean life and a clean home are two of the most important things that I can teach you." Even though their house in Norway was very small, with only three rooms, Karin kept it immaculate. The kitchen had one small table whereupon she prepared meals and the family ate. The bedroom that Karin and Anna's father, Bjorn, shared had room for a bed and not much else. The other room, the children's bedroom, was the same size, but it seemed smaller when crammed with Anna and her brothers and sisters. The banal house had two small windows and a large garden space, of which every inch was used. Karin had a green thumb, as did Bjorn, and gardening was one of the few things that they enjoyed doing together.

Anna also had enjoyed working in the garden and often stopped for a moment to enjoy the view. That view was the best part of their home, and Anna took it in with an intensity that almost felt surreal. Their home was located on an island in the North Sea, just off the coast and west of Bergen, Norway. From their garden Anna watched the waves rolling in off of the ocean, forming sculptures of foam that were continually being rearranged and re-sculpted.

All the way from her earthen and rock prairie home in South Dakota Anna could close her eyes and visualize it, and viscerally smell the salt water breeze. She could still see the ships and boats in the harbor and hear the men visiting excitedly as they worked on the docks. She had dreamt of the lands far away that those ships ventured to. She had watched the sea gulls land on the little wooden fence around the garden meant to keep the rabbits out, waiting for Anna to dig up a worm for them. Anna loved all animals, but the birds especially intrigued her. She envied their ability to fly off whenever they wanted and go wherever they desired.

Anna recalled her cherished trips to Bergen for supplies When her father would let her go along with him, which was seldom. These trips were great adventures to Anna, and they formed some of her fondest memories of Norway. She would help him load their small sailboat with everything that they thought would make some money for the family. Depending on the wind speed and direction and how rough the sea was they could usually make the trip in less than an hour. Anna was always a little apprehensive when the sea was angry and the giant waves pounded their boat, but her dad never seemed to notice. To her he almost seemed happier when the sea was a challenge so that he could prove his seamanship skills.

Upon arrival at the dock their first stop was always the huge fish market, where Bjorn would sell any fish that he had caught that morning. He fished almost every day, but he always went fishing early on the day of their trip to Bergen so that he would have a little extra cash from the fish sales…if he caught any that morning. After selling his fish and Karin's fresh butter and cream, Bjorn and Anna would roam the market—Bjorn looking for bargains and Anna drooling at the sight and smell of the fresh baked bread and pastries, the fish stews and ready-to-eat dinners. Dozens of vendors sold everything from fishing supplies to food to clothing. Anna loved the colorful clothing and had dreamt of owning one of the woolen, hand-knitted Viking style head covers that tied under the chin and could keep you warm from the cold wind sweeping in off the ocean. To Anna, Bergen was both a wonder and a delight, although she didn't think that she could ever live in such a busy and huge place. Too many people and not enough animals for her—she liked the open spaces better.

Anna's dad was strict and didn't have much use for Anna or her sisters. In his mind they were good for cooking and cleaning and not much else. He worked hard to put food on the table though, primarily from their small farm and garden and from his fishing trips into the

North Sea. Bjorn definitely was a hard man, but Norway required that of him. Nothing came easy here, and a man in this country had to do things that men under other conditions couldn't imagine possible. Bjorn was up to the challenge, and he took care of his family, even loved them if someone could see under that tough Norwegian crust. He put Anna and her brother Peder to work cleaning the fish he brought home, keeping the good ones for market and the others—those too small or undesirable to sell—for their table. When there were no fish to clean he would put the children to weeding the rows of vegetables and grain on their small, stony farm. The ground seemed to have more rocks than dirt, but the rain was plentiful and the crops usually did well. Karin thanked God for that, since a good crop meant the difference between starving and having food on their table.

It was also Anna and Peder's job to butcher the small animals like chickens, rabbits, and squirrels. When it came time to butchering larger animals like wild game or a hog or a steer, it was a family or even a neighborhood affair. Anna was thankful that the men had to do the killing and the gutting. She knew that killing for food was a part of life, but it didn't come easy for her. She didn't like the repugnant, foul smells that came with butchering either. Once these jobs were done much of the rest of the mundane work was left to the women. One of Anna's tasks was to strip all of the fat off the carcass and cut it into smaller pieces that could be ground with lean meat to make it tastier and go farther. Sometimes the fat was rendered into lard (a job that made Anna hold her nose) or made into soap with the same lye that they used in their beloved lutefisk. While Anna didn't enjoy eating lutefisk, she did love lefsa, which was usually only made for holidays and special occasions. Anna often wished that she still had one of those special Norwegian waffle griddles that were used to make the delightful pastries.

Nothing was wasted when her modest family butchered. The blood was made into sausage; the tongue, heart, liver and other organs were delicacies, as was the headcheese and suet pudding, which was made from almost pure lard. The hide was tanned and made into all sorts of winter gloves, coats, and boots. The intestines were cleaned, boiled, and used to stuff their homemade sausage into. Her family had their own special sausage recipe, and when they fried it for dinner noses turned to follow the fragrant aroma.

Anna was tall for her age, and all of the boys and most of the girls in her school had to look slightly up to talk to her. When her mom was alive she had been at the top of her class in all subjects, but after her mom's passing, Anna began doing poorly. She had been the person in school that everyone asked for help, not only for school problems but also for life problems. She had been the optimist, the one with the eternal smile on her pretty pre-teen face. Full of faith, she told everyone that things would get better. The boys, especially Edgar, tried to sit beside her in class or maybe be so brave as to try holding hands with her. Anna used to enjoy her friends and her position of leadership, but things changed after her mother's death. Anna, only 14, was missing her desperately when her father remarried without even letting his family know first. His new wife Marion already had three of her own children, so it meant more mouths to feed from their already meager existence.

At first Marion acted like she would learn to love and take care of her new family, but Anna soon figured out that it was just a show for Bjorn. When he was out fishing or working the farm, Marion would put Anna and Peder to work at the worst jobs and let her own children boss them around and tell them how to do their work. This especially irritated Anna, who was much more mature and competent to do farm work than Marion's lazy children. When Anna confronted her dad about this, he told her to grow up and quit complaining—"just work harder." Marion was her new mother, and if Anna didn't like it her dad couldn't do much to help it. One day Marion's children left the chicken coop door open and all of the hens escaped. It had been their job to collect the daily eggs from under the hens, and when they got tired of doing this "dirty farm work" they decided that they would just turn the laying hens loose so they wouldn't have to pick the eggs any more. When Bjorn came home and found out that the chickens were gone, he demanded to know who the guilty party was. Marion conspiratorially put the blame on Anna, who got the thrashing of her life while Marion's children made faces at her and taunted her. Anna found an anger that she hadn't known before her step-mother and her family had arrived. She vowed to leave this life behind and never look back.

It was a typical blustery spring day, not knowing whether it wanted to snow or to rain or to be sunny. Anna decided to stay in the little one-room schoolhouse over recess and read a little more about America. She prayed a lot, and her main topic with her creator was "how do I escape from Norway and get to America?" She had been obsessing about this distant Eden, where everyone had freedom and the land was abundant and rich. She dreamt and prayed that one day she would travel to this distant and sublime land of opportunity and live happily there, away from her hated stepmother and her estranged tyrant of a father. Anna's furtive goal was to secretly stow away enough money for the trip from the meager jobs that she could find. She knew that if her stepmother or dad found her hidden money they would take it from her, so she was careful to guard her secret, her dream. She was young and strong and resilient and knew what she had to do.

2

Iver Olson

Iver was running as fast as his stout little Norwegian legs could take him, trying to keep up with his older brothers, John and Martin. It was chore time on the Olson farm and they were late. Iver knew that being late for chores was inexcusable, and he and his brothers didn't want to face the fury of their father if he found out that they had wasted their time playing on the mountainside rather than bringing in the milk cows. It had just rained and the air was fresh with the smell, as it often was in this majestic mountain valley town of Tenold. Below their vista lay the fjord town of Vik, a small fishing village and seaport. Iver's family often traveled down the valley to sell their milk and eggs, or to take their small fishing boat out into the bay. They were a rugged, self-sufficient family, cutting their own timber and sawing it into lumber for their homes and barns. They butchered their own chickens, cows, and pigs, and planted their own crops, even though land good enough for planting was hard to come by. They also made their own cheese, butter, and soap. Everything they had, it seemed, was made by their own hands and ingenuity. It was all a part of surviving the harsh Norwegian way of life in the late 19[h] century.

Iver loved animals even more than he loved the soil and the mountains. His father finally gave in and let his children have a puppy, which Iver named Buster. Buster was a German Shepard who loved the Olson children almost as much as Iver loved him. Unfortunately Buster also liked the neighbors' dogs, and at night Buster and his dog buddies found out that it was fun to chase sheep together. After a few of their escapades the neighborhood got together to put an end to their raids, which had already left four lambs and a couple of ewes dead. Buster was discovered in one of the neighbors' sheep pens one morning and was shot before he could make his getaway. Iver was heartbroken, but he knew that the outcome was necessary. His dad had explained to him that the neighbor's sheep were their lifeblood, and Buster and his friends couldn't be allowed to kill any more of them.

Three days later a little sorrel pony was mysteriously found in the Olson shed. Iver's dad had walked seven miles to get the horse for his mourning children and had led it all the way back. The horse was love at first sight for Iver, and before long he was spending every spare minute with his new pal, which he named Buster Brown in remembrance of his dog and because of the horse's brown coat. Iver even slept with his horse, and before Buster Brown knew what had happened Iver had started riding him. Soon all of the Olson kids were on his back. Olav almost regretted getting the horse for his kids as some of their chores got neglected more than once because of Buster Brown, but he secretly had to smile at the joy they had with the horse. Iver didn't know it at the time, but living with and learning from Buster Brown would turn out to be an invaluable life lesson for him.

Iver grew rapidly, and before he was 10 he had caught up to and was passing his brothers in height and strength. Life could be very harsh on their mountain, and Iver was eager to meet the challenge. Many of the children his age tried to avoid their chores and balked when they were asked to do something to help the family, but never Iver. This was especially true when it came to his mother. He knew how hard Eva worked to keep them fed and make their house a real home. He could see the worry on her face and her tear-stained cheeks when things weren't going well or they couldn't provide essentials, let alone luxuries like Christmas presents. His heart was already big for his age, and he tried to do everything in his power to make things a little easier for her. Iver loved his father too, but in a different way. His father could be tough on him, but they worked together well, being able to communicate what needed to be done with only glances and nods and gestures.

The Olson family was a family in the truest sense of the word. Whatever task they had before them was usually tackled by the entire family if possible. Their family structure never resembled a hierarchy. What they did they did as equals, each doing whatever job they were capable of. They worked well together, and very seldom did Iver or any of his siblings have to be asked twice to do something. Their limiting factor was their acreage, which was barely enough to support one family. They often needed to supplement their income by doing additional work—Eva sold handmade products in town, and Olav worked jobs for neighbors along with fishing and lumbering. It got to the point, as Iver and his brothers got older, that Olav depended almost entirely on them to work their farm so that he could bring in more outside money to keep things going.

Even at the young age of 12, Iver knew what his other brothers also knew. The farm was only big enough for one family, and it would one day go to his eldest brother John. This Norwegian tradition was never questioned among the Olson family, and even at this age Iver was already wondering what he would do to make a living when that time came. Iver's only wish, his only dream, was to become a farmer like his dad, but he knew that more land was not to be found. Along with the land shortage, the Norwegian farm economy was currently at another low, as was most of the Norwegian economy. Fishing had been a good source of revenue for the Olson family, but even the fish market was slowing down. Norway's fleet of sailboats, once one of the world's greatest, was being slowly replaced by the newer modern steamships. Iver was painfully aware of all of this. Even though he felt that his destiny was to be a farmer he knew that he would never have a farm here. And even if he did, there was no money in farming in Norway.

Iver was intelligent and liked learning but schoolwork couldn't hold his attention. "Wake up Iver!" his teacher yelled as the ruler came down on his hands. "Your school work is terrible. How will I be able to pass you on to the next grade?" Iver didn't say anything, but he didn't care, as he had no intention of going to school any longer. He would take a job as a fisherman or a farm laborer and start making his own money so that he could buy his own farm someday, somewhere.

Iver had been to the docks the day before and had heard about a faraway paradise called America. A land of milk and honey, they said, where farm ground was so abundant that the government just gave it away. Iver had made up his mind on the spot that this new country was where he would go as soon as he had enough money to travel there on his own. Iver wasn't like his brother Martin, who liked working with wood and wanted to learn the carpentry trade. Iver's heart was mated to the land, animals, hard work, and fresh air. His best moments were watching the newborn calves and piglets run in their pastures or seeing the crops grow to maturity. He was a farmer at heart. His roots were deeply imbedded in the soil and nature. And America had an abundance of this.

As much as he loved his family, as much as he loved the valley of Tenold and the Olson farm, he had already made up his mind to leave. He would have left even if he had known that his mother would stand at the dock in Vik for months afterward, crying for the son she knew that she would never see again. He would have had to go even if he had known how much his father's heart would ache to see him just one more time. Once Iver's young 15 year old mind was made up, there was no turning back.

3

Rasmus Johnson

The Johnson family prided themselves as master craftsmen, especially in the ship building industry where they had made most of their money. But sales were slowing in the 1890's, and Knut Johnson could see storm clouds on the horizon. A new steamship was floating proudly in their harbor, and it didn't bode well for their family since they built sail ships. Knut wisely started expanding his business to home and furniture building. He boasted that if it could be built by Norwegian hands and was made out of wood, his family could do it—and do it better than most. He instilled this love of wood and craftsmanship into his three sons, of whom Rasmus was the youngest.

Knut started building a new home in Oslo for a family friend when an unexpected accident happened. It was a windy, rainy day and one of the rafters they were hoisting up by rope slipped out of the loop and fell, hitting Knut in his right elbow after glancing off his shoulder. Knut's arm was broken, and his oldest son, who had been helping with the project, was away in Oslo taking care of another family member, leaving only Knut's youngest son Rasmus to get the home finished before their winter deadline. Knut quickly saw the potential in his youngest, until then overlooked, apprentice. Rasmus soon was able to cut and hammer faster than his older brothers, and he could lay a floor straight as an arrow with hardly having to check his level. He selected each piece of lumber as if it were a labor of love and as if he was building the grandest mansion ever to grace the bedrock of Norway. Rasmus was born to love wood and to create not just homes or pieces of furniture, but works of art and family heirlooms.

Rasmus's reputation as a master carpenter grew quickly. He was now a young 18 year-old man, and the ladies all took a second look when he walked by. Although only average height, he had a commanding presence and was, by any standards, handsome. But Rasmus only had eyes for his childhood friend and sweetheart, Astrid. They took long walks and held hands, often going on picnics with their parents. They climbed trees and sat and watched the clouds form visions in the sky, pictures of their future life together. Rasmus was smitten by this petite, shy girl that he cherished, along with her family. To no one's surprise, he proposed and asked for her hand in marriage. Astrid happily accepted, but what Rasmus said next gave her pause and secretly troubled her heart. He told her that his dream wasn't to have a family in Norway, but in America. Rasmus said that he had been thinking about their future for a long time and that his thoughts always led to a new land—a land where fortunes could be made and everything in life wasn't hand to mouth; a place where he could build a grand mansion for his family and they could live like aristocrats; a place where he could not only dream dreams but live those dreams as well.

As their wedding day approached, Astrid grew increasingly more fearful. Rasmus had already purchased and paid for their transport to America, which would be leaving the day after their wedding. Her honeymoon was to be on a ship in steerage class, which she was less than thrilled about. But Rasmus failed to see the trouble in her eyes and eagerly went on with his plans. Astrid's family also failed to see her trepidation. They were proud of Rasmus and thought of him as their own son—he was strong, talented, and handsome. They were so anxious to have Rasmus as their son-in-law and the father of their future grandchildren that they missed the subtle but sudden changes in Astrid's demeanor.

On the eve of their wedding, Astrid, with her eyes full of tears, told Rasmus that she could not travel to America with him. Her dream was to be Rasmus, but it also was to raise her family in Norway. Her heart wasn't strong enough to leave her family and friends behind. She loved him, but not enough for such a leap as to leave the known for the unknown. It sounded like foolishness to her, and she wasn't about to have her home torn from her and replaced with dreams that might not come true, even if they were with Rasmus. If he wanted her, he had to stay in Norway and accept life and his future here.

Rasmus felt like screaming, but no words came. He tasted the salt from his tears as he listened quietly to what she was saying. Her words crushed him. He was torn and heartbroken. How could Astrid have sprung this on him at the last minute? She was his dream, but so was America. How could he choose? How could she let him down like this and make him pick one dream over another? He had already spent a good part of his savings on their passage to America. In his mind he could see and almost touch this distant land, but he had always thought about it with Astrid at his side.

With only a soft "good-bye Astrid" that he was barely able to whisper through his grief Rasmus left Astrid and went off to think this harrowing new development over. He had never touched alcohol, but this had him crazy enough to try anything. When he woke up the next morning, which was supposed to have been his wedding day, his heart still ached, along with his head. He had bragged to his friends that he would strike it rich in America. He had said (with a little help from the ale) that no woman would stand in the way of his dreams and that if she chose Norway over him that was her concern, not his. Now he regretted some of those alcohol-induced statements, but he had still said them. And most of it still rang true for him. It was Astrid, not him, that had made the demands. She should have spoken up sooner. He already had his ticket paid for. He was going to America.

4

Leaving Norway

Anna finished her chores at home and then went to the neighbor's house to do their cleaning and to make another batch of bread for them. She did this for several families. They all loved her and paid her as well as they could, even a little extra as they could afford it. Anna was strong, maturing into a young woman, and was innovative in her work. When she left their houses, their loaves of bread often had some special ingredient, such as apple slices or raisins, in them. Their table might have a fresh bouquet of wild flowers, or that chip in their door may have been fixed.

Anna went to the docks whenever she could to help the fishermen scrub out their boats and get ready for their next fishing trip. She also gutted their fish and got them ready for the market. Between cleaning all the fish and her childhood training with cutting meat and cleaning and scraping hides, Anna was getting quite efficient with a knife. The word on the docks was that she could scale and clean a fish faster and better than most men. When Anna was through with a fish, all that remained were big beautiful fillets, a thin layer of fish skin, and a skeleton. The men appreciated this assiduous young girl who was so industrious and had so much energy, and they paid her as much as their meager budgets could afford. Sometimes more because they liked her so much.

Her stepmother Marion soon found out about Anna's work and demanded that Anna give her the wages she was earning. She told Anna that it was her duty to do this, because when she was working outside of the home Marion's precious children had to take up some of the slack. Anna partially complied, secretly keeping most of her wages in her hidden stash. Marion even suspected that this was going on but kept it to herself in hopes that Anna would make enough to leave. Marion didn't want this pretty, hard working girl in her home. Anna made her children look small and lazy, and she wanted them to be the apple of Bjorn's eyes, not his own children. Besides, they could use one less mouth to feed, and Anna was independent enough to be out on her own. Marion told her children, "Good riddance to that girl who has never appreciated her stepmother. I hope that she leaves."

Going on 16 years old, Anna had saved about 50 kroner, enough money for her steamship ticket, but she knew it wasn't enough for the trip. One of her best friends in school was Monica Jensen, and Anna had let it slip to her that she was thinking of going to America as soon as she could get enough money put together. Monica's uncle had already made the trip around four years earlier and was sending for his family members as he saved enough money for their tickets. Her uncle Eldon had told Monica that America expected immigrants to have some money and to be strong and healthy. If a passenger wasn't healthy, the ship would refuse them because they were responsible for the immigrants' return trip to Norway if America didn't accept them. Eldon had also said that his arm ached for a long time from all of the vaccinations, but that they weren't nearly as bad as the stench of the disinfectant that they doused people with.

Furthermore, his family had all started studying the American language so that when they got there they would know what was going on and could understand the language and ask questions. Anna had thought of this, but until now she didn't know how to go about it. Since Eldon's family was already studying English, Anna asked them if they would help her learn English too. She even promised to clean their chicken coop, among other chores, if they would teach her. Anna hated chicken coops, as did almost anyone that ever had to clean one. The air was foul and the dust so fine that it would penetrate the skin and leak through any mask. Anna wore a cloth around her head and over her face to help her breath and filter the stench, but she still coughed that miserable chicken coop dust out of her lungs for days.

The information Anna learned from the Jensen's proved to be worth every bit of work that she did for them. Her English was improving over time, but the language was quite a challenge, even for someone as bright as Anna. Why did they have so many words that had more than one meaning?! The next ship to leave Bergen for New York was arriving in a month, and she was determined to be on it whether or not her English was perfected. It was the White Star Line. Anna had originally researched the Norwegian American Line but found it to be a little more expensive. Fortunately for her, competition among the lines was bringing prices down.

Anna knew that her English would not be great, but she studied it day and night. She had also confided that she was covertly planning to go to America with another family she worked for, the Knutson's. They were, to Anna, a beautiful family that all loved each other and all worked together toward common goals—the kind of family that she would want to have some day. They were a family that she could trust not to tell her dad or her family about her secret. They had even saved up and bought her a small trunk for the voyage. All Anna owned to put into it was one dress, a sweater, a jacket, and some socks and under garments, but she would be eternally grateful to this family for their kindness. They, along with the Jensen's, had become her second families, and she would miss them as much as her own family. The Jensen's had given Anna the address of their uncle in America and had written to him that Anna was hard working and could be trusted, hoping he might be able to help her should she ever need it.

Anna's last month in Norway was brutal. It seemed like she was working day and night. She became tired and edgy. Every time her dad even looked her way she cringed, thinking that he may have discovered what she was up to. She tried to be extra nice to Marion and her kids; she didn't want to do anything to upset the routine that she had established. She did her best not to be seen or heard. The days seemed to last forever and she crossed each one of them off her calendar, praying harder than ever that she wouldn't be discovered and that she would safely escape.

Finally, after what seemed like an eternity, the ship was leaving the next day. Anna had her money and her trunk packed and hidden in the Knutson chicken coop—she preferred it over the Jensen's as it hadn't been cleaned and nobody would go snooping in a dirty old chicken coop. She would sneak away from home that night, tell her best friends good-bye, and be on the dock bright and early in the morning. Now that the time was so close, Anna was even more terrified that her dad or her step mom would find out and steal her money and make her stay in Norway. There would be no sleep for her tonight, but it would be worth it. She figured that her family wouldn't even miss her at breakfast in the morning unless Marion wanted her to do the cooking. Anna had made a couple extra loaves of bread at the Knutson's that day to leave Marion for breakfast, hoping that would suffice. If they didn't want her for anything at breakfast time, they wouldn't miss her until chore time.

Rasmus's day wasn't going much better than Anna's. Although his hangover was dissipating and his headache was going away, he still had a lot to do. He had been so busy preparing for his wedding that he hadn't even considered what he would pack for America. Would they let him bring some of his carpentry tools? He only had work clothes and one nice coat, so packing his clothing would be easy. How much money would he need? All that he could do was to bring everything he had in hopes that it would be adequate for the voyage and enough to show the Americans that he was capable and self-sufficient. If they wouldn't accept him and he had to come back to Norway, he would be a disgrace. Rasmus slowly got his wits about him and went to packing his most cherished possessions: his wood-working tools. After the important things, he packed his clothes. Then came the hardest part, which was saying good-bye to his family and friends. Astrid already knew that he was leaving and she hadn't done anything to find him and convince him to stay, so he didn't feel that it was necessary to say good-bye to her again. Still, he left her a note early the next morning, just before leaving for the ship. He had made his mind up not to tell her family. He didn't want to face them and was worried that they might try to shame him into staying. Telling them would be Astrid's duty.

Dear Astrid,

It is with a heavy heart that I write this. I truly wish that you were leaving with me today for America as my wife. I just want you to know that I respect your decision not to marry me and to stay in Norway rather than go to America with me. Maybe it was too much for me to ask of you. Please say good-bye to your parents and the rest of your family for me. I love all of them and will miss them almost as much as I will miss you.

I will say a prayer for you that you find someone else to make you happy.

Kindest regards, with love,
Rasmus Johnson

Anna walked through the night until she could see the White Star Line steamship docked in the harbor under the bright and clear Norwegian star-filled sky. It was early but there was already some activity, so she hid behind one of the crates in the shipyard and waited for the morning sun to come creeping onto the horizon. She dozed for a short time, only to awaken from a nightmare that her stepmother had captured her and imprisoned her in the chicken coop. Too afraid to go back to sleep, Anna nibbled the last of the bread that she had stowed under her jacket. The harbor was slowly coming to life, and she could hear the sounds of fishermen making their way to their boats. She was intently watching the ship when someone behind her yelled "Get out of the way. We have to move this crate onto the ship." Relieved that they weren't authorities looking for her, she quickly found another hiding spot. She remained there for another two hours, until hundreds of other anxious passengers had gathered by the dock. Figuring that there was safety in numbers, Anna slipped out of her hiding place and tried to lose herself in the crowd. By now the morning sun was fully up and all that Anna could see were the faces of strangers. Some of them seemed as poor and lost as she was. Others looked wealthy and were dressed in fine clothes that appeared to be tailor made for them. The one thing that they had in common was that all of them were eager to get on board that ship. Once they had gotten this far, they were all anxious to get aboard the Star and start the journey.

The line to the ship was long and slow, but Anna was gradually getting closer to the boat and to her freedom. Despite being the most exciting day of her life, she was trepid with fear that her dad had found her missing and would show up and try to prevent her from leaving. At the same time she was amazed at the size of the ship, and her heart was pounding from the mixture of fear and excitement. Her head on a swivel, she furtively looked forward at the line in front of her and the massive ship, while also checking behind her in fear of being found out. In the process, she kept noticing a handsome young man ahead of her who looked and acted like he knew what he was doing, and she secretly hoped that he would notice her too, even though he seemed a few years older than she was.

Rasmus indeed had noticed her—the tall and beautiful young lady with the gorgeous hair and big blue eyes. How could anyone miss her? He slowly worked his way closer to her so that he could hear her talk to the others in line around her and get a better look. She was pretty enough to be from a royal family, but her clothes and the fear in her eyes were telling a different story. She was a mystery. Maybe he could learn to forget Astrid with someone like her on board.

5

The Proposal

The line slowly moved forward and swept Anna and Rasmus along with it. Rasmus had let some of the passengers move ahead of him in line just to be a little closer to that magnetic young lady in line behind him. When he was close enough, he smiled at her and she smiled back. Rasmus kept thinking what a wonderful voyage this might turn out to be. Just looking at her was helping his broken heart heal, but he knew that he needed to guard it closer this time. He didn't want any more broken engagements in his future. His plan would be to get to know this mysterious and alluring girl while on the trip of his life, the voyage to his destiny, to America. Sharing it with someone would make it go so much faster and make it much more enjoyable.

Anna was starting to get over her fear of being detected by her family, while her newborn fear of not getting admitted on board was starting to take over. Some in the line ahead of her had even thrown up, so great was their fear. The stories of those getting turned down at the last minute were rampant, and everyone in this line desperately wanted to get on that ship. A thousand harmonious minds had one similar thought: get on the ship and leave for a new life. One of the men in line behind her seemed especially apprehensive. Anna couldn't understand his language, but she would later find out that his fear was indeed life-threatening. He looked like Daniel in the lion's den at the moment the lions were about to be turned out. Anna couldn't help but to privately share his anxiety so she said a silent prayer for him...and for herself.

From a distance it looked like a column of ants marching up the anthill. Anna wondered how all of these people could possibly fit onto this ship, even though it seemed enormous. The hours of waiting in line, which seemed like days to Anna and even made those long and boring church sermons that her early childhood memory evoked seem short, were finally about to end. With her heart in her hand and some help from Rasmus, who had finally gotten next to her in line, she handed her ticket to the ship's steward. He seemed to scrutinize her closely but he hardly gave Rasmus a second glance. Having both made it on board, they were so excited that without thinking Rasmus gave Anna a hug. It was a bit embarrassing, but they both secretly enjoyed it, more than either of them let on. Their new adventure was about to unfold; both of them were beginning to taste and feel a newfound freedom.

The ship was large but not as big as Anna had thought—or at least not as prodigious as she had made it to be in her mind. All Rasmus could do was admire its construction. He wanted to see every beam of wood and explore every plank. It brought him back to his family and their love of boat making, of wood and creating wood products. It somehow made him think of Astrid and her family again. Little did he know the tongue-lashing she was getting back home in Norway from her family. They had taken Rasmus's side and had told her that she should have honored her engagement and went with Rasmus to America. To back out on such a fine man as Rasmus was dishonorable to them; now that he was gone forever, she should be ashamed of herself. Astrid was in tears again, and she truly did miss Rasmus. But she thought that she would never see him again, so she cried even harder.

Rasmus was still feeling a bit lonely when he spotted Anna. Both Anna and Rasmus had tickets in steerage. His heart skipped a beat and his homesickness dissipated at the sight of her. "Hey Anna, where have you been?" They had at first hoped that someone had made a mistake when they were taken below deck and were shown what looked like large barracks with tiny, stacked cots. The straw beds had no blankets and not even a pillow. They had imagined that they would have small but at least private rooms of their own. This was more like cramming a large herd of cattle into a small barn. Rasmus learned that it was called steerage because of the steering tackle that ran through this area to connect the rudder to the tiller, or helm. It was actually the cargo hold and would be used for cargo on the return trip to Europe. Even this seemed exciting at first, but their first night proved it to be almost unbearable. Anna had virtually no privacy. The young girls were crammed on one side, but there were no curtains or walls. Rasmus had done what he could to help her be comfortable, like moving a couple of the men farther from her cot.

The air just kept getting thicker, and the first night seemed to last forever. Anna longed to get out and to see what was happening on the deck above and to taste some fresh air. So did Rasmus. Apparently some of the people were used to these sorts of conditions though, as there was a lot of snoring and heavy breathing. Someone was screaming, probably having a nightmare about not getting on the ship or of dying of asphyxiation. To make matters worse all of the babies seemed to be crying.

When the eternally long night was finally over, Anna and Rasmus were at last permitted to go above and replace the stale air in their lungs with some fresh air. The ship's crew had delivered buckets of what they called food and left them for the fittest passengers to eat first. It was more like a battle than a meal, and the conditions made it feel like a charity food kitchen. Despite not sleeping at all, neither Anna nor Rasmus was hungry enough to fight the food line, but both were exhilarated to be breathing real air and to be together again. They realized that they could get through this. It was just another trial for them, another mountain to climb, one last hurdle to get over.

Although they couldn't easily mix with the first class passengers, they could see that they had it a lot more comfortable. Some were even bragging about the good food and the comfortable bed. Anna knew that even if she had had enough money for first class she wouldn't have spent it. Every Norwegian kroner was cherished, and having a few of them in her pocket made her feel better. Rasmus actually did have enough money for first class, but he too preferred the less expensive passage. They had both been brought up in a way that stressed the importance of saving everything possible, of wasting nothing, of living as frugally as possible.

Even though it was their first full day together, Rasmus and Anna felt like they had been life-long friends. Rasmus was easy to talk to, and Anna had a gift for listening with compassion and kindness. At first their conversations were light and introductory. They were both a little bashful, especially Anna. She had never visited with a man other than her brothers or her dad before. Rasmus seemed so different. It was like Anna had found another person within herself when she talked with him. It was a feeling she truly enjoyed, and she soon cherished every minute she had with him. Although Rasmus had been in love and had had many conversations with his fiancée, this seemed different to him. Anna's eyes lit up when he talked to her. Her strength and her beauty were apparent, and he sensed that she was someone he could count on—someone strong enough to do almost anything, someone who would never give her word and then change her mind like Astrid had. Perhaps Anna was even a little intimidating to this strong young man.

Before long, their stomachs started growling, and even though they didn't want to go below they realized that they would need a lot of resilience and energy for this trip. They knew how important it was to stay healthy. Their biggest fear was to get sick and not be accepted by the Americans. If that happened they would be shipped back to Norway in disgrace and shame. Anna vowed that this wouldn't happen and that if it did she would never face her stepmother again. If she had to go back, she would lose herself in Oslo and hide in shame there.

Rasmus volunteered to fight the line and get their dinner pails filled (the ship supplied these pails to the passengers), but Anna refused his offer. She wanted to prove her worth and show everyone, Rasmus included, that she was capable of helping herself. As they went through the line, Rasmus admired her strength and realized that Astrid would never have been able to take the journey unless she had been in first or second-class. Anna was independent, strong and ambitious-- Astrid wasn't as self sufficient and depended on others for her security.

After they made it through the line, they sat down together to taste the mystery food that they had been served. Anna tried to make light of it, saying that the hog on their farm might have enjoyed this stuff. Rasmus laughed and again admired this new person in his life. Astrid would never have been able to eat it, let alone joke about it.

Anna and Rasmus started getting to know the other folks that were on board with them. There was the Anderson family with the twin girls. Their father kept them herded together, protecting his flock. His name was Anders, and they had lost their fish market business in Oslo. Their family and friends had chipped in to help them pay for passage, and they had promised that once they struck it rich in America they would send money back to Norway to repay their debts. Then there was a young man, Arne, from Vik. He was married but couldn't afford to pay for two passengers. He worried how he would take care of his young bride and where in America he would take her. He worried about learning English and about finding work. He worried about everything, and the only solution seemed to be to leave her behind until he had made enough money to alleviate his concerns. He had promised his bride that once he found work and had sufficient money he would send for her. When she arrived they could start their life together as Americans. The one thing that all of the immigrants seemed to have in common was that none of them even thought about keeping their nationality; they were all going to America to be Americans.

Anna again noticed the mysterious man she had seen behind her in line—the nervous Daniel in the lion's den. He now seemed a little less apprehensive, but it was clear that he needed a friend. Always the compassionate and caring person, and remembering what she had been taught in church, Anna wanted to help if she could. She pointed him out to Rasmus and asked him what they might be able to do. Rasmus made it a point to smile at him, but the man's eyes seemed vacant. Whatever he was running from couldn't, or wouldn't, be easily left behind.

The next day Rasmus noticed him again and, knowing how much Anna wanted to help, he made it a point to bump into him (which under their crowded conditions was easy to do). Rasmus apologized and though he had precious few cigarettes, he offered the man one of them. This seemed to bring him around, as he was overwhelmed that Rasmus would offer this kindness. If they could bridge the language gap there would be a new friendship for both of them.

Rasmus pointed at himself and said "Rasmus." He gestured toward Anna and said "Anna." For the first time, the man's face turned up into a modest smile.

He pointed to himself and said, "Ivan."

Anna felt her heart warm up. They would help this man and show him some friendship.

It was now the third day of their voyage, and already there was talk of a storm brewing in the Atlantic, which made the passengers nervous. They had been told of the terror of ocean wrecks such as the S/S Atlantic and the S/S Danmark. Rasmus told Anna that it was nothing to worry about and that steamships were much more reliable and storm worthy than sail ships. "After all, we are in the first year of a new century," he added. He had no idea if they really were more seaworthy, but it sounded good, even to him. He already cared enough for Anna to try to protect her, even though she seemed so independent. That afternoon the wind started kicking up and the waves got bigger and more foreboding. Anna had been on small fishing boats, but they always kept fairly close to shore. When clouds developed they could usually make it to land and shelter ahead of the storm. But this was different. There was no place to hide out in the open sea, and this could be a life or death situation. They had no choice but to go with the flow and ride the storm out, hoping for the best.

The crewmen issued orders for everyone to go to their cabins or below deck to the steerage area. Many of the passengers in steerage tried to stay above. They said that they would rather risk going overboard than have to go below into the pestilential air there, feeling like rats drowning in a barrel. Rasmus knew the danger of this and helped convince those who would listen that if they wanted to survive they needed to do as they were told. Going overboard into seas like this would mean instant death, and the possibility of it happening was very real. The stench below was bad, but risking your life to avoid it wasn't a good idea. After shepherding the others, Anna and Rasmus were among the last to go down. The doors were shut behind them and there was little light to see with, so all they could to do was hold hands and smile at each other and do more planning for what lie ahead.

Rasmus was interrupted by a tap on his shoulder. Ivan stood by with an anxious smile on his face. Another gentleman was with him, and with sign language they seemed to be asking if they could share the cot that Anna and Rasmus were sitting on. Rasmus and Anna smiled back, and Anna gestured for them to sit down, getting up herself and then sitting down again while motioning to them. Ivan's companion told them in fairly good Norwegian that he could speak a little of Ivan's native tongue, which was Russian. His name was Thomas, and his parents had lived near the border between the two countries. His dad was Russian but had married a Norwegian woman he had met on a trading trip to Norway. As Thomas was growing up, his mom spoke Norwegian while his dad spoke Russian. The two languages were both used brokenly, and Thomas still remembered enough of his boyhood Russian to do a little interpreting for the group.

While a brief surprise to Anna and Rasmus, it was natural that Ivan would be from Russia, since Ivan was a popular Russian name. History had taught them about Ivan the Terrible, a Russian Tsar. It was somewhat comical to watch the puzzled look on Thomas's face as he tried to interpret Ivan's story. Some of it may have been lost in translation, but they found out that Ivan had a good reason to be fearful. He was wanted by Russia for treason against his country, and he had a bounty on his head there. He had hated the way common

Russians were treated by the ruling class, and he desperately wanted freedom for his people. He was engaged in the revolution and had been caught smuggling revolutionary literature into Russia. At one point they had captured Ivan and set an execution date. Only through good luck and help from a pretty Russian girl that he knew did he escape death. He had hidden in the Russian countryside for weeks and finally had a chance to sneak across the border into Norway. From there he had made his way to Bergen and had sought a ticket to America…or anywhere as far from Russia as he could get. He had even indentured himself to get the money for passage. His biggest regret had been leaving behind that pretty girl who helped him. He was fearful that she had been found out, which would have meant death preceded by torture and continual raping by the Russian military. He had told her that if he possibly could he would one day send for her. Poor Ivan—what horrors he had come through! And now he had to leave his native country, with virtually no hope of helping his countrymen in their fight for freedom again.

Every once in a while the ship would violently lurch amid the continuous up and down motion. Most of the people in steerage had become sick, and the stench of the vomit was beyond horrible. The ship's crew made an attempt to bring them a few buckets of food, but only a handful of them had stomachs strong enough to eat. They were all anxious about the storm and wanted to know what their chances of survival were. The crew tried to assure them that they would be fine, but these people were used to being lied to and no one seemed to believe that they would make it through the storm. Except Anna, of course, who sang songs to the children and soothed the old folks. Although Thomas and Ivan had never prayed before, Anna assured them that her God would never let them down and that they would live through the storm. She stood up and started reciting the Lord's Prayer aloud, which she had memorized and could say backwards or forward. Some of the others joined in, and a semblance of peace came over the steerage area. Even though many were still sick and the ship was still creaking and groaning, the steam engines were running and the storm had to run its course sometime. Anna's recitation of the Lord's prayer, along with her confidence, gave them all hope again.

The storm pummeled them for another twelve hours, but just as day was breaking so did the storm. They were given their buckets of "food" and were allowed to go back above. The sun had never felt so good; the sky had never been so sublime. Many said prayers of thanks that morning, and just as many said prayers for the rest of the journey to be storm-free. It was chilly out, which Rasmus was thankful for, as it gave him an excuse to put his arm around Anna. Was he falling in love with this girl after only a few days with her? He certainly felt proud to be with her, as most everyone in steerage had by now gotten to know her and admired her attitude and her ability to think straight when bad things were happening. They no longer looked at her as just a pretty, young girl but as a responsible young woman, a leader. Rasmus was strong and assuring, but Anna had the respect of everyone. Rasmus admired her and wondered if she was feeling the same way about him as he was about her. Only a few days before this he had thought that he would never feel this way about a girl again, but now he was questioning that notion. His feelings for Anna were developing from somewhere deep inside his soul, someplace he hadn't known existed. With Astrid it had been more of a family friendship, a relationship that seemed expected of him. Because Rasmus was so fond of Astrid's parents and the feeling was mutual, he would have felt guilty—like he was letting them down—if he hadn't proposed to her. What he was feeling for Anna, however, didn't have any expectations from others. He alone was responsible for what he felt about her.

"A kroner for your thoughts?" Anna interrupted his daydream. "What's on your mind today, Rasmus Johnson?"

Just then Mr. Anderson came running up to them and asked for their help. One of the twins was missing and they couldn't find her. Anna immediately took charge and told Rasmus to find Ivan and to look here on the top deck and she would go down and search steerage. "Remember," she said quickly, "little girls can hide in the smallest of places. Don't leave anything unturned."

Anna ran back down to steerage and tried to get everyone's attention. "Please help us find little Kari, the Anderson twin," she hollered.

Those within earshot started looking immediately, and Anna began by crawling under the cots. Sure enough, in the far corner with her rag doll as a pillow, little Kari was curled up under a cot where she was concealed from view.

"Over here!" Anna yelled to Mrs. Anderson, who had the other twin, Kristine, in hand.

It was a joyous family reunion, and the Andersons repeatedly thanked Anna and Rasmus for their help. Kari and Kristine were already playing again, but with stern commands from their mother to stay within eyesight.

By now it was time for the evening "meal", which to everyone's surprise had some recognizable food in it: boiled potatoes and beets and onions. Anna would have liked some butter to put on them, or some cream, but such luxuries were nowhere to be found on this ship—at least for those in steerage. They ate happily, celebrating the defeat of the storm and the finding of the little Anderson girl. Rasmus and Anna, even under such circumstances, were quite content just to be with each other and to be alive.

On the 13th day, the ship's captain announced that they were about half way through the voyage and that they were making great time. With good luck they would complete the voyage in less than 4 weeks. Even better, there wasn't any news of more storms in their path. This put the passengers in a better-than-usual mood, even though the stench in steerage was getting impossibly worse. Anna remarked that her nose was starting to get accustomed to it all, comparing this to a family of skunks living together. "If they can get used to their smell, we can get used to ours. We might even miss this smell some day!" she joked.

By now Rasmus was certain that he wanted to marry Anna. At first he had thought that some of his emotions were coming from the fact that he missed Astrid and her family, and that he just desperately wanted to replace them. But every day and every new adventure with Anna reinforced his feelings for her. It wasn't just her beauty. It wasn't just her ambition and intelligence. It wasn't just the way she walked and her easy manner. It wasn't that he was missing Astrid and her family. It was this amazing and alluring person that he was getting to know. It was Anna. Rasmus wasn't a very religious man, but he decided that maybe there was a reason that things hadn't worked out with Astrid. She never would have been able to take this journey. The toilets alone!—their repugnant odor was so awful that she would have wanted to turn back after her first trip to the toilet.

He knew Anna prayed a lot and that her conviction in her faith was impenetrable. Maybe, he decided, there was something to this faith. Her loyalty to that faith and to her fellow passengers made him certain that she would never turn her back on him. Then and there he came to the conclusion that he would spend the rest of the voyage trying to win her heart and that he would ask her to marry him when the time was right. As soon as the ship got to New York and they had made it through Ellis Island and become Americans, they would find a church and be properly married…if Anna was willing. Rasmus prayed that he could convince her to marry him, and promised Anna's God that if he did he would love and honor her forever.

Anna sensed the change in Rasmus. He had become even more serious, even more attentive. He shared more of his dreams with her and spent every minute of his time with her rather than smoking and chatting with the men. Because Anna had never had a real boyfriend, these were new feelings for her. She had heard about love and sweethearts and had more than once dreamt that some prince charming would take her away from her Norwegian life and her stepmother. But this was real. It wasn't a fairy tale. Was she falling in love with Rasmus? Or was she just lonesome and wanting companionship during her journey? She determined that she would give this her utmost attention and would pray about it. Before Anna made any important decision she asked Jesus if she was making the right choice.

It happened gradually at first, but then more and more of the passengers started getting ill. There weren't any doctors in steerage, but the ship arranged for a doctor from first class to make rounds there and see if anything could be done to help. No one had died yet, but it was getting serious. Anna did what she could, taking cold rags to help cool down the fevers and making sure that those in bed got something to eat and drink if they were able. The doctor said that it was probably some sort of viral flu, that there wasn't anything else he could do. He said to watch the young and the old especially close, as they were the most susceptible and usually the first to die. "Keep them hydrated and do what you can to keep their fevers down," he instructed.

Rasmus was a little jealous of all the attention Anna was giving those in need, as he wanted to spend every waking minute with her. With any luck they might be in New York in eight or nine days, and he hadn't proposed yet. He hadn't even told Anna that he loved her, hadn't even kissed her. He had wanted to a million times but was always afraid that she might reject him and embarrass him. He knew his feelings, but he didn't know hers and wanted to be sure. Anna was sitting at the bed of an elderly lady, holding a wet cloth on her head. Rasmus sat down beside her and took off his hat and asked her, very seriously, if she would go on a date with him. "Would you have dinner with me tonight?"

Anna started laughing at the thought of this absurd idea, but then her wits took over and she humorously answered, "Of course I will. What restaurant will you be taking me to? In which dining room shall we dine? Shall I wear my evening gown and my pearls, or my new fashion dress? Will you be in your tux or just your suit?" Even the sick old lady laughed with them.

"You'll just have to wait and see," Rasmus smiled. "Pick you up tonight about 6?"

Rasmus had found a candle, which he hid in his pocket for the occasion. And he confiscated two boiled carrots and a potato from their noon ration. That evening, he walked over to Anna's cot and held his arm out all prim and proper. "Is madam ready for our date?

We must not be late or we will lose our reservation at the captain's table."

"Yes, we must hurry," Anna replied. "Does my gown match your suit? Are the captain and his crew waiting for us?"

Rasmus escorted Anna to a little table where they sat together. He lit the candle and got out the carrots and the potato. Anna said a short prayer of thankfulness for the food and for their safe voyage thus far. And to his amazement Anna thanked her God for him too.

Neither of them had taken the time to really look out over the vast ocean and enjoy its beauty, its breathtaking enormity. "Look," Anna cried, "those must be dolphins! They are following us. I think they are wishing us well, and that they are a good omen that the rest of our trip will go smoothly." They ate their meager portions and Rasmus asked if he could hold Anna's hand. She had been through this in her mind and happily obliged. They visited about nothing in particular, and watched the dolphins playing in the ship's wake. They even saw a few birds, another sign that they were getting closer to land.

Rasmus sensed a little urgency at this and took Anna's other hand and looked deep into her big blue eyes. "I've been doing a lot of thinking, Anna. Not just about what I would do when we get to America or where I would go or what would happen to me. I've been thinking mostly about you. I can't even walk across the deck without thinking about you. As a matter of fact, all I think about is you and I can't imagine not thinking about you. I've been attracted to you since I first saw you. At first I thought I was being foolish and that I was just excited about going to America, but the more I've thought about it the more I've come to realize how much you mean to me. I want to just hold you, and to steal a kiss if you would allow it. Anna, I think…I know that I've fallen in love with you. We don't have a lot of time left, and while you don't have to answer me right now I need to know if you feel the same way about me."

Anna was a little taken back by this sudden baring of his heart. At first she just sat there in thought. Then she said a silent prayer and looked back into Rasmus's eyes. "I've dreamed the same dreams you have Rasmus. I've had the same thoughts. I've never had anyone dependable in my life, and at first I thought that my feelings for you were just that: someone that I could lean on and depend on, someone strong that could help me with my voyage. I'm only 16 and I've never even had a beau. My life has been so busy just trying to get by at home and I've been totally preoccupied with working and saving all I could for my passage. I've never dared to imagine what love might feel like or what it would look like. But in the time that has passed since I met you, my life has changed immeasurably. I've gone from wondering what it would be like to be with you to wondering how I could get by if you weren't here. I don't need another night or another day to make up my mind, Rasmus. I feel the same way about you as you do about me. Your confession has lightened my heart. And I would love to have you give me my very first kiss."

Rasmus got up and took Anna in his arms. They hugged and kissed and they cried. They both now had something more to live for. This would be the beginning of a new life for both of them.

Rasmus stayed mostly hidden the following morning. He had found a nice oak stick and was busy carving engagement rings for Anna and himself. Today he would give Anna an engagement ring, and he would promise to get her a real wedding ring when they got to America and were married. Anna was still busy nursing sick patients and was especially worried about two babies. She had asked the doctor if he could visit again, as she was afraid that they might not make it through their sickness. She also noticed that Ivan seemed to be getting ill. Poor Ivan, after all he had been through, he sure didn't need this.

The ship finally offered more help and some better food. They realized that if these passengers didn't get better America might not take them in. For the ship, this meant an obligation to take them back to Norway, and that would detract from their profits. So they dug into the food meant for first and second class passengers only and begrudgingly gave some it to the passengers in steerage. Anna gave her portion of meat to one of the large families to divide amongst them. There were eight of them in the family, and three were quite ill.

Anna was very exhausted with all the nursing and other chores that she had taken upon herself, and she wanted to steal a moment on an empty cot to just shut her eyes for a moment and relax and maybe dream of her time with Rasmus and the home they would have. Just as she was thinking about him and was ready to close her eyes, he came into view. He had a colossal smile on his face. Anna thought something extraordinary must have happened on the ship. He got down on his knees and took Anna's hand. "Anna, will you marry me?"

"Of course I will, Rasmus!" Her bright eyes were wide and expressive. "I thought we had gone through this last night," she said smiling.

"But it wasn't proper," Rasmus replied. "I didn't formally propose, and I didn't have rings. Here are our engagement rings."

Anna looked at them and tried hers on. It was beautiful and fit almost perfectly. "I know it isn't a real ring," Rasmus said, "but as soon as we get to America I will buy you a proper one."

"No you won't, Rasmus Johnson," Anna immediately replied. "I will always cherish this one, and it will mean more to me than a thousand store-bought rings. I love it, and I love you. These rings will forever be a reminder of our voyage to America and how we fell in love. Just as you carved out these rings we will carve out new lives in America."

Meanwhile, the virus seemed to be dissipating, and most of the afflicted were getting better. A few of the older folks had died, along with some of the infants. It could have been a lot worse according to the ship doctor. Anna only had one patient left to tend to—Ivan. He didn't seem to be getting any better, which was strange for a man his age.

The captain announced that they would make New York in three days. They would probably arrive late in the evening and start disembarkation the next day. Anna and Rasmus were so excited and there was so much to think about! They spent the next entire day— when Anna wasn't tending to Ivan—dreaming about the life that they would have together. Both of them wanted a large family. Rasmus especially wanted sons to help him in the construction business he planned to start. But the first home that he built was going to be Anna's. She wanted two stories and maybe a basement, with lots of bedrooms for her children and a good efficient kitchen. After all, a kitchen was a woman's territory and it had to be just right. She also wanted oak trim and cupboards and a built-in pantry for china and silver...if they ever could afford such luxuries. She had seen photos of fancy homes in a magazine and was only teasing Rasmus when she asked for these things. But Rasmus took her requests seriously. He looked at Anna and told her that he could build anything—that was his gift, his talent—and nothing would be too good for her. If she wanted oak trim and built-in cabinets and a pantry, she would have them. He solemnly told her, "If I never do another thing in my life, I will build you a home worthy of your love, Anna Ingevich. That is my promise to you."

6

Tragedy And Triumph

Rasmus and Anna were sitting with Thomas, talking about Ivan. He had had an even worse night, and the ship was to arrive in New York Harbor in less than 24 hours. The ship's doctor had visited twice now and he said that Ivan's life was out of his hands. Additionally, Ivan seemed severely depressed, which surely wasn't helping him recover. Anna remembered how apprehensive Ivan had been when they were boarding the ship—how he had looked like a caged animal and continually scoured the surroundings for police or authorities. "Why don't we all try to cheer him up a bit?" she offered. "Maybe if he is happier it will help him fight the fever and his cough."

Nothing seemed to console him. They stayed with him all night and tended to his fever. Under the spell of his high fever, Ivan said a lot of things that he probably would never have otherwise revealed. Of course only Thomas really understood him, and even Thomas didn't understand it all. Most of all, Ivan was ashamed that he had been foolish enough to get caught by the Russian authorities and therefore had hurt the cause of the revolution. Because of his mistakes, his father had been executed when he refused to help the communists find Ivan. It could have been worse, he was told. They usually assassinated the whole family. But Ivan's dad had outguessed them and had moved his family before they caught up with him.

Had Ivan been there, he would have seen his father die proudly in defense of his son. But now poor Ivan could only see heartache. He had thought that his hope was America. But now that he was this sick, he had even lost that hope and decided that he had nothing left to live for.

It didn't help when the doctor made his rounds the next morning, the day they were to arrive in New York. He took one look at Ivan and told him the truth. "In your condition, they won't even let you off of the ship. You have no chance. Your only choice is to stay on the ship and go back to Norway. If you recover, you can find another voyage and come back again. I wish I could give you better news, but this is the way it is."

Anna, Rasmus, and Thomas stayed with Ivan all morning. His fever had broken a little, but he was still severely depressed, now knowing for sure that he wouldn't be allowed to leave the ship. He felt that his life had been cursed, that he was good for nothing. Anna continually reassured him that he had done nothing wrong. If anything he had been a hero and should be treated as such. She told him that he was now a dear friend and that she and Rasmus would wait in New York until he made another voyage back to America when they would help him find work and a new life. Ivan weakly smiled at Anna and Rasmus; it was all he could do.

With Thomas's help interpreting, he said, "How did I ever become so honored as to find friends like you? I have done nothing for you, yet you've tried to help me, even on my sickbed. You are one thing in this world that I have found to be good and pure."

He closed his eyes for a while, but then opened them and spoke to Thomas again. Thomas translated, "He wishes that he could go to the top deck again and be in the open air. He is asking that we bring his cot topside and stay with him in the sunshine and fresh air for a while."

They all agreed immediately. "Why didn't I think of this?" said Anna. "Maybe the sight of the ocean and breathing some air that isn't foul will snap him out of it. Maybe the sun on his face will help him recover. I have been praying for a miracle, and maybe this will bring some healing to Ivan."

The men helped him up the stairs, mostly carrying him, while Anna brought the cot behind them. They found a spot with a great view of the ocean right by the rail and placed Ivan on the cot. He had a modest smile on his face.

Anna and Rasmus sat by him and discussed the disembarkation procedure. Because they were in steerage class, they would be the last off the ship, but that didn't matter at this point. They had survived and they had found love. They had each other, and that was immensely more than they had when they left Norway. Save for Ivan, the trip had gone as well as could be expected. As they conversed, they heard Ivan whispering to Thomas but they didn't mind—he could keep his thoughts from them if it made him feel any better. Maybe he was planning his return trip and wanted to keep it a secret? Thomas got up and moved several feet away and pointed to another ship out on the sea. He asked Anna and Rasmus if they would come over and look at it with him.

After a few minutes of discussing what the ship was and guessing that it was another ocean liner bringing passengers from Europe to America, they returned to Ivan's cot. He was gone! Thomas had tears in his eyes, and all he could do was point at a diminutive figure in the immense ocean. Ivan had used the last of his strength to silently slip overboard. He knew that his friends would try to keep him from doing it, and he knew that he could never survive another trip. By now the Russian authorities would have tracked him to Norway and to Bergen. They would contact the ship and tell the captain to place Ivan under arrest so that they could execute him as a revolutionary traitor when the ship got back to Bergen. Maybe they already had contacted the captain. To Ivan, dying at sea was much better than having to go back to Russia for execution. His last instructions to Thomas were to explain all of this to his friends, to ask for their forgiveness, and to give Anna a farewell kiss from him. He hoped that Rasmus wouldn't mind this request.

After Thomas explained about Ivan's request for forgiveness they all solemnly joined hands. Each of them said a few words as they looked out over the vast ocean, wondering if he was home and at peace yet. Anna said the Lord's Prayer through tears as they all murmured their final good-byes to Ivan.

The captain interrupted their thoughts and announced that they would be at their destination, near the entrance to New York harbor, in less than two hours. Since it was already after five 5 p.m. they would have to anchor and stay overnight before any disembarkation procedures could start. Anna and Rasmus were equally excited and sad. They had never experienced so many emotions in such a small amount of time. They would have loved to help Ivan discover America with them and to put some of the happiness they felt into his sad eyes. Saying good bye to him had dampened their joy, but Ivan's life had also shown them how much they had to be thankful for.

After more disembarkation announcements and instructions the captain told the passengers how successful their voyage had been. He said that sometimes as many as ten percent of the folks in steerage died before reaching America. He boasted that less than three percent of this steerage group had perished and that all of the first and second class passengers had arrived "fit and ready for America."

The low number of steerage losses was partly due to Anna and Rasmus's continual encouragement and assistance. Anna's attention to the ill and her nursing skills had probably saved many lives, and her cheerfulness and prayers helped all of them get through their struggles. The captain didn't mention this.

It was a festive night; everyone was celebrating. There was singing and dancing and hugging and laughing and crying. They had been let out of their prison-like home in steerage and allowed to crowd onto the small allotment of deck space that steerage class had been given. Anna and Rasmus made their way through the crowd, saying good-bye and good luck to the many passengers they had met during the voyage. They felt like a large family. So far they had survived, they had persevered. But the rumors about Ellis Island were running more rampant than before, and even with all the cheer this last cloud still hung over the entire steerage crowd. Would they pass the final test tomorrow? Their dream now seemed closer than ever, but somehow farther than ever. Tomorrow was Judgment Day. Would it be heaven or hell? Anna prayed with many of the families and encouraged everyone. She was brave on the outside, but on the inside she had her trepidations. It all seemed too good to be true, too good to really happen, almost transcendental. Would she really be Mrs. Rasmus Johnson in a couple of days? Would she soon be an American? Her life had been one of disappointment, and too many bad things had happened. If only she could share this with Karin— how her mother would have smiled at seeing America with her! How happy her mother would have been to see Anna make this journey. How proud she would have been to see her daughter marry such a fine man. What were Bjorn and Marion doing now? Had her father even looked for her or missed her? She would never know the answer to these questions.

Rasmus gathered Anna's trunk and his tools. He wanted to be alone with Anna, but it was impossible in this environment. It was too noisy, too raucous, too crowded. He wanted to have Anna all to himself. He found her and put his arm around her and ushered her to the least crowded place he knew of, back to steerage. They sat on Anna's favorite cot—the one farthest from the stench of the toilet— and held hands. Anna suggested that they rehearse the dreaded questions that were asked of all the immigrants. She had been trying to teach Rasmus a little English and also wanted to practice her own some more with him. Every word, every phrase, was so important. Even the little things could be misinterpreted if they were said wrong. It could mean the difference in being allowed into America or not. English had so many different words that meant the same thing. How would she ever know the meaning of all of them? In this manner they passed the hours: rehearsing, practicing, singing, laughing, crying, and just holding each other, letting their love for each other grow, until Anna finally fell asleep in Rasmus's arms.

When they woke, their final breakfast of some unknown mush was being distributed into their pails. It was six a.m., and they were told that the medical inspection team would board sometime around seven or eight. Steerage class passengers were avoided, as this service was only for first and second class passengers. The doctors even went to their rooms so the exams could be private. Only those with serious illnesses were sent to Ellis Island for further testing. Traveling with a first or second-class ticket was like having a get-out-of-jail-free pass. Their inspection was brief and easy. Money answered their questions for them. Steerage class was different. Those passengers were looked down on. Surely these poor people had more diseases and more mental conditions, more fleas and lice? They were considered to be less desirable so they needed closer inspection and were more apt to be turned down and deported. But in reality these people would become the heart and soul of America. They were accustomed to hard work, and they paid their own way, building America right along with their dreams.

It was almost ten a.m., and the doctors were already leaving the ship. In such a short time, they had tested the first and second-class for cholera, plague, all sorts of fevers, diphtheria, smallpox, scarlet fever (which was what their ship's doctor thought had spread through the passengers), measles, mental disorders, lameness, eye disease, and all the other things that could get them deported. Now that the first and second-class passengers had been tested the ship could proceed to the bay and into the harbor.

Anna and Rasmus had found a small box to stand on so they could take in the first sighting. Just as the Jensen's had told Anna, the Statue of Liberty came into view first. It was breathtaking. A Norwegian next to them exclaimed that it had to be one of the Seven Wonders of the World. Surely she would guide them through the harbor and welcome them into the new land. Seeing the landscape was absolutely heart-warming after being at sea for almost four weeks. It made them feel good to their souls and gave them renewed hope. The Manhattan skyline went on forever. This new land seemed infinite, beyond grasp. After the vastness of the ocean and these new sights, Anna and Rasmus felt small and insignificant. Of all things to wish for, Anna wished only for a new dress. She wanted to look her best for this new world, but she had nothing. It was enough for

Rasmus though. He was admiring her. As alluring as the new sights were, he couldn't take his eyes off Anna. She was all he had ever dreamed of and so much more. He would always have the best view in the world if Anna were in it.

Finally they were docked. It was time for first and second-class to officially be released. The ship's crew tried to organize the chaos but was having a hard time of it, as everyone was in such a hurry and wanted to be among the first ones off. Those in first or second-class were so fortunate—they were already Americans, having passed the medical exams. They didn't need to go to Ellis Island and go through the trials there. They were already free to do what they wanted, go where they wanted, and live the rest of their lives as they were able.

Those in steerage were getting more apprehensive again. They knew that their turn was coming and that within twenty-four hours they would know their fate. They were so happy to be where they were, but they just wished that they could skip their next test. To fail it would seal their fate, would close their doors and tear their hearts out. The ship's captain brought them out of their thoughts and back to reality. He announced that they were next. He told them to listen closely and do what they were told and everything would go easier and faster. They were to go to a waiting area where they would start the process, each receiving a manifest number and a nametag. Then they would be loaded onto barges for transport to Ellis Island. They would have to leave their luggage, but they were assured that they would get it back. Anna didn't have much to lose, but Rasmus worried about his precious tools. They stashed their money in their pockets, left their luggage, and waited. Rasmus held Anna's hand and informed the ship's crew that they were together and had to be placed on the same barge so that they could go through Ellis Island at the same time. There were some objections, something about men and women, but Rasmus prevailed and they were crammed onto the same barge. Anna wondered how it could stay afloat with so much weight. Shoulder to shoulder, they were literally too crowded to even turn around.

Finally they arrived at the dock and could move onto dry land.

They could hardly walk, wobbly with sea legs. The land kept rocking back and forth and wouldn't cooperate with them at all. Their legs were like uncontrollable appendages that didn't want to take orders from their heads. Anna and Rasmus laughed and teased each other about having to learn to walk on land again. Their ears were assaulted with what seemed like a million languages and endless chatter. Their eyes saw strange people with strange attire. There were people everywhere. Getting off the ship was almost as difficult as getting on had been.

Someone was looking for them, for their manifest number and their names. They hadn't realized it, but they had been assigned an interpreter. His name was John, and he could speak at least seven languages. He was friendly and didn't seem to be offended by their poor clothes and their lack of bathing. He was an American, the first they had met. If all Americans were this nice, they would get along just fine, much better than they expected. John was surprised that Anna could already speak pretty good English, enough to easily get along on her own. Rasmus was a different story, but he apparently had started learning and seemed like an intelligent and proficient person. John told them that they were way ahead of most of the people who arrived at Ellis Island. Some of them had proved to be almost beyond help, but he had tried his hardest, no matter where they were from or what their circumstances had been. John, along with most of the interpreters, were among the unsung heroes of the great immigration of the early 20th century and often meant the difference between an immigrant getting deported or not. Figuring the immigrants out was often like trying to solve a puzzle with a million pieces. Just getting their names right could prove to be almost impossible. John promised to stay with Rasmus and Anna all through the day and to help them with the entire process. He had a family in New York, and as long as he was home by seven p.m. for supper they would be happy.

Anna and Rasmus were on their way to the dreaded registry room. John told them that millions had gone through this room prior to them and that he would do everything he could to help them. He also told them that just going up all of those steps ahead of them were a part of the health tests prior to "the room," but the test was supposed to be a secret. There were observers on top of the stairs watching the immigrants climb them, looking for people who were lame or were breathing hard or had to stop and rest. Once they made it to the top, a doctor looking for any signs of illness or mental disease examined them. If he deemed it necessary, they went to another room to be bathed in disinfectant. One of the most crucial tests was for an eye disease that Rasmus and Anna had never heard of before. Something called trachoma, which could lead to death or blindness and meant certain deportation. It was prevalent in Europe, and the Americans wanted to make sure it wasn't imported into their country. The test was somewhat painful, but both Anna and Rasmus passed with no problem. As a matter of fact they both had passed all of the health tests, as shown by the chalk mark that they received indicating that they could move on into the dreaded registry room. Some of their fellow passengers received other marks, indicating that they had to undergo further testing in other rooms.

Shortly after, they had to face the infamous thirty-one questions. Judgment time was upon them. The ship's manifest had already told the examiners many of the answers, but they had to go through every one of them again: their names, their marriage status (Anna blurted out that she was soon to become Mrs. Rasmus Johnson, but the examiner didn't even look up), had they ever committed a crime, where were they going, what would they do, and on and on through the list that they had rehearsed and rehearsed and rehearsed. The final question, of course: did they have any money and how much?

After answering all the questions satisfactorily, they had passed the examination. The interpreter, John, had a huge smile on his face; Anna and Rasmus were welcome to stay in America. It was such a huge relief that they both started crying—tears of delight, tears of relief, and tears of happiness. After all they had been through, they had persevered. They were finally Americans!

7

The Telegram

John escorted Anna and Rasmus to the money exchange room, where they waited in line for a teller to exchange their Norwegian Kroners for American dollars, or "greenbacks" as they had heard them called. And at last, if they could find their luggage and Rasmus's tools, they would be on their own. To their great relief, they did find them, just as they had been left. With the procedure complete, they were now free to leave Ellis Island and explore America.

John asked them if they needed a place to stay tonight, something they had entirely forgotten to think about. A few inexpensive boarding houses were nearby. If needed, he would help them find one. They greatly appreciated this and took him up on it. On their way out, John received word that Rasmus had a telegram message waiting for him. Since it was so late, the message would have to wait until tomorrow when he could go to the telegraph office and get it. They were ready to leave when they noticed a family that they had met on the ship sitting in the corner of the room. They were huddled together, and all of them were crying. Anna and Rasmus could tell that these weren't tears of joy. Even though they needed to get going, Anna decided that they should stop and see if they could help.

Mrs. Dangerud was sobbing almost hysterically. Anna ran over and gave her a hug and asked her what had happened and if she and Rasmus could help her. "Please tell us what is going on," Anna asked.

Mrs. Dangerud couldn't bring herself to talk, so her husband explained for her. Their daughter still had signs of the fever, and the doctors had said that she was a health risk if they let her into the country. She had undergone several tests, and the officials decided that they had to deport her back to Norway. This posed all sorts of problems for the family. Their daughter was only eight years old, which meant that one of her parents would have to go back to Norway with her. It was a governmental requirement that they wouldn't let children under the age of ten travel alone.

Mrs. Dangerud (Tove) didn't want to leave the rest of her family in America while she traveled back to Norway with her daughter. She wanted them all to go back to Norway together and give up on their dream of America. Mr. Dangerud (Nils) thought differently. He wanted Tove to take their daughter back to Norway until she was over the illness, and in the meantime he could find work and put together enough money for their passage back to America again. He would stay with the rest of the family in America, where they would find jobs and a place to live and wait in New York until all of the family was together again. Then they would all decide if they wanted to stay in New York or to move somewhere else, perhaps to Dakota where Nils had friends who wanted them to come and live. The Dangerud family had argued most of the afternoon about what to do and they were still at an impasse. It was tearing their family apart.

Anna and Rasmus could see the logic in what Nils wanted to do and knew that he could probably never get enough money together for all of them to come again, at least not in Norway. Anna had met another family with similar circumstances earlier in the afternoon and suggested that Tove visit with them. Perhaps they could travel back together and help each other out? If Tove and Nils decided that it would be best for them for Tove and her daughter to go back, traveling together might make it easier for both families. The women would have traveling companions and could help each other. If it worked out they could even travel back to America together to reunite with their families. Tove quit crying almost immediately. After all she had been through, it was just too much for her to think about having to go back alone with her daughter. Having traveling companions with the same circumstances would make all the difference in the world.

She and Anna went and found the other family, who had by then decided that the wife and sick son would have to go back to Norway. Anna explained the Dangerud situation to them and asked them if Tove and her daughter could travel with them back to Norway. They were delighted to have companions as well! They hugged and got acquainted, and all of them, especially Tove, thanked Anna over and over for helping them in their time of need, for giving their family hope and answers. Anna said another of her silent prayers, thanking God that she had run across the other family, and thanking Him that she was able to help the Dangeruds. Rasmus just smiled. Anna had come through again. She was amazing. Who else would have put the puzzle pieces together and made it all work out for the best?

Anna and Rasmus still had to find that boarding house—John had given up on them and had left for home, but not before giving them directions to the boarding house that he thought was the best. He also gave Rasmus directions to the telegraph office so that he could go and get his message in the morning. Rasmus and Anna would have all night to plan their wedding, which they wanted to take place the next afternoon. Anna had agreed to a justice of the peace so that the wedding would go faster and cost less, but only under the condition that they do it proper and in a church when the time came that they could.

It was a nice enough evening, so they enjoyed the walk to the boarding house. Rasmus had thought about asking Anna if they could just get one room, but before he could get his thought out he realized that it wouldn't be the honorable thing to do, or the Christian thing. They had waited this long, they could wait one more night. Besides, he knew that Anna would never agree to it anyway. She wasn't the kind of lady that would sleep with a man before she was married.

Anna brought him back to reality and said to Rasmus, "I'm starving. I just now realized that we haven't eaten all day. Are you hungry too?" When they got to the boarding house they asked the lady there, Donna, if there was a chance that they could get something to eat. She said that it would be no problem and that she could rustle them up a little grub. What was "grub," they wondered? Was it some sort of worm? Anna hoped that "grub" was tastier than the slop they received on the ship.

Donna continued, "And while I am rustling up some food for you two, you can go to your rooms and bathe if you want. I won't have time to heat enough water for full baths but there is enough for sponge baths if you want."

Anna almost cried with joy. She had been afraid to ask about bathing and was worried that it would cost extra. While Anna was beaming with joy, Rasmus stood there sharing her happiness. Donna added, "If you want, I can even have your clothes washed while you clean up." Anna told her that she only had one other dress, which wasn't much cleaner, so Donna offered to wash both of them and lend Anna a bathrobe to wear while her clothes were drying. Americans were great; it was like living in a dream.

As it turned out, the "grub" was delicious. Donna apologized that it was only some leftover hot dish from their earlier supper, but to Anna and Rasmus it was food fit for kings. It had been a long time since they had had a good homemade meal, and especially something that actually had some vegetables and real meat in it. America was truly a bountiful and gracious place. Donna was being as kind to them as John, their interpreter, had been. They told Donna of their plans to get married tomorrow, which excited her. She liked nothing better than weddings (she was still single and only a little older than Anna), and seemed a bit disappointed when they told her all they could afford was a justice of the peace.

It had been such a long day and all of a sudden Anna and Rasmus realized that they were exhausted. Tonight they would sleep in real beds, in clean clothes, in clean skin, and in air that smelled fresh and fragrant. Rasmus looked at Anna again. If it was possible, she was even more beautiful. Her now clean and freshly washed hair was so long and had such a shine. It was almost blonde, but with a brownish-red tint in it. It went so well with her big blue eyes, the deepest and most sincere eyes Rasmus had ever looked into. How did he ever find such good fortune as to meet this girl, this stunning and incredible woman?

Anna's room was next to his, and the night seemed almost unbearably long as he laid there anticipating what it would be like to have a woman like Anna in his house, in his bed, and in his life. It would be an intense night of waiting for tomorrow to happen, the day that he would finally call her Mrs. Rasmus Johnson. It would certainly be the best day of his life. Anna was thinking the same thoughts, and when they did sleep they probably dreamt the same dreams. Although they had not been together for very long, it seemed like they had been together forever. Anna had found her true love, and she already felt that life without Mr. Rasmus Johnson would be impossible. Rasmus felt the same; they were meant to be together.

They were both up early, and Donna already had breakfast ready for them. It was another American feast with bacon, eggs and sour dough bread with wild berry jelly and fresh butter. Anna and Rasmus wanted to tell John, if they ever saw him again, what a good boarding house he had delivered them to. During breakfast they made plans for the day. Anna's job was to find a justice of the peace and make a reservation for their wedding. If she wanted a new dress for the occasion she should buy it. Rasmus gave her five dollars in hopes it would get her what she wanted. While she was dress shopping and justice of the peace hunting, he would go to the telegraph office and get his message. It was probably his parents, wishing him well in America and wondering if he had arrived safely. He and Anna would meet around noon, back at the boarding house, and then be off to their wedding. They had a room reserved again for tonight, but this time it was only one room. Tonight they would be Mr. and Mrs. Rasmus Johnson. Today they would start their life together. If ever there was a couple in love, it was Anna and Rasmus.

Anna and Rasmus decided that they had time for one more cup

of coffee, which they both loved. It had been nearly a month since they had had a real cup of coffee, and it tasted heavenly. It gave them time to go over their morning agenda once more and to rehearse their wedding and honeymoon plans. They thought that after the wedding they would splurge and find a real restaurant and maybe even go to one of those fancy New York plays. Their honeymoon would be two glorious days of seeing the sights and hearing the sounds of New York. Then the work would begin.

Rasmus had skills that were in high demand in any growing city, and even with his broken but improving English he wouldn't have any problem finding an employer. His real goal was to have his own construction company, just as his father had, but he knew that he first had to work for someone and get to know the area and the people and improve his ability to communicate. Anna, on the other hand, had never been formally employed, but with her charm and good looks Rasmus figured that she could find something fairly easy, even if it was being a waitress in a hotel or restaurant. Of course when his business started growing and he started making a lot of money, her job would be to raise their family. Before they could do that he would build her the house that he had promised her.

Anna headed north toward the business district while Rasmus headed east. Donna gave him better instructions than John had, and he figured that he could be at the telegraph office in under an hour, almost at opening time. He couldn't wait to see what his parents had to say and to hear some news from Norway. But what he really couldn't wait for was his wedding, his marriage to Anna. They had had a long, serious hug and an even longer kiss when they left each other this morning. It brought out the feelings Rasmus had been trying to keep under control for the past weeks. This morning he had felt like he was going to burst with love for Anna. He almost asked her if they could just skip the rest of their plans and go straight to the justice of peace. But he had waited this long; another few hours wouldn't kill him. And to see Anna in a new dress, radiant for her wedding, would be worth it all.

Anna noticed a small church as she was looking for a dress shop.

Donna had told her where the justice of peace was, in the courthouse, but they wouldn't be open for a while yet. This was her chance to have a few moments with her Lord. She hadn't been in a church for weeks, so this would be special. She walked into the empty building and found a pew close to the altar where she sat with her eyes closed, her heart open, and her mind overwhelmed with prayer and thankfulness. In her prayer she went over all that she had been through with Rasmus: how they had gradually fell in love and what their future life together would look like. She looked up at the cross and thanked God that the worst of her trials were over. She thanked Him for life, for health, for getting her to America, and for Rasmus. She asked Him to help her be the best wife and mother that any Norwegian girl had ever been. Rasmus deserved it.

The courthouse was easy to find and open by now. It was the biggest and grandest building in the area. The marble steps looked brand new, as did the hand-carved, massive wooden doors. She stopped at the first office she came to and asked where there was someone who could perform a marriage.

"Judge Wellington is in today, honey," she was told. "Why don't you ask him if he can fit it in? Go up one flight of stairs and then his office is the first door on your right."

When she got there the secretary told Anna that the Judge wasn't in yet but that she had his schedule, and yes, he could probably fit a marriage in around three o'clock, as he didn't have court this afternoon. Three was a bit later than they wanted, but Anna agreed immediately and thanked the lady for her assistance. Anna asked if she owed any money but was told that the judge usually did this for free. He was, after all, a public servant. But the secretary did need their names for the judge. Anna smiled all the way down the stairs. "Mrs. Rasmus Johnson" was all she could think of.

By now the dress shop was open too. They had so many beautiful colors and new styles to choose from. The lady helping her asked what she was going to use her new dress for, and Anna happily exclaimed, "I'm getting married."

"Well that changes everything, darling," replied the clerk. "Let's look at the wedding gowns."

The wedding dresses were stunning. To Anna they weren't dresses; they were gowns, fit for royalty. The first thing Anna noticed was, of course, their prices. For that much money she could buy both a dress AND new shoes and have money left over. And what would she do with a wedding dress after they were married? It would be way too classy and way too nice to wear for any other occasion. Anna's practical nature took over, and she asked the clerk if they could go back to the other dresses again.

"Are you certain, dear? You would look like a New York high society model in one of those wedding gowns."

Anna blushed and said that she was indeed certain. She needed some new shoes too, as her only pair was worn through. She tried a few dresses on but decided to get the long, blue-green dress with the white lace trim. It could be used for almost any occasion after their wedding, and Rasmus would like that the color matched her eyes. New shoes would be much better to have after the wedding than a pretty wedding dress folded up and put away in her trunk to never be used again.

It wasn't even 11:30 and Anna had already finished her errands. She thought about stopping at the church again on her way back to the boarding house but instead decided to walk straight back in case Rasmus was there waiting for her. Besides, she could hardly think straight with the excitement of her wedding coming up in less than four hours. She couldn't wait to get Rasmus to Judge Wellington.

The telegraph office was already open when Rasmus arrived. He announced his name and told the operator that he had been given a message by the interpreter at Ellis Island that he had a telegram waiting for him.

"You sure do Mr. Johnson," said the operator. "I have it right here. I think that you are going to be very happy as you have some great news from Norway." He handed Rasmus the telegram.

Rasmus read it. Then he read it again. It couldn't be real. He read it a third time. At first he thought that he was having a nightmare, but the telegraph office and the people in it didn't seem like a dream. Rasmus had never in his life fainted, but he fell in a heap on the telegraph room floor. The telegram fell crumpled beside him:

Dear Rasmus:

It is with heavy hearts that we send you this message. When Astrid told us what happened, we couldn't believe what she had done. We were devastated, and we felt like our family honor had been taken. We love you like our own son and we have had a long visit with Astrid. She feels badly about her decision and has been miserable ever since. We found another passenger ship leaving for New York. Astrid has a second-class passage and she should arrive in New York within three or four weeks. By the time you get this she will probably have been to sea for at least four days. Can we get an address where we can reach you? We will send another telegram when we know exactly when she arrives so that you can meet her and be married in America. We wish the wedding would have been here with all of our family and friends, but that can't be changed now. We pray that this will repair our honor and our friendship.

Lovingly your family,
Magnus, Liv, and Astrid.

Rasmus woke with water being splashed in his face and the clerk fanning him. He was hoping that it had all been a bad dream, but he saw the message lying beside him. He was embarrassed, so without thanking anyone he picked it up and went outside. He found a bench and stumbled onto it, tears streaming down his face.

It took several minutes to compose himself. This was the worst news he possibly could have received. Why did he even go to the telegraph office? He should have just stayed at the boarding house with Anna and taken her to the justice of the peace right away this morning and gotten married. How could he have been so stupid, so foolish? How was he going to show Anna this message? He hadn't even told her about Astrid and her family. He had never told Anna that he once had been engaged, only a month ago, and how it had ended. He had intended to, he really had, but every time he approached the subject something had happened or he had just plain chickened out. He wanted to spare Anna those details of his life; he didn't want her to feel second best or to think that he had proposed to her because of anything that had happened with Astrid, because it hadn't. If he had known the two of them in Norway before any of this had happened, he would have chosen Anna easily. Yet it wasn't that easy now. The circumstances were entirely different. He walked slowly and hunched over all the way back to the boarding house, wishing he would get run over by a wagon or hit by a train. Anything would be better than showing this message to Anna. This was to have been the happiest day of their lives. It was now the worst day of their lives, especially of his.

All the way back he kept thinking of ways to escape. What if he didn't tell Anna anything; if he just said that the telegraph people made a mistake and that they didn't have a message for him? Or maybe he could tell her the truth and they could just run away together and leave Astrid standing at the harbor. He could have the telegraph people send Magnus a letter back that they were sorry but they couldn't find a Rasmus Johnson to deliver the message to. Or they could say that he had died on the ship with the fever. He could even just tell the truth, that he had met another woman that he loved more, so much more.

When he got back he was exhausted with worry and pain. Anna was sitting there waiting for him, and the instant she saw him she ran to him to tell him what all had happened with her this morning and that their wedding was set for three p.m. As she got closer to him she could tell instantly that something was wrong. Rasmus was crying, and his eyes were red and swollen. He tried talking to her but no words would come out. After several attempts, he just dug into his pocket and got the telegraph out and gave it to Anna.

Anna read through it slowly and carefully. Just as Rasmus had, she read it again. She didn't know any of these people, but it was fairly easy to understand what had happened. Rasmus had been engaged, and probably still was, to the daughter of this family. She had apparently backed out, and Rasmus had left for America. But now she had changed her mind and wanted to marry Rasmus. This Astrid was in fact heading for New York to marry Rasmus at this minute. Anna's face went from wild happiness to bewilderment to fear in the span of a few breaths. How could this be happening to them? She instantly hated this Astrid and her family. She asked herself, why hadn't Rasmus told me about this family and his engagement? Did he ever even love me or was he just running from a broken heart? A million questions went weaving through her mind, but most of all she just felt broken. Heart, soul, and mind—all broken. This was too much, even for Anna Ingevich. Tears were streaming from her eyes too.

They walked over to Rasmus's room and sat there without speaking for a long time. Rasmus finally broke the silence. "I love you so much Anna. I should have told you about all this, but I thought that it was over. I really did try to tell you several times, but it never seemed right. Astrid didn't love me enough to come to America with me, so I left without her. I was broken hearted, but believe me I love you so much more than I ever loved her. Now I have no idea what to do. Her family believes in me and is counting on me to marry Astrid when she gets here. Astrid has none of the strength that you do, Anna. She will never survive on her own here, and I know her well enough to be positive that she would never go back to Norway. Her family is one of honor above everything, and to them she has already broken that honor by not marrying me in Norway and coming to America with her husband. She will have too much pride to go back, and if she did I doubt that they would take her back into the family anyway. Knowing Astrid, I would be willing to bet that she will sit at the harbor waiting for me until her money runs out. She isn't resilient enough to pick up the pieces and go out on her own and make her way. She will end up destitute. What can I possibly do, Anna? Can you ever find it in your heart to forgive me? You always have the answers, Anna. Please, tell me what to do?"

Anna didn't have any answers. She didn't know what to say or what to do. They were supposed to be getting married in two hours, but she knew that that wouldn't be happening. She briefly thought about walking to the courthouse to cancel their wedding appointment, but she didn't have the strength. If she went she knew that she would just end up standing there in tears anyway. She finally confronted poor Rasmus. He looked like he had aged twenty years since morning. She took his hands, which were shaking, and looked into his eyes.

"Rasmus, I think that this is just too much for either of us to handle right now. We should both have some time alone to think it over. When we have had enough time to gather our thoughts and be logical about this, we need to decide what to do. We need to make this decision together, as a husband and wife even though we aren't married. Would you please ask Donna if my room is still available for tonight? I don't think that I can face her right now, I just want to have a place to sit and think and pray."

Rasmus went to the office, and Anna went to the room she had stayed in last night. Fortunately it was still vacant. Her trunk was even still in it. She fell on the bed and started crying again, lost in thoughts about why this was happening to them. It just couldn't be real. She wanted to wake up to find that it was all just a terrible dream and that she was still going to marry Rasmus today.

After sobbing herself to sleep, Anna had bewildering dreams. She dreamt that the ship had sunk and they all had drowned at sea. She dreamt that Ellis Island had deported her and that her Dad had picked her up and made her go back to work for Marion. She dreamt that Rasmus had gone off with another woman. When she woke up she was too terrified to go back to sleep; she didn't want to go through another nightmare. She just wanted some peace. She went through their situation for hours and from a hundred different angles, but it always turned out the same. There really was only one solution. She saw that the light was still on in Rasmus's room, so she went over and knocked on his door.

"Could I come in for a while, Rasmus?" His eyes were still red, but she could tell that he had recovered sufficiently to talk this over, or at least listen. "I have to get this off my mind or I'll go crazy. I've changed my mind a thousand times tonight, but I think that I know what we have to do. I think that in your heart you know what you have to do too. There is only one solution that will leave you with an honorable outcome, and even though I don't think that it is the right answer for the two of us together, I think that it is the right answer for each of us individually."

She had his attention. He was listening intently and nodding his head. "Rasmus, I have gotten to know you, probably better than I know anyone else in this world. Maybe better than I know myself. Above all, Rasmus Johnson, you are truly a man of your word and a man of honor. If you went off with me you would look over your shoulder all of your life, wondering what had happened to Astrid. You would feel that you had let her family down, and that anything that might have happened to them or to her was entirely your fault. You would live in shame. I don't think that you could live with that, and I don't think that I could live with myself if I asked you to run off with me and forget her. I would feel just as shameful as you would. I don't know why this has happened to us, and I have no idea what will become of us. But I do know, deep in my heart, that we must go our separate ways."

"I have only one thing to ask of you, Rasmus. Could you please pay for my room for another night or two, and could you please move to another boarding house, far enough away that I won't have to see you again while we are here in New York? I will love you forever, Rasmus Johnson, but my heart is so broken that I don't think that I could take seeing you again. I don't know what I will do or where I will go, but I want you to always know that I will be fine. I am strong and I will have the help of the Lord. Please don't worry about me. My love will follow you, and above all I want you to be happy. You asked for my forgiveness, Rasmus, but I see nothing to forgive. This wasn't your fault and neither was it mine. Please forget about me, and please have a wonderful life with Astrid. I would feel even worse if I dreamt of anything less for you. Good-bye, my dear Rasmus."

Rasmus knew that she spoke the truth, and he knew that the kindest thing to do was to simply obey her wishes. In his heart he had come to the same conclusion, but he didn't have the strength or courage to tell her. He didn't want to disappoint the most amazing woman he had ever met. But here she was protecting him from having to say it. She was being the strong one. Even in this act she was proving her love for him. He gave her salty cheek a soft kiss and mouthed, "I will always love you, Anna" and left. He went to his room and composed a short note in broken English to Donna.

> *Dear Donna,*
>
> *Here is $50 for you to give to my dear Anna. Please let her stay with you as long as she wishes, and please take care of her for me while she is staying here. Before I leave New York, I will check back with you and see if I owe you anything more. You have been so kind to us and we are in your debt for this. Anna is the love of my life, but unforeseeable events have caused us to part.*
>
> *Your friend,*
> *Rasmus Johnson*

In the morning Rasmus was gone, and Anna was alone.

8

Iver Tenold

Iver Olson's mom and dad had helped him pack and make preparations for his journey to America. They were so proud of him, yet they were so afraid for him. He was just a boy, yet he was acting like a man. That was how Iver had always been. It didn't matter if his dad gave him a job that should have been for someone much older than him. Iver was always up for a challenge, and he always came out on top of it.

When he had been only ten years old, the Thune family from their village needed someone to herd their sheep from the other side of the mountain to their farm near Tenold. They couldn't afford to pay top wages and couldn't find anyone willing to herd sheep that far over mountainous terrain to their village. One day Mr. Thune asked Olav if one of his sons might be interested in the job. Olav told him that his older sons already had work, but if the pay was right he might let Iver do it.

"Iver!" said his neighbor. "He's only a boy. This is a man's job."

Olav replied, "You apparently don't know my boy, Iver."

Mr. Thune didn't want to trust the herd to a boy. But Iver was all he could find, so he gave Iver instructions on how to find the flock. Olav and Eva gave their son a jar of water and some sandwiches and sent him on his way on foot. It took Iver six days to get to the herd of sheep. When he found them, he discovered that the herd was larger than he had been told. Undeterred, he rounded them up, re-filled his water jug, and started back up the valley to the mountain pass toward home. The first day up the mountain wasn't too bad, as he had a stream to follow and open meadows. Slowly the herd wound its way up to the top of the mountain, with Iver moving back and forth behind the sheep, letting them know that he was in charge but also making sure that he didn't push them too hard.

The first night out he found a little clearing and moved the sheep to the middle of it. This way if any predators were near he would be better able to protect the herd. There was a small haystack near the edge of the clearing, which made a perfect bed for Iver and added a better vantage point. At the break of dawn he heard the sheep blatting and jumped down to see if anything was wrong. Sure enough, a big grey wolf was stalking the sheep. Iver had dealt with wolves before and wasn't the least afraid. He grabbed a few rocks and a big tree limb and took off after the wolf, yipping and yelling at it. It took off into the woods, and that was the last Iver saw of it.

For the next four days he traversed mountainous country, which took him through a couple of passes and over some rough trails. Sometimes he had to take the sheep single file, but usually they could travel as a flock. Two of the sheep went over a steep embankment one day, and it cost Iver hours of precious time getting them back to the herd. A lesser herder would have just left them there, but not Iver. One at a time, he hauled them back up to the flock. It took another three days to reach the summit, but from there the hardest work was over. The air was getting warmer, and one night he found an old cabin to stay in. It had a little fireplace, which he took advantage of to roast a cottontail that he had snared.

None the worse for wear, a few days older and a few days wiser, Iver arrived in Tenold with the flock of sheep. He had left the other side of the mountain with 83 head and he arrived with 83 head. That would have been an amazing feat for anyone, but for a ten year old boy it was almost miraculous, and it certainly won Iver the admiration of the local farmers, especially the Thune family. Olav wasn't the least surprised though. He had a lot of faith in his youngest son.

By the time Iver was fifteen, the only thing he wanted in life was to be a farmer, but he knew that their small farm would go to his oldest brother John. His family knew it too, and they felt bad that Iver might never have his dream. Four years earlier Olav's younger brother Christian had immigrated to America. Like Iver, he had wanted to have some land of his own, but there was none to be found in Norway. The Olson's hadn't heard from him all these years and had feared that he had been killed or something bad had happened to him.

Eventually, the Olson family heard back from Christian. Communication wasn't easy from where he was living in America. He wrote to his family that he had found free land in the middle of the wild American prairie. This wide-open prairie had grass as tall as the wagon wheels, and the sea of grass stretched in every direction. The deer and wildlife were abundant, and white faced cattle could be purchased at a reasonable price. It was everything Christian had dreamed of, and he was on his way to becoming the owner of his own farm, which was called a ranch in this wild country. A railroad in North Dakota was close enough to ship cattle and bring in supplies, and a nice settlement called Dickinson had started where the railroad stopped. Christian made it sound like paradise, which it certainly wasn't. He conveniently left out the parts about rain being in short supply and the winters being hard and long. He also left out the Indian wars, smallpox, rustlers, lack of health care, and train robbers.

When Iver read his uncle's letter he proclaimed without hesitation that he was going to America to become a rancher like his uncle Christian. He would be free to have his own land there, and with that land he could make anything that he wanted out of his life. It was as if God himself had written that letter and had instructed Iver where to go and live the rest of his life. Olav and Eva were happy for their son, but they were sad for themselves. America was a far off land, and they knew that if they let Iver go they may never see him again or his children if he found a wife there. The only good thing that they could see was that Iver would have some family there, Uncle Christian.

The town of Vik was at the head of their mountain fjord and only a few miles from Tenold. Ships came in and out of the sea port routinely. From the mountain top above Tenold, where Iver had herded the sheep, down to the valley and the sea port was one of the grandest vistas in the world. Iver would have to remember it well because once he got to the interior of America there would be no such sights. Olav learned that a passenger ship from the Norwegian-American Line (NAL) would arrive in Vik in about a month, and he told Iver that his family would raise the thirty dollar fare that he would need. Iver gave all of the wages he made from fishing and helping neighbors and other odd jobs to his family, but Olav told him to keep his spring and summer wages so that he would have enough money to make a start in America. It seemed a fortune to him, and it was virtually all the money that his family had, but fifteen year-old Iver left Norway with the equivalent of seventy-five American dollars in his pockets (of which thirty were spent for passage).

That month passed slowly for Iver, but too quickly for his parents. Iver was very much loved in his home and in his village. When the day came for him to leave, most of Tenold was there at the dock wishing him well. It made it a little easier for Olav, but Eva cried for hours. She cried until he was on board, and she cried while the ship left port. For nearly three months she went down to the docks almost every day and said a prayer for Iver, and shed a few more tears. One of the townsfolk remarked that the sea water in Vik must be saltier than anywhere in Norway from all of the tears that Eva had shed there for her son.

Iver's ocean voyage was one of the few that were fairly uneventful. Even still, steerage class was horrible, toilet conditions were wretched, and the food was, well, it certainly shouldn't be called food. Iver wasn't a person to complain about anything, but he did notice how hard it was, especially on the older folks. He got to know several other young men on the ship and organized them into a sort of community outreach program. They fought the food lines to get older folks and children something to eat, they helped them with navigating the stairs when they were allowed into their allotted space on the deck, and they brought them water to wash with. The only water available to them, except for a small rationed portion of drinking water, was salt water from the ocean. The salt water dried out your face and hands pretty fast, but it was a step better than being filthy.

About ten days out, some of the men on board were starting to get a little edgy. Between the stench in steerage and the small amount of allocated space on deck and the terrible food, they were either like caged lions ready to pounce on anything that crossed their paths or they were just the opposite, spending all of their time on a cot without even bothering to try to get out of bed. One morning two of the more vocal men started arguing about which one of them was the best fisherman. Their argument turned bitter, and they started throwing punches at each other. Space was limited and one of them backed into an old man nearly knocking him overboard.

Iver was watching and became furious that they had jeopardized the life of an old man. He jumped into the fray and told the two men to grow up. This just turned their rage toward him, and they both started swinging at Iver. Iver wasn't extremely strong, but for his age he was strong enough and his biggest asset was that he was quick and agile on his feet. He could move like a cougar and pounce just as quickly. He dodged a couple of one man's punches. Then the guy's feet slipped out from under him, which caused him to fall hard on the deck and knock his wind out. The ship was continually pitching one way or the other, which worked in Iver's favor as his feet could move so much faster than his opponents' could. The other guy threw several more haymakers at Iver, but he easily dodged and ducked them and kept out of harm's way. The poor fellow ran out of steam, and Iver won the battle without even throwing a punch. Later, when their tempers had quieted and they had mellowed out a bit, they gave Iver a congratulatory hug and held his arms up saying that he was the boxing champ of the Norwegian fleet.

One of the ship's officers, Tor, was taking note of Iver's abilities and his ambition. He befriended Iver and eventually offered him a junior officer job on the ship, telling Iver that with his capabilities he might someday command a ship of his own. Iver didn't need a lot of time to think this over. He said that he was very thankful for the offer, but that his goal was to have land and a cattle herd of his own. The ship's officer was disappointed; young men like Iver didn't come along every day. Iver told him with a wink that if he got tired of steering the ship he could come out west and help Iver on his cattle ranch.

They reached America four days ahead of schedule. It was nearly record time for an ocean voyage from Vik to New York. Everyone on board was thrilled. The doctors had quickly completed their slack examination of the passengers in first and second class, and the steerage passengers were ready to get off of the ship for their exams. Iver's Mom and some of her friends had given Iver a crash course in English before he left, and Iver had also been practicing it with Tor, the ship's officer. Tor could speak both Norwegian and English fluently, and he was happy to help Iver, especially since Iver had made his job so much easier. He also coached Iver on what he would be expected to say and do on Ellis Island, but he assured Iver that he would have no problems becoming an American. He was strong, his health was great, he was intelligent, he had unique abilities, and he even had some money. If there ever was the perfect immigrant for America, it was Iver Olson. Tor and Iver had become good friends, and it was hard to say good-bye when it was time for the steerage class to get off the ship and onto the barges to Ellis Island. Iver had arrived in America.

1900 marked the turn of the century. The Civil War was over and the Spanish American war had just ended with America winning, making it a new world-class power. People were still reading Huckleberry Finn, and Custer had been killed in the battle of the Little Bighorn in Montana. William McKinley was the President and was having a re-run of his 1896 campaign against William Jennings Bryan. It was into Ellis Island and this infant American landscape that Iver and his fellow Norwegian travelers were thrust.

Iver and a few other single men were grouped together and given the same interpreter. Like most of the interpreters, he was a patient fellow and knew several languages. Iver was the only one in his group that spoke any English at all, so their interpreter had his work cut out for him. Everyone wanted to know what was expected of them and what they had to do to make sure that they didn't get sent back to Norway. They had come this far, and now they only wanted to become Americans. Some of them had relatives and jobs waiting for them, and they were anxious to start making those American dollars. They threw out a hundred questions at their poor interpreter, who spoke fluent Norwegian and patiently tried to answer each question, but only after he had figured out each of their names.

When it came time to climb the stairs, the secret fitness test, Iver ran up them three steps at a time. He was used to climbing the mountain behind their farm house, so this was nothing. One of the doctors observing the immigrants made this note about Iver: "This one certainly isn't lame and looks like he could run from New York to Kansas without breaking into a sweat." For Iver the health tests were easy, and even the dreaded thirty-one questions that they had rehearsed went well. At least until they asked his name. "Iver Olson," he told them. The questioners then asked Iver where he was from, to which Iver said, "The village of Tenold in Norway." They told Iver that there were just way too many immigrants named Olson from Norway already, and that his American name would be changed from Iver Olson to Iver Tenold. Iver was puzzled, but Norwegians were used to changing their names and being named after villages or farms. Some of the men even took their wives' last name when they got married, so this didn't bother Iver in the least. He could be Iver Tenold to please these bureaucrats if it helped him get into America. Maybe a new name would help him get a new start?

After finding a boarding house to stay in, Iver and his shipmates decided they should have some ale and celebrate their good fortune and their first night as Americans. After all, it was the best night of their lives, and they were now free to go where they wanted and do what they wished as genuine American citizens. Although he would have liked to celebrate all night with them, Iver decided to call it quits early.

"Sorry lads, I can't afford any more ale and I certainly can't afford any trouble. Tomorrow I'm going to look for a train that will take me to Chicago, then on to Minnesota and Dakota. My uncle has been there almost five years and he will be waiting for me, maybe even in North Dakota at the train station. I will be working on his farm until I can afford my own. If anyone wants to go west with me, they are surely welcome. They say that there is free land there just for the taking, and I intend to have my own farm someday. I will be heading out tomorrow morning, so if you want to go along let me know before I leave."

When he returned to his room, Iver cleaned up, had a good meal, and then, best of all, he slept in a nice bed with clean sheets and no stench in the air. He slept soundly for the first time in a long while. The folks at the boarding house were good to him even though he was a total stranger. He felt safe and secure in America. In the morning, after a steaming hot cup of coffee and toast and eggs, he got directions for the railroad ticketing office and left on foot. New York and the big city were too alluring for his ship mates to leave so soon. They wanted to drink some more American beer and find some pretty American girls. If they could find good jobs, they might even stay here and make their fortunes in New York City. They tried to talk Iver into staying with them, but they couldn't change his mind. He came to America to own a farm of his own, and nothing would deter him. Once Iver had made up his mind, there was usually no talking him into changing it.

It was about a two hour walk to the train station. Once he got there it was quite confusing, especially for a Norwegian lad with limited English. But with the help of a few strangers and some luck, Iver managed to buy a ticket to Chicago. The train wasn't leaving until noon, so Iver had some free time to roam around the huge train station complex. He had never seen anything like Central Station (the Grand Central Station Terminal wouldn't open until 1912), and he had never seen anything like New York. At home he had felt like the king of the hill and everyone knew him and they were all proud of his accomplishments. Here he felt small and insignificant. There were hundreds of people coming and going, all so busy and in such a hurry, and all of them seemingly knowing exactly where they were going. They didn't even acknowledge him. Iver hadn't had time to feel homesick until now, and it hit him really hard. He sat on the bench waiting for his train and thought about his mom and dad, his family, his horse, his friends, Mom's cooking, Dad's encouragement and pride, the beloved mountain in his backyard, the village of Tenold and the seaport of Vik, the beautiful fjords of Norway, fishing in the sea and hunting in the valley. It flooded over him like a tsunami, all those beautiful memories from Norway. For the first time in months, Iver questioned his judgment and his will. He had never felt so alone, so small. Tears welled in his young eyes.

The station loudspeakers were announcing that they were boarding the passenger train to Chicago in fifteen minutes. Iver dried his tears and packed his memories back up. Besides an extra shirt, socks, overalls, and a few dollars, the memories were all he had, at least for now. In his heart he knew that somewhere out there in America there was a place for him.

Iver didn't realize it, but he had found one of the nicest trains in America, the 20th Century Limited. It would take him from Central Station in New York to LaSalle Street Station in Chicago along what the railroads called their water level route. What he also didn't realize was that it would be so expensive, taking nearly one-third of his travel money for the 1000 mile trip to Chicago. But it was extremely fast and would get him there in just under a day. Iver looked out of place amongst the businessmen in their fashionable suits and fancy ties. He did his best to make himself look presentable, but he couldn't help but notice the stares. Once he got to Chicago, he was determined to look for less expensive travel options. He would try to travel with others who were poor like him rather than rich and snobbish folks that wouldn't even look his way.

Chicago was a lot like New York, but Iver didn't like it as well. He could smell the smoke from the factories and the stench of the nearby slaughter houses. Immigrants were everywhere, and they didn't seem to be doing very well. Some had been indentured and were little more than slaves for their new bosses/owners. One poor fellow told him that he had no bed at night and just slept on the street, where he was afraid that he would be robbed or murdered. Chicago looked dirty and dingy to Iver. It made him feel like turning around and going back to the beautiful valley of Tenold that he had left behind for his dreams.

He didn't want to spend any more money than he had to, so his lunch upon arrival was an apple and water from the fountain. He found out that the passenger train from Chicago to Minneapolis was also quite expensive, at least for him, so he started looking for other options. He left the station to eat his apple and walked out amongst the trains. An old guy with tattered clothes said to him, "Looking for a ride? Where are you going?"

"Minneapolis and on to Dakota, but tickets are pretty expensive."

"Why buy tickets? I'll show you how to ride for free if you get me something to eat. I might even travel with you if I get the urge."

Iver went back in and bought his newfound friend two apples and some candy, and before he knew what was happening he and his traveling companion were in an empty cattle car heading northwest for Minneapolis, Minnesota, which was a short day away. It was smelly, but fresh air flooded the car once it got to moving. Iver's new friend, Bill, told him all about travel in America and the Wild West where Iver was heading. The freight train was slower than the Limited, but Iver was still making great time as he had hardly had any layover at all in Chicago. He would reach Minneapolis around 2AM, and according to Bill he would have no problem finding another free ride to North Dakota.

From what Bill had told Iver, he could take the North Pacific railway into North Dakota and at Fargo he could hop on the Great Northern railway and travel southwest to Dickinson, North Dakota, which was about 18 years old in 1900. That would be the end of the line and the closest that the train would get Iver to his final destination, which was his uncle's farm in northwestern South Dakota. If Iver's uncle wasn't there to meet him, Iver would have to buy a horse or walk the final distance, which he guessed was around

150 miles. Iver hoped that horses were cheap in America, as he didn't want to waste time walking that far.

In Minneapolis, Bill was right again. There were two empty freight cars in the train heading west. The only problem was that they were hog cars and they made the cattle car that they had hopped from Chicago to Minneapolis smell downright rosy. Bill decided that even though he liked Iver's company he would turn around and head back toward Chicago or possibly spend a few days in Minnesota with the Swedes. Iver didn't know it at the time, but in about twenty-nine years, during the Great Depression, he would be using the railroad again, and maybe even the same car, to send his own hogs and cattle to Chicago in hopes of finding a decent market for them there. He would send a load of hogs to sell in Chicago, but a telegraph from the railroad would be sent to him saying, "The good news is we got your hogs sold, the bad news is that they didn't bring enough money to pay for the freight." Iver would telegraph the railroad back: "I don't have any money, but I've got more hogs," to which the railroad would never reply.

It took another day to reach his final destination of Dickinson, North Dakota. He had traveled through what appeared to be the richest farm ground he had ever seen. Hundreds of miles of it spanned from horizon to horizon, with the land as flat as the lefsa his mother made him at Christmas. In Minnesota fields of corn and small grain were still unharvested, and it looked like there was enough grain there to feed the entire world. Small towns were starting along the railroad tracks, and the train slowed down for most of them and stopped a couple of times to pick up and drop off freight. The people at the stations seemed to be mostly of Scandinavian descent and were well dressed and appeared clean. Iver immediately liked Minnesota a lot better than Illinois. He was so attracted by the fertile looking farm land that if it hadn't been for his uncle in Dakota he would have stopped and looked for a farm in Minnesota.

The towns got farther and farther apart once the train reached Dakota. The rich farm ground gradually turned into prairie grassland, especially after crossing the huge Missouri River that ran from north to south dividing the Dakotas into western and eastern regions. Iver's sharp eyes spotted abundant wild game. He was familiar with deer, coyotes, and turkeys, but the rabbits here were huge compared to those at home and looked like they could out run the train. He had never seen pronghorn antelope so he could only guess what those creatures were. The landscape went on forever, mostly a sea of rolling hills and grass that waved with the wind, much like the waves on the ocean had. Iver heard the conductor call out, "next stop is Dickinson, North Dakota."

Iver was surprised to see that Dickinson wasn't a city but rather a pretty small town. There was a general store, a stockyard, and a few dozen homes, and everything looked fairly new. Like most of the newly started towns, the railroad was the primary reason for their existence. Dickinson was located along the Great Northern Railway and, like all these small, newly founded towns, had high hopes of becoming a city someday. It had formerly been called Pleasant Valley as it was located in a pleasant little valley in southwestern North Dakota, but the Dickinson family moved in and re-named it. Dickinson was located right on the southern edge what would later become known as the Bakken oil field, one of the world's largest. If Iver had settled there his great grand children might have inherited some oil.

Iver's uncle wasn't in Dickinson when he arrived, but Iver didn't expect him to be as it was a long ride just to meet someone. It was either walk or find a horse, so Iver did a little snooping around to see what a good horse and saddle might cost him. He had saved quite a bit of money by using livestock cars for most of his journey, but he didn't want to waste it on a horse when the money could be put to better use buying land. Iver stopped by the blacksmith shop and explained his situation to the blacksmith, who just laughed at him and told him to get a horse. "This is big, wide open country, and a horse is an integral part of it," he told Iver. "A man won't last long out here without a good horse. As much as you've been told how good this land is for farming, it isn't really so, young man. We don't get enough rain for farming. This here is cow country, and it takes horses to handle cows. If I were you, I'd save my legs and get a horse right away. You can get to Reva, South Dakota in three or four days with a horse; otherwise, it'll take you at least eight. You'll need those extra days to get ready for winter, which is coming whether we want it to or not."

Iver could see the wisdom in his newfound friend's comments and asked him where to buy a horse. He told Iver to check the stockyards, but that if he didn't find anything there he just might have a prospect. One of the ranchers had not been able to pay his bill, and the blacksmith took a two year-old filly as payment. "She's an average looking sorrel with two socks, but she is big and sound and don't seem to have much buck in her. I'll take $40 for her and that old saddle on the fence. It has a new cinch and good quality leather. Might even throw in a rope."

The stockyards wanted a minimum of $75 for a broke gelding, and the saddle would be extra. So how hard could it be to break that sorrel filly? "By the time I get to Harding County and find my uncle, she'll be gentle broke." Iver went back and told Ted, the blacksmith, that he'd like to try the filly. Iver had never really broken a horse, unless you considered his childhood pony. Buster Brown, his pony in Norway, couldn't have been called a real horse, although Iver learned a lot from him. With Ted's help he got the filly saddled, and to Ted's surprise the filly didn't even throw off this "tinhorn." She crow-hopped and hunched up a bit, but that was it.

Ted had pointed the general direction that Iver should travel and told him that "There are a couple of small streams, one called the Cannonball and the other Cedar Creek. The north and south forks of the Grand River are farther south and should be a good spot to camp for the second night when you reach one of them. From there you are on your own, but there might be a few homesteaders along the way to help you find your uncle's place."

Iver asked Ted, "If my uncle, Christian Olson, happens to be in Dickinson looking for me, please tell him that I headed in that general direction."

"What's your name?" Ted asked.

"Iver Olson to my uncle, but my new American name is Iver Tenold."

"You got it, Iver Olson. Tenold. One last thing," he asked, "are you really going out into the wilderness without a gun? What if you run into a wolf pack or a horse thief? What if you get stranded somewhere and need a little meat for the campfire? It's been ten years since the last of the Indian Wars down at Wounded Knee, but you never know."

Iver hadn't even thought about needing a firearm. In Norway he had always used his dad's rifle when he went hunting, but other than hunting there was no need for a gun. He could see, though, that he was going to be riding out into wild country alone and that some protection could possibly save his life. He thanked Ted again for all of the help and asked him if he would keep the filly for him for another hour or two while he looked for a gun to buy.

"Sure," said Ted, "it will do the filly good to be tied up with the saddle on for an hour or two anyway. Try the general store; they usually have a couple of rifles and some six shooters."

Iver headed down the dirt street and into the brand new general store in Dickinson. He asked the clerk what they had for guns, and the clerk asked him if he wanted a pistol or a rifle. This presented another problem for Iver to solve. A pistol would be a lot handier to carry and use, but Iver had never shot one of them as he had only hunted with a rifle. After a bit of thought, he decided that he would get a lot more use out of a rifle, especially for hunting.

"I was afraid that you'd want a rifle because I am out of new ones, and the two that I have on order won't be here for another week or two. I do have a pretty good used model 1873 .44-40 that I took in on trade for groceries last week though. I reckon it'd cost about twelve dollars new, but I could let you have it for ten."

Iver thought a bit, then said "If you throw in a couple of boxes of shells and let me see how it shoots first, I'll take it."

Iver went out behind the store with the clerk to test the gun. Other than a couple marks carved into the handle and a nick or two, it was a very fine rifle. When Iver inspected the barrel, it had good rifling and looked like it hadn't been shot very much, maybe only used for a few hunts. "I'll take it," he said. "How much for a dozen of those wormy, almost-spoiled apples?"

Iver went back over to see Ted and get his filly and show off his model 1873. "Good choice," said Ted. "The '73s are my favorite gun by far. If this little filly doesn't do you in and you don't get lost, you should make it to your uncle's in three or four days. If he shows up poking around here, I'll let him know that you're probably out there lost or something. Lots can happen. I had a neighbor die from a broken arm just 'cause there was no doctors and it got infection or something."

For the second time that day, Iver walked around the filly and talked to her while scratching her legs and back. Then he slowly eased back into the saddle. The filly hardly flinched. "You certainly have a way with horses," said Ted. "Have you broken a lot of them?"

"My first," replied Iver, and off he rode, southwest, easing the filly into a nice steady walk. He leaned down to the horse, "I think I'll call you my little Prairie Princess, Prairie for short. You and me are going to get along just great. I just hope that when we get to this Grand River we can find a place to get across. It sounds awful big to me, and the rivers back in Norway were mighty hard to cross." Prairie didn't answer, but Iver kept talking to her anyway.

Iver was in a hurry. He had gotten a late start, and he wanted to get to water before dark so that he could camp by it like Ted had suggested. Prairie was being really good for a green, mostly unbroken, filly. She had only acted up once when a grouse flew up beside her. Iver was a bit afraid to step her into a higher gear but thought he'd give it a try, so he nudged her with his heels lightly. She didn't really know what he wanted, but finally she broke into a trot. Iver nudged her again and she started to gallop, but not before taking a few jumps and attempting to buck. Iver quickly pulled her back into the trot position and off they went, a little bit slower than the gallop but faster than the walk.

It was early fall and one of those beautiful "blue bird" days on the prairie. The sun felt warm on his face, and the temperature was perfect for making good time—not too warm and not too cold. As far as Iver could see, there was grass and more grass. The landscape was studded with hills, but they were mostly gradual rolling hills among this landscape of grass, which could be as tall as Prairie's belly. Every once in a while they kicked up one of those large rabbits (Iver later found out they were called jackrabbits). There was also an abundance of small rabbits called cottontails. He saw antelope (Ted had told him what they were), grouse, prairie chicken, and a few deer. Iver had never seen so much wild game and was tempted to try his luck on one of those antelope, but at the same time he was afraid that Prairie might not be used to shooting and run off with him. Besides, the antelope could run like the wind. They ran as one unit, all with their heads down and effortlessly covering the prairie landscape. Still, his mouth was salivating at the thought of some real meat cooked on an open fire.

It was nearing dark, and the sunset was glorious with a few scattered clouds showing off their colors. Iver truly felt like he was in heaven. His homesickness had vanished in the excitement of the day and all the new experiences it had brought. He was breaking his first real horse, carrying his first rifle, and heading for what would become his lifelong home while riding through the unknown prairies of the Wild West. He was both exhilarated and frightened at the same time. He felt very alone, yet somehow very secure in this strange new land.

Prairie spotted the creek first. There were a few small sand dunes and some taller tufts of grass along its banks. It wasn't the crystal-clear mountain water that Iver was used to, but both he and Prairie were thirsty and stopped for a drink. Since it was nearly dark and some nice cottonwood and cedar trees stood nearby, Iver decided that it would be a good place to stay for the night. He figured it was probably Cedar Creek. He made a small driftwood corral for Prairie and unsaddled her, putting some hobbles on for extra good measure. She had all the grass she wanted within reach. Iver made a small fire along the water's edge and formed a nice soft bed in the lush grass. He munched two apples, saving the rest for tomorrow, and fell asleep listening to the water drift by and watching a million glorious stars in the huge, western sky. For the first night in a long time, Iver didn't dream of his family and his home in Norway. He dreamt of his own ranch and a herd of fine horses here in this wide open country that seemed like it was his just for the taking.

Iver woke up early and Prairie whinnied at him softly. Iver had never felt so sore, especially in the areas where his behind and legs met the saddle. He wasn't used to riding and could now understand how the cowboy term "bow-legged" came to be. His soreness soon gave way to wonder again as he saddled up Prairie. They had already formed a strange and wonderful friendship; Prairie seemed to be sharing the new adventure right along with Iver. She had been from the North Dakota badlands, so she had never seen this country either.

They headed southwest again in hopes of finding civilization and that "Grand" river. Iver had been told that there was a wagon trail to the south that went from east to west and that his uncle lived very close to that trail. He and Prairie walked up a small butte to get a better view of the country and were met with one of the most amazing sights on this earth. A large, lumbering herd of bison were grazing near another small creek. The herd seemed to go on for miles, leaving what looked like a giant road behind them. Like an enormous harvester, they inched along the prairie, devouring the grass in front of them and leaving the earth nearly naked in their wake. Iver let out his breath slowly in amazement. He never dreamt that such a sight was possible on this earth. This was not the land of milk and honey, it was the land of milk and meat and honey. He was probably in the vicinity of Hettinger, North Dakota, which would be founded and served by the railroad five years later. Hettinger would be the scene of the last great bison hunts of North America many years later. Indians would be let off of the reservations to join in with these hunts.

Iver was making great time. Prairie moved with grace and ease and could cover what he figured was around three miles per hour when she was in her running walk or faster trot. She seldom shied or made any unsuspected moves. She was sound and steady. Iver once suspected that she had jumped over a rattlesnake, but he didn't see it. He would find out that rattlers were shy creatures that did their best to avoid humans. It was almost sundown of their second day, and good fortune found them another creek. This one had a few large bluffs in places and more cottonwood trees. There were also some sand dunes, so it was the perfect place to make a small fire. With Prairie watered and hobbled he found some firewood and made a bed beside the creek. His apples were about gone, so he walked around looking for a rabbit. He was soon roasting one of the cottontails over his campfire. Iver was one happy and contented man. Life was good, and this American prairie was proving to be his newfound best friend.

They got up early the next day, before the sun poked its head up over the eastern horizon. He and Prairie were both eager to get going, hoping to find some civilization and reach their final destination. They didn't stop for a noon rest, but just kept pressing on, putting mile after long mile behind them. Prairie was taking it better than Iver, whose behind and inner legs were rubbed almost raw. Late in the afternoon they saw another herd of Bison and watched a smaller herd of antelope skirt around them. Beyond the herd, along the bank of the stream and a few miles to the west, was what appeared to be a cabin? Iver decided to make his way around the herd and investigate, since this was the first sign of civilization that he had seen. He reached it in a little over an hour and found a small, round corral with some horses and a cowboy riding one of them. A lady came to the door of the combination wood, earth, and rock cabin and said hello...surprisingly in a Norwegian accent. Iver was never so glad to see and hear a fellow Norwegian. They were the Larson family, a family who would become lifelong friends of the Tenolds. Two Norwegian families together on the prairie of South Dakota, from what seemed like a million miles and another planet away from their native Norway.

The woman's name was Reidun, and she introduced her husband, Odd, in the same broken Norwegian that Iver knew. It felt like a family reunion to Iver, and even Prairie seemed a little excited. Iver asked them if they knew of his uncle Christian Olson.

"Of course we do!" Reidun said. "We wouldn't be here if Christian hadn't told us about this land. He is your uncle? He never even told us he had relatives coming."

Reidun asked if Iver would like to stay for supper since it was already dark. It was an hours' ride to Christian's place, and Iver could get an early start in the morning. Iver said he would really like that, and his horse could use the rest too. He got off and tried to walk normally, but Reidun burst out laughing at him. She apologized when Iver seemed a little bit embarrassed, explaining that they had the same problem when they first arrived.

"Once you get used to it you can ride forever and not get sore," she said. "You just have to toughen up that tender hide on your rear end."

Reidun turned to go back inside. "I'm going to fry up some fresh antelope steak for supper. Odd just got him yesterday and he is as fat as a butterball. Their meat is even better than our Norwegian fresh caught cod."

She was right; Iver had never had such a good steak in his life. Maybe it was because he was truly starving after only having a dozen apples and a cottontail in three days, but it was indeed a feast fit for the king of Norway. He couldn't believe his grand fortune, finding such good people way out here in the middle of nowhere. This "grand" thought brought to mind the river.

"Where is this "grand" River?" he asked Odd. "I've been watching for it, and I have to admit that I'm glad I missed it as river crossings can be pretty hard and dangerous. I don't even know if my horse is a good swimmer."

Odd and Reidun laughed again. "Well, Iver, you've crossed it twice already. You crossed it about a day south of Dickinson and you crossed it again just now to get to our house."

Iver had to laugh at this too, all that worrying about crossing the two forks of the "Grand" River; which turned out to be a small stream about three feet deep. "In its defense," Odd said, "it can be a lot wider and deeper in the spring when the ice breaks up and the snow melts."

With his belly full of steak and his horse happily in the corral, Iver now knew for sure that he had found his home here on the prairie. God had made it just for him it seemed, and he went to sleep on their porch feeling safe, contented, and thankful.

In the morning Reidun made Iver some biscuits to take with him on his ride to his uncle's and asked him to give some of them to Chris. Iver said over and over how thankful he was to have met the Larson family and that he would be most pleased to repay their kindness (which he did many times throughout their lives). Odd said he wished he had time to ride along and visit Christian (Reidun and Odd called him Chris), but he just had too much to get done before winter set in. Iver wondered to himself, how bad can winter be in this nice country? He would later find out that winter in this land could be a matter of life or death and that it wasn't anything to take lightly. Odd took Iver to a bluff above the Grand River and pointed to what he called the Slim Buttes a few miles to the southwest.

Odd told him, "If you find that wagon trail, follow it west and you can't miss Chris's place, right there at the base of those buttes that look like great big ships sailing on an ocean. Come and see us again, Iver. We will be happy for the company. We get together with Chris once in a while but it is never enough. This land may seem gentle as a kitten right now, but it can be very harsh and can roar like a mountain lion. This time of the year is mostly spent in preparation for winter."

Iver thanked Odd once more and guided Prairie toward those battleships in the middle of the ocean of prairie.

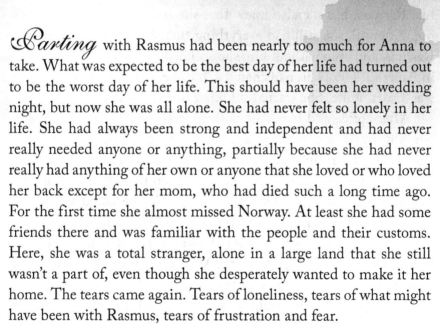

9

Good-Bye

Parting with Rasmus had been nearly too much for Anna to take. What was expected to be the best day of her life had turned out to be the worst day of her life. This should have been her wedding night, but now she was all alone. She had never felt so lonely in her life. She had always been strong and independent and had never really needed anyone or anything, partially because she had never really had anything of her own or anyone that she loved or who loved her back except for her mom, who had died such a long time ago. For the first time she almost missed Norway. At least she had some friends there and was familiar with the people and their customs. Here, she was a total stranger, alone in a large land that she still wasn't a part of, even though she desperately wanted to make it her home. The tears came again. Tears of loneliness, tears of what might have been with Rasmus, tears of frustration and fear.

After an awful night of terrible dreams and sleeplessness, Anna went to visit Donna to ask her if she might be able to stay another day. She had virtually no money, but she would ask Donna if she could pay her back for the lodging after finding some work. What else could she do? She didn't want to beg or to be a bother, but she didn't want to sleep on the streets of New York either. Donna saw Anna's red eyes and tear-stained cheeks. She saw the strain on her beautiful young face. Donna ran to her and gave her a huge hug.

"Don't worry, honey. Rasmus left me a letter with some money and instructions to take care of you and let you stay as long as you want. Come, I'll show it to you. Then we can decide what you'll do after you've had some hot coffee and breakfast."

Donna took Anna to the office and showed her the letter from Rasmus and gave Anna the $50. Anna started crying again after reading it, knowing that it was the last thing she would ever have to remind her of Rasmus. He had done the last thing that he could for her out of his love for her, and had probably given her the last of his money. Anna knew that she would never meet another man like Rasmus, but she also knew that she had to move on with her life. After all, she still had everything that she had before meeting Rasmus, and even without him she still had her dreams of a new life in America. Her plans had changed, but she understood that change was a part of life. She started thinking like the old Anna again.

After coffee and breakfast with Donna, Anna asked her if she had any work or if she had any friends that needed help. Donna had already been thinking about this. "I'm so sorry," she said, "but I couldn't possibly afford any help here, even though I could use it. Tell you what; if you make the beds and do the laundry you can stay here for free until we find you a good job. That café down by the courthouse had a help wanted sign in the window yesterday and we can start looking there, ok? Why don't you take a nice walk downtown and see if they still have that sign in the window? The walk and the fresh air would do you good and help you clear your mind. Let's get together for dinner and maybe one of us will have some good news, ok?"

Anna thanked Donna again. "Donna, I was so fortunate to have met you and to have you as a friend. I don't know what I'd ever have done without you."

"I think you would have survived just fine, Anna, but thanks. I needed a friend too."

Anna put on her new dress, the one she had planned to get

married in. She was so thankful that she had just gotten a nice dress rather than some fancy wedding gown that she wouldn't have any further use for. As it had turned out, she wouldn't have even used it. This thought made her sad again, but she combed her long hair, but it in a bun as she always did, and tried to put a smile on her face. Today was the first day of the rest of her life, even if it wasn't what she had planned it to be. On her way to the café, Anna passed the church again, the same one she had prayed in a couple days earlier. Anna hadn't prayed since then, and she needed to. Many in her position would have blamed God for what had happened and would have been asking Him why He had let her down, but not Anna. Her faith was deep and wide, not shallow enough to blame God for her circumstances. She again thanked God for getting her to America and asked Him to look after her. She asked Him to forgive her if she hadn't been all He wanted her to be. And she said a prayer for Rasmus that he would receive the happiness he deserved and that he would find work and be able to make a new home for his family in America. Anna wanted him to be happy and successful, even if she couldn't be a part of it.

The café was almost empty as the breakfast customers were gone and the dinner crowd wouldn't show up for another hour or two. The help wanted sign was still in the window, so Anna went in and asked about it.

"Hold on a minute, honey," the lady behind the counter said. "I'll get the owner and he can tell you all about it."

The owner seemed a bit frustrated as he was short-handed and had to help with the cooking. He came out of the kitchen and looked Anna over. "You got any experience in the restaurant business? What's your name? How old are you?"

Anna blushed a bit and started with her name. "I'm Anna, and no, I've never worked in a restaurant. But I can cook and I can clean and I can bake. My English is getting pretty good and I can write some, so I could also take orders. I am honest and I work hard." Then she added, "I am eighteen years old," which of course wasn't the truth but Anna was desperate.

Tom doubted that she was that old, but he was having a hard time finding good help. "I'll train you in the business if you work for half price until I can depend on you," he said. "When you show me that you are worth it I'll promote you to full wages."

Anna looked squarely at Tom and asked what "full wages" would be.

"I can give you twenty-five cents an hour, and you can keep your tips if you turn out to be really good and dependable. Until then I will give you 15 cents an hour and keep your tips for myself."

Anna thought it over, and to Tom's relief she took him up on the offer. She added that if she wasn't pulling her weight and getting full pay within one week she would move on. "When can I start working?" asked Anna.

"How about right now? We'll see what you are made of this very afternoon. You can either take orders or wash dishes, your choice."

Anna didn't want to get any dishwater on her new dress so she chose taking orders. She just hoped that Donna would forgive her for not keeping their noontime dinner date.

Tom only had three things on the menu for supper, so taking orders was easy for Anna. The customers, especially the male customers, took to her immediately and even helped her with their orders. Anna was her usual cheerful and pleasant self, with that made-to-order smile that a good waitress needed. She got a couple of things wrong, but was quick to correct her mistakes and apologize. The men left some of the best tips Tom had seen. In fact, just about all of them left tips, which was very unusual. He put them in his pocket and didn't let Anna know that she had done so well. No sense in spoiling the new employee right away, he thought to himself. When the supper crowd had left, Anna helped clean up and asked when she should be there in the morning. Since she was being hired mainly as a cook she offered to come in early and bake some fresh bread and make some pancake batter for the breakfast customers.

Tom encouraged it. "Come in between four and five and we'll see what your bread turns out like."

Anna left for the boarding house and couldn't wait to tell Donna the good news that she had found a job and to apologize for missing dinner.

When Anna returned with her job news, Donna was happy for her even though she had been looking forward to having Anna help her at the boarding house. They visited until late in the evening about the plans both of them were making. Donna wanted Anna to make New York her home forever, but Anna wasn't so excited about it. She could see the hurry and the worry and the indifference on most of the New Yorkers' faces. Anna decided that if she ever found a place to stay for the rest of her life it would be someplace in the country where people appreciated each other and where you were a name, not a number. In the back of her mind, she could remember what the Dangerud family had said about a wild and free land out west in the middle of America where someone could make their own destiny. That was more of the reason why she came to America. That would be her goal and her new dream. And right now, Anna desperately needed a new dream.

Four a.m. came fast. Anna had put her good dress away and walked to the café in her work clothes determined to show Tom what she could do. When she arrived, she had to wait a few minutes for Tom, but he soon showed up and unlocked the door. "I wasn't sure you would come," he admitted.

"Let's make those customers of yours some food they will look forward to," she replied. "I need the milk, cream, eggs, butter, sugar, and baking powder." She frowned when she saw the cream and eggs, and gracefully requested, "I will need thick, rich farm cream and fresh farm eggs with bright yellow yokes from now on, Tom. If you want good bread and pancakes, you have to start with good ingredients."

Anna soon had bread in the oven and had pancake batter mixed up. Tom's face brightened when he smelled the bread baking. Hiring Anna might've been the best decision he had made in a long time. "I think we will have pancakes and eggs with some bacon for our breakfast special today, Anna. What do you think?"

Anna agreed and added, "If pancakes are the special, why don't we slice up some of those apples and put them in the batter. That way they will be really special."

About then the cook, Roberto, and the waitress/till lady, Evilynn, came in. "What smells so good in here?" they chimed in unison. Anna brought the first loaves of bread out of the oven to cool and showed Roberto the pancake batter that was to be used for the breakfast specials.

"I ain't ever seen the like," he said. "These pancakes are going to be more like apple pie!"

Tom wanted Anna to try the waitress position too, so she put on a clean apron and waited by the door for their first customers. When the first three of them arrived Anna greeted them with that huge smile of hers and welcomed them to "Tom's Diner" as she showed them to a table. "We have a breakfast special of pancakes, eggs, and bacon, or you can just have some fresh bread and butter and jam with breakfast if you don't feel like pancakes."

The three customers had never been greeted at the door before, nor had they experienced this kind of special treatment. Instead of being their usual gruff selves, they took another look at Anna and smiled back. Old Tom was even smiling to himself.

"Tom's Diner, huh? This place needed a name, I reckon."

The pancakes were a smashing hit, along with the fresh bread. They made the eggs and bacon a lot tastier. One customer who had never said a word to anyone in the café before commented that these were the best pancakes in New York. In fact they were the best he had ever eaten.

"If you think these were good," Anna replied, "come back tomorrow and they will be better if I can get the boss (she winked at him) to buy me some premium eggs and cream."

"I'll be here. You can count on it. Matter of fact I might just eat all my meals here from now on. Got no cook at home."

"We'll be here again, too," said two young men in the corner. They had been giving Anna the eye since arriving. "The food and the scenery are a lot better than the last time we ate here."

The day went by quickly—never a dull moment. Anna was

like the new princess in town, and just having her there seemed to make the food smell and taste better. The customers all seemed pleased, even those who had been indifferent in the past. Tom wasn't the brightest candle on the block but he noticed. Even Roberto and Evilynn took note and complimented Anna on how tasty and wonderful the fresh bread and pancakes had been.

At the end of the day, Anna was really beat, especially since she had been up most of the night worrying about how the day would go. Tom asked her if she would sit with him for a minute, so she poured them both some coffee and they sat at the counter. "I'm not too good with words," he started. "I suspect that you figured when I hired you that I would keep you at half pay for as long as I could, and that's why you kept me to a week. I guess I'm kind of stingy, and you were right to think that. Truth is you've only been here a day, and I already don't know what I'd do without you, Anna. I kept your tips and half of your pay yesterday afternoon, but I intend to give it back. And I'm gonna put you up to full pay right away. Just wouldn't be right any other way. Now you get on home and don't worry about cleaning up the dishes. You deserve a good night's rest. I'll fetch you some fresh thick cream and some better eggs for the morning. I was thinking of some good ol' beef stew for dinner tomorrow. You ever made stew?"

Anna couldn't wait to get back and tell Donna about her first day at work. She was pleased with herself and knew that she had done her very best. Working hard wasn't unique to this immigrant, and knowing she had done well and had helped others a little along the way made Anna feel good. Donna was all excited and made Anna go over every minute of the day with her. "I want to live it with you," she exclaimed. "Your little café makes my boarding house seem so boring. I almost wish I could work there with you."

Anna smiled at Donna. Having a friend again was really nice. "It isn't that exciting Donna. And it can really wear you out, speaking of which I am very tired and had better get to my room. I have an early date tomorrow."

"A date?" asked Donna expectantly.

"You betcha," Anna replied forgetting her proper English, "with a really good looking batch of cream and eggs."

"Darn," replied Donna, "I was thinking of something a little more interesting."

The next morning, Tom was at the diner early, waiting for Anna. He couldn't wait to show her his purchases of the thicker, fresher cream and huge eggs he had found.

"You did good boss," Anna smiled. "The bread and the batter'll be better than ever. Did you find some fresh veggies and beef for the stew? I'll make extra bread. Nothing better than fresh bread, butter, and good beef stew. I've got a few special spices that my mom taught me to use. They make the broth just burst with flavor."

The same breakfast crowd that was there yesterday showed up again, and this time they brought friends with them. Anna had to rush into the kitchen to make another batch of 'cakes to keep up with the demand. Today she had added a few blueberries to the batter.

"I thought those apple ones were the best I'd eaten, but these are even tastier," said the old bachelor. "I'm gonna get fat you keep feeding me like this!"

Dinner and supper were the same, and even Roberto remarked that he had never made better stew in his life and asked if Anna would teach him how to use the spices. Anna went around and asked the customers if they would like a little more stew, and none of them turned her down.

At the end of the day, Evilynn took count of the till and said they had the best day since she started working there, up nearly 50%. "What're we gonna do, Tom? At this rate you'll need another diner, or at least you'll have to add another room."

Tom chuckled and went out back to retrieve a new sign for their building. It read

Tom's Diner
Best 'Cakes in New York

They all cheered and Evilynn said, "'Bout time this joint had a name. Makes it feel more like a real eating establishment. Why don't you and Roberto go hang it up above the door while Anna and I clean up?"

"No way," said Tom. "Anna is up at least three hours before the lot of us. She needs her beauty rest so she can keep all those big tipping young men coming."

Anna blushed and gave her apron to Evilynn. "Sorry Evilynn, bosses orders. By the way, what's tomorrow's special? How about some of those—what're they called?—you know the cooked ground meat in tomato sauce mix on fresh buns served with pickles? They seem to be an American favorite. We'll include some potato soup and something sweet. I might even find time to bake one of my mom's favorite desserts. She could bake the best apple pie in all of Norway. Her crust alone made many a Norwegian's mouth water. When she made a pie for the Sunday social, it always brought the top kroner—I mean, top *dollar*."

The week turned into a month, and the weather turned cloudy and colder with winter's approach. Anna asked Donna if she could stay there until spring, which pleased Donna. "Please don't EVER leave, Anna," she said. "I'd never find another friend like you in a million years."

Anna didn't make any promises, even though she had grown really fond of Donna too. Her heart was still set on living in the country, and the land out in Dakota sounded more exotic than ever. Anna had inquired about Nils Dangerud and learned that he was living less than a day away. She wanted to visit with him about how his family was doing, especially Tove and their daughter Heidi, whom Anna had helped get back to Norway when they were forced to leave Ellis Island. She also wanted to find out about Nils's friends in Dakota and see if there was a way to contact them. She was determined to ask her boss for a couple of days off so she could go visit Nils and his sons. Anna knew that winter travel wouldn't be easy, so she asked him the first chance she got.

Tom told her, "I know you need a little time for yourself, Anna, but truth be told business has gotten so busy I'd fall on my face without you here. Those two guys from the factory keep asking me if you would date one of them. Like I'm your father or something." He paused and thought for a second. "Guess I do feel sort of like that sometimes. Let's try to find another waitress and get you some time off, ok?"

He reluctantly gave Anna the next weekend plus the following Monday off. She asked Donna if she wanted to ride along, but Donna wasn't able to get away. Anna checked around for transportation and discovered that she could take a bus to the edge of town and that the bus stop was within a couple of hours of where Nils lived. Early Saturday morning, she started on her way to another new adventure. Anna enjoyed being at the diner, but she was long overdue for doing something else and getting her mind off of her work. This trip to the edge of New York to see Nils and his family would be just what she needed to keep her spirits up during the coming winter days. She arrived mid day and walked from where the bus stopped to Nils' home, breaking into a run when it was in sight. The house was small but neat, and Anna guessed correctly that Nils and his family were doing well. She knocked on the door, whereupon little Nils junior appeared, looking like he had grown an inch or two. He remembered Anna right away and was excited to let her in.

"Is your papa home?" Anna asked. "I'm sure hoping he is 'cause I've come a long way to visit with you and see how your family is doing."

Just then Nils came around from the back of the house. He was both shocked and delighted to see her. "Why Anna dear, I thought you'd been long gone with that good lookin' Rasmus fellow of yours by now. Did you two get hitched?"

Anna's smile faded at the mention of Rasmus and she replied, "We have a lot of catching up to do Nils. I'm sorry I didn't have a way to let you know I was coming today and I really want to have some time with you. Are you busy now?"

"Of course not, my dear Anna!" he replied. "I'll always have time for you, child. We feel like you saved our family and you are the one that gave us hope for the future. Because of you I am here and have found good work and am making a real home for my family, one that we never would have had in Norway. Come on in dear Anna, we must catch up. Did you see how Nils Junior has grown?"

"Where is that Erik?"

"He has grown too and is working along side me at the construction site. He should be home pretty soon."

"Do you like it here?" Anna asked.

"We love it here. I don't think the wood is as good as we had in Norway, but the business is boomin', as they say in America. I hope to have our own Dangerud homebuilding business soon."

Nils was full of good news and couldn't wait to tell Anna that Tove and their little daughter Heidi had made it safely back to Norway. Heidi had almost fully recovered by the time the ship reached their homeland, and Nils had already nearly saved enough money for their return passage to America.

"For your kindness and quick thinking we are in debt to you, Anna," he continued. "I am hoping to build Tove a house of her own, maybe even start on it before she comes back. Do you think she would mind? I know how you ladies like to plan your houses."

Anna assured Nils that she thought that Tove would not only not mind but that she would be delighted that he had started building it. "Just make her a nice kitchen and a bedroom of your own and rooms for the kids." She paused for a moment. "Maybe a screened in porch for a place to sit and read. That's all we women need, Nils. I know you will make it warm and comfortable."

Nils smiled and changed the subject. "And how about you, Anna. Do you and Rasmus have a home of your own yet? I know a little about his family. Master builders, right? I'm guessing that if he has started building the house you two talked about it will have only the very best wood and the best workmanship of any home in America."

Anna slowly began telling Nils what had happened, and that she didn't even know where Rasmus and his wife were living. It brought tears to her eyes, and Nils apologized for not knowing what had happened and for bringing it up. "I thought I detected a little sadness when I first mentioned his name upon your arrival."

"It's ok, Nils. I have to get on with my life and it's for the best that I don't even know where they are living. I might be tempted to visit and see how he is doing, and I doubt that my heart could take seeing him with his wife. I need to confess to you that I didn't just come here to see how your family is doing and to find out if Tove and Heidi made it safely back and if Heidi had recovered." She looked away as if dreaming of someplace else and continued, "I don't want to live in the city all my life, and I was wondering if you could tell me about your friends in Dakota? Have you been able to find out how they are doing and what life there is like? It sounds wonderful to me, like a place that I could start a new life and build a real future in."

Nils started telling her what he knew about the Wild West and the lands of Dakota. His friends had indeed made it there and had found the land to be very cheap, but it was wild and untamed and dangerous. He explained, "I don't think that it's a place for a beautiful young woman like you Anna. You need to find a New York congressman or doctor or a lawyer and make a life here as the fine lady that you are. I don't think that Indians, outlaws, and wild creatures should be your future."

Anna was undeterred by these comments and asked Nils to tell her more about this wilderness. So Nils continued to tell her what he knew about Dakota. "The best way to get there is probably by train from New York to Chicago to Minneapolis and west from there," he explained. Nils didn't know if there really were still Indians and outlaws, but he did know that there was an abundance of wild animals like wolves, coyotes, mountain lions, and bear. He told her that his friends that were living there really hadn't told him a lot about what they did and how well they were doing. "I've only heard from them once," he said, "but they promised to write again. There is hardly any mail service from that desolate place, and I think their nearest post office is over a hundred miles away in North Dakota. Come to think about it, they did say there was a brand new railroad station and settlement starting up two or three days from their homestead. I think Odd said that a new railroad was working its way west through southern North Dakota. He may have called it the Milwaukee line."

Nils scratched his head in thought and continued, "The Larsons are fine, hard-working folks, and if any family can tame a country like that it's people like the Larsons. Odd was always one of those adventurous types that enjoyed making things out of whatever he had. His wife Reidun even reminds me of you, Anna—a tall, pretty, and independent lady who can do almost anything that any man can. You would enjoy them Anna, but I still think that you should stay here. How Tove would love to see you when she arrives."

Anna made Nils promise that he would write to the Larson's and get more information about South Dakota for her. Then Nils wanted to hear all about her new friends and her job in the city. It was getting late in the afternoon and Anna asked Nils if there was a boarding home or hotel near by that she could stay the night in before returning to her boarding house.

"Oh Anna," he said. "If you can stay over, please do us the honor of staying here. You can have the boys' room and they can either roll up a bed on the floor or stay in their tree house that I made them in the backyard. They love it and they won't have many more nights to stay there before the end of fall. I'm afraid that it will be an early winter from the way the boys on the job site talk." Nils paused and looked toward the kitchen. "We aren't much for cooks, but we can see what we have. We truly would love to have you as our guest for the night, and I will walk you to the bus station in the morning. You will be our first guest in this house, and the kids will love having company. There is a little spot near that bus station where we can have a cup of coffee while we wait for the bus in the morning. Please, Anna. One of the things I miss the most is being able to visit with folks from home."

Anna stayed the night and visited until late with Nils and his boys. She got their address and gave them the boarding house address where she was staying. She made Nils promise to get in touch with the Larsons for her, and she in turn promised to come and visit them again and let them know what she had decided about leaving or staying.

Nils kept his word and walked Anna to the bus station. He

even offered to buy her ticket, but Anna refused saying that she was making good wages and tip money at the café and that Rasmus had left her a little money to help too. "Besides," she told Nils, "you need to save every penny so you can get your wife and daughter back to America as soon as possible. You must miss them desperately, as they must miss you. If anything I should give you some of my savings to help pay their passage." She paused and thought about it. "Tell you what Nils Dangerud; I will pay for Tove's passage if you can pay for Heidi's. That way you can get them here even sooner, as soon as the ocean is safe for spring travel. When you get your business going—and I know you will—you can pay me back if you want to. I also think that you should see what second-class costs to make sure that Heidi doesn't get sick again, and as I remember second-class passengers don't even have to go through Ellis Island. They get into America much easier than we poor steerage folks did. If we can get enough money that is exactly what we must do Nils."

Nils could see the old Anna coming through, trying to save them again. Here she was, needing every penny to start a life of her own, yet offering to help them out. He said, "Anna Ingevich, you are nothing short of being an angel. I will check on second-class for my ladies. I wouldn't have even thought of it, but how I would love to have my girls travel in style. I would die if Heidi got sick and they were deported again." Nils stopped and fancied a thought. "I wish one of my boys was your age, Anna, so I could have hopes of getting you as my daughter-in-law. I think you may just have saved us Dangeruds a second time."

They both saw the bus pull in and start unloading passengers; it would be leaving to go back into town again in fifteen minutes. Nils gave Anna a big hug, and Anna made him promise to look her up when he needed the money for passage tickets. Nils had tears in his eyes when Anna got on the bus, and Anna had a happy heart.

When Anna returned to the boarding house, Donna was excited to see her. "I missed you so much. I know, I know—you've only been gone a little over a day but it seemed like a month to me. Why don't we take a walk to the park and watch the birds and ducks for a while?

We won't have many more chances before winter hits and it will do us both good to get out. I'll wear my best dress and you can wear yours too. How about that? It's too late for the service or I'd even go to that church of yours with you."

"Will you?" asked Anna. "I'd love that. And yes, let's go to the park and stretch our legs. That was a long bus ride."

"Mine could sure use stretching, Anna, but those long legs of yours don't need it." Anna was easily eight inches taller than Donna.

When they got to the park, one of the boys that came to the diner daily noticed Anna and asked if he could have a word with her. She was always so busy at the diner, so he never seemed to get the chance to talk to her. Donna got the hint and asked if she might be excused so she could go feed the ducks. David almost lost his nerve, but bashfully asked Anna to sit on the park bench with him. Anna hadn't been with a young man since Rasmus, and she was a little reluctant. But at the same time, she felt a little sorry for David, who she could see was having trouble getting his words out.

Finally, he spoke: "Anna, I see you at the diner every day, and I think that you are the most beautiful girl in New York. I've said this a thousand times but only to myself or in my dreams. I'm sure that you haven't even noticed me, but I just had to tell you what I thought. Anna, would you possibly go on a date with me sometime? Would you ever consider someone like me? I know you'd have to get to know me better, but I feel like I've known you forever. Would you please just give it some thought?"

Anna sat there for a minute, a little taken back by all that David had to say. She felt bad, but it wouldn't be right to string this boy on. "Can I call you David?" she said. "I have to say 'No.'" David was obviously crushed and looked down at the ground. Anna continued, "It isn't you, David. You see, I've just been engaged to get married and had to break off the engagement. My heart is still broken, and I'm just not ready to put it on the line again. I have noticed you, and I think you are a fine young man from what I've seen of you in the diner. You are handsome to boot. I think that any young lady would be lucky to have a date with you. And if my heart hadn't just been broken, I would have jumped at the chance."

David picked himself up a little at these words. "I still think you are the most beautiful and wonderful girl in New York. If you change your mind please let me know. It would make me the happiest guy in the world to have a date with you." David gave her a shy smile and Anna gave him a little hug. "Will I see you at the diner tomorrow, Anna?"

"Of course, David. I'll cook up something really special, just for you."

Donna couldn't wait to hear the news and was disappointed when Anna told her that she had turned David down. She said, "You can't pine your life away dreaming of Rasmus, Anna. You need to start dating again."

"Maybe you are right, Donna, but my heart just isn't up to it yet. Rasmus was the love of my life, and it will take a lot of time for me to get over him. I might never, unless of course another handsome Norwegian comes along again," she teased. "Let's start back, Donna. You've made my day wonderful, and I even enjoyed sitting with David. You didn't put him up to asking me out when my back was turned, did you Donna?"

"Not on my life, Anna! I would have kept him for myself."

Over time, work was getting even busier and more and demanding. Anna was beginning to feel the stress. Her pie and bread and pancakes, along with those long legs and her smile, had made her something of a celebrity in the area. Tom's business had doubled and tripled, to the point where he had to move into a bigger building and hire extra waitresses and another cook. He had put Anna in charge of nearly everything, so she roamed from the kitchen where she still made her famous goodies to the dining hall where she helped take orders and greeted all of the customers.

"I swear, Anna," Tom remarked, "you seem to know every one that walks through those doors and they all know you. I'm glad you aren't in politics, or you'd be the mayor by now."

"Well," said Anna, "I have been asked to run."

Her boss gulped but then saw the twinkle in her eyes. "Pullin' the boss's leg again, eh? You know though that I'd be the first in line to give a big political donation, all that you've done for me. I was a broke, old hash-slinger when I met you, ready for the poor house. You've made me into one of the up and coming businessmen in the city in just a few months. Hiring you was the best thing I've ever done in my entire life. I must be smarter than I thought? Winter hasn't even slowed our business down."

It was almost the end of February when Anna had a visit from Nils. He had found a ship with second class passage for Tove and Heidi, and if Anna could still lend him some money he would pay for their passage right now so that he would be sure they got a ticket. He would need thirty-five dollars, and if she couldn't loan him that much he would surely understand. Anna went to her savings stash in her bedroom. She knew that she would need about seventy-five dollars to get her train tickets and the other items that she would need when she left for Dakota. It would be close, but she still had another month before she planned to leave, provided the weather cooperated.

She got out the thirty-five dollars and gave it to Nils. She said that she hoped she would still be here when his ladies arrived, but she wasn't sure since she was planning to leave as soon as the weather broke in the spring. Nils thanked her again and again for the money saying that he would pay her back with interest as soon as he possibly could. Anna smiled and nodded in agreement, then asked if he had heard from the Larsons yet. He said he hadn't but was sure he would soon and he would let her know when he did.

"We are going to have the grandest family reunion ever when Tove and Heidi get here, Anna. You would sure make us proud if you would be there too. You are just as much our family as our own flesh and blood. Without you, we'd be back in Norway starving with no hope for the future." He hugged Anna good-bye. She was too teary-eyed to reply.

Anna made a couple of trips to the train station early in March and inquired about ticket pricing and how the weather would be for the trip. The ticket agent told her, "You just never know, young lady, but I think it would be safe for you to leave pretty soon. Both Chicago and Minneapolis can get bad spring storms. March and April are totally unpredictable. We can even get storms in May. But by and large it should be ok. The worst that can happen is a few days' delay. It will cost you extra food money but won't affect your tickets. They will have been paid for and we will get to your destination…as soon as it is possible."

Anna hadn't told Tom or Evelynn or anyone at the diner. She knew that she would have to break it to them sooner or later, but later seemed easier. It would be hard to do. Donna suspected that Anna was thinking about leaving but was still holding out hope that Anna would stay at least for another year. She had even offered to help Anna start a restaurant of her own. Maybe they could go in together fifty-fifty and run a hotel with a fine dining room? Anna was grateful for the offer and for Donna's confidence, but she still had that crazy Dakota dream in her head. Besides, she had seen Rasmus from a distance one day, and even though it had been months her heart seemed to break all over again. New York just wasn't big enough for both of them.

Later that week Nils paid another visit. He had heard from the Larson family, and they were anxious to meet Anna if she came to Dakota. Of course Nils had told them how Anna had saved his family and helped the Dangeruds through the worst time of their life. The Larsons promised him that if they could be of any help to Anna they would do everything in their power to do it. They would even meet her at the new train station in Hettinger if they could get her train schedule.

Anna went to the train station the next day and bought her tickets through to Minneapolis. She figured that she would be a bit short on cash and planned to work for three or four months in Minnesota before continuing to Dakota. While there she would learn to shoot a rifle and ride a horse if possible. She was going out into the wilderness, and she was going to go prepared.

The hard part was saying good-bye to her friends in New York.

Anna knew that this would include Rasmus, even if he wasn't aware of it. Leaving New York would be her final good-bye to him in her heart. There would be no more chance sightings or no more hoping that he would come see her. She would finally be able to start a new chapter in her life. Maybe it wasn't really the lure of the west that was moving her. Maybe it was as simple as trying to say a final good-bye to Rasmus.

She was leaving in two weeks and needed a day or two to get another change of clothes for the trip. A better trunk would be nice, but her old one would do. It was stamped Ellis Island and meant a lot to her. She knew that she had to start saying her good-byes and that most of all she had to tell Tom. He had grown to count on her for almost everything, and she knew that he would feel like it was the end of the world.

She broke it to him that morning, and he sulked all day. Anna tried to convince him that it was for the best, that he could find even better help than she had been, but he was despondent. "I might as well sell out now," he complained. "You practically do everything; all I do is watch you take care of the place. Without you, Evilynn and the rest of the crew might even quit me."

"Tell you what," Anna said. "I think that Evilynn has more gumption and more brains than you give her credit for. Why don't we give her a chance to run this place? She knows the customers as well as I do, and she has run the register honestly since I've been here. I will give the cooks my secret recipes and then oversee Evilynn in her new capacity until I have to leave. My money is on that girl, Tom. I think she has what it takes to keep this outfit going if we help her get started."

Tom gave it some thought and then shouted across the diner, "Hey, Evilynn! Would you come over and have a talk with Anna and me?"

It wasn't any easier with Donna, but Donna understood what Anna was going through, and deep down she knew that Anna had to leave New York and Rasmus behind. "We would have been good together, Anna. I'll bet that we would have had the best hotel and fine dining in all of New York."

"You have that right," replied Anna. "Don't you think for a minute that I'll ever forget you and your kindness. Without you, I might have just gotten on that ship and went to back to Norway. I hope you'll come and visit me in that Dakota wilderness some day, as soon as I get it tamed down of course. You have been like a sister to me since I arrived in New York. How will I ever get by without you, my dear Donna?"

Anna had made arrangements to say good-bye to Nils and the boys, and he had promised to take her to the train station in the morning after staying the night with them. She was so sorry that she couldn't stay long enough to welcome Tove and Heidi, but ships were unpredictable and it might be another few weeks before their arrival. "Besides," she told Nils, "leaving would be even harder for me once they arrive. Now is the time to go." Nils understood, but it was still going to be a long and teary-eyed trip to the train station in the morning.

Anna had packed all of her belongings and her new outfit, along with new socks and shoes in her trunk. Nils had made her sandwiches and had bought some apples and other fruit for her trip. He also put five dollars in the bag with a little note that read: "I still owe you $30 and will pay you the rest as soon as possible." Nils reluctantly but admiringly said good-bye, as did Anna. He stood on the platform waving as the train departed and was still waving when he disappeared from Anna's sight.

Anna looked out the window and dried her eyes as she whispered her final good-bye to Rasmus.

10

Grandfather Williams

On the train, Anna introduced herself to the lady sitting across from her. The older lady looked up and told Anna in a strained voice that she was Gertrude but her friends called her Gert. She seemed nervous and went on to tell Anna that she had never traveled by train before. She was going to Minneapolis, too, to visit her younger sister and her family. Gert was terrified that she would get lost in the Chicago terminal and not be able to find her train connection there. "Don't worry, Gert. I'll help you and we'll get there together, ok?"

A huge smile of relief appeared on Gert's face, and she thanked Anna. What Gert didn't know was that Anna had never traveled by train before either, and that she was also apprehensive about Chicago. But now she had committed herself to helping Gert. Anna knew she had a day to figure it out and that someone on the train could explain what they needed to do once they got there. She dug into the lunch bag that Nils had packed and offered Gert an apple.

"Oh my goodness, you are a kind one," said Gert. "I'd love an apple. I've been so worried all morning that I haven't eaten anything."

Apples—and any fruit—were really hard to get this time of the year. "I also have some lefsa if you would prefer that, Gert."

They both watched businesses and homes go by their window until they became sparser and sparser and the city turned into country.

It was a marvelous way to travel. A dining car offered food (if you could afford it), and some of the passengers even had a place where they could lie down to take a nap or sleep for the night. Neither Anna nor Gert had these accommodations, but they both were fine with sleeping in their seats. Since train travel was new to both of them, everything seemed exciting and adventurous. Even the noise of the steel wheels on the tracks and the smell of the engine smoke didn't deter their ebullience. Anna told Gert about steerage on the ship and how horrible it had been. Compared to steerage on the ship, sleeping in a seat with fresh air, some food in your stomach, and listening to the steady pounding of the rails was a pure joy. Anna thought that she could get used to this; even the rocking motion as they banked into turns was a thrill. They were offered free water to drink, and they even had toilets to use. This was traveling in style!

After some time, Anna noticed that Gert was closing her eyes for a nap, so she decided to rest too. Before long, she was dreaming. It was a grand dream about open prairies and her new life. She woke up smiling, which she took as a sign from God that this was going to turn out all for the best. She started to close her eyes again, not to sleep but to say a nice, long prayer of thanks. After all, Anna had a lot to be thankful for and a lot to look forward to. Just then she saw a porter walk by.

Gert was still sleeping, so Anna whispered to him, "Would you be so kind as to explain to me what we do when we reach Chicago and how we make sure that we get on the right train to Minneapolis?"

"Of course, young lady," he replied. "It's a large station, but not quite as big or as complicated as New York. All you have to do is to read the schedules when you get off of this train and look for the passenger train to Minneapolis and when it departs. There will be loudspeaker announcements and directions to your train. If it all seems too complicated or if you have a hard time reading, I will be glad to be of assistance."

"Oh, thank you so much," Anna said. "You have taken all of my worry away! I had offered to help another passenger without really knowing how to do it myself."

Gert opened an eye and said with a smile, "I heard that, Anna."

Anna thanked the man again for his help and asked him about when they would be getting into Chicago.

"About one p.m. tomorrow, Miss. Can I get you two ladies a blanket and a pillow for the night?"

Anna went to sleep easily, letting the motion rock her to sleep. She was hoping to start the same dream that she had awoken from during her afternoon nap, but that didn't happen. She woke up during the night and just sat for a long time staring out into the darkness, wondering about life on the prairie, praying that she would get there and be able to survive and truly start a new life. Then, as always, her thoughts turned to Rasmus. She tried so hard to keep those thoughts from her mind, or at least deeply buried, but try as she might they always seemed to come to the surface again. At least now when he crept in, she was able to smile and pray that he was happy and doing well. She was determined to have shed her last tear over what could have been. She had so many happy times with him, and from now on if he popped into her mind those good times would be what she would dwell on.

Anna was lonely, and more and more often her thoughts drifted back to Norway. She really had loved the North Sea and the city of Bergen with its huge fish market and all sorts of vendors. She dearly missed her mother and maybe, just maybe, Marion had some justification in the way she had treated Anna. After all, she had her own children to think of and worry about. Anna had actually been begrudgingly thanking Marion for pushing her out of her home when she had been with Rasmus. If it hadn't been for the way she was treated at home she might never have gotten on that ship and would never have met him. Now that Rasmus was gone, Anna wasn't so sure. She started missing her home, her friends, and her country. Doubt about her choices and her future entered her head.

The smell of breakfast coming from the dining car brought her out of her deep and insecure thoughts. Gert was looking around and commented, "My goodness that sure does smell good."

"Nothing smells better than fresh coffee and bacon frying in the morning," replied Anna. "I used to be a cook and a waitress in New York in a place called Tom's Diner."

"I always wanted to go there," Gert replied. "I was told they had the best food in New York, especially for the working man. Some lady there made pancakes that were legendary. Let's go splurge on a cup of coffee and see what an egg or two costs?"

Anna only had one sandwich left that Nils made her. "Let's do it, Gert. Let's go have some coffee and maybe an egg and toast. Then we can come back here and split my last sandwich. We should feel fat and sassy coming into Chicago. Then, since I have done this so many times and know exactly what to do and how to do it, we'll find our train to Minneapolis."

Gert and Anna laughed together and headed for the dining car.

Upon arrival in Chicago they found out that they would have a three hour wait for their train to Minneapolis, so Anna and Gert decided to stretch their legs and see a little of the city. They passed a row of vendors, and since the vendor prices were so much less than the dining car prices were they filled a bag with some fruit and bread. The hot dog vendor was busy and the dogs smelled so good, but the two ladies were able to resist the temptation and walked by. They went far enough to see a few buildings and some stores but turned around quickly, afraid that they might miss their train. Anna said, "All of these buildings in the city look alike to me anyway Gert. I sure don't like the odor of the stockyards, and the people here seem poor and unfriendly. This sure isn't a place that I would like to live."

"I agree," declared Gert, "and someone should clean some of this garbage off of the streets."

On their way back they both looked at each other as they passed the hot dog stand. "I think my willpower is gone," said Anna. "They smell so good. I may never come this way again, and I might forever regret not having one of them."

Gert agreed wholeheartedly, and they got in line. Anna loaded pickles, mustard, catsup, and onions on hers. Gert did the same. They went into the station and found a bench where they could wait for their train and enjoy the delicious hot dogs, a real American treat for Anna. Their train was almost on time, and being the old pros that they were they got to the front of the line so they could find seats together. They soon were off to Minneapolis and to another state. Anna was indeed a world traveler at the ripe old age of 17.

Anna enjoyed Gert. She had never married, but her sister had a large family. When Anna told her that she planned to stay in Minneapolis for a few months before heading to South Dakota, Gert offered to have Anna stay with her at her sister's house. "Really, Anna, she wouldn't mind. She will give me a room of my own anyway, and I sure wouldn't mind sharing it with you. That way you could save every penny that you make for your travels rather than waste some of it on boarding houses."

This idea really appealed to Anna. Having friends there that knew the area and could help her find a job, not to mention the savings on a room, would be really great. "That is so kind and considerate of you, Gert! I would truly love that, but only if you ask your sister first and she and her family approve. The last thing I would want to do is to intrude on your family time. If they agree to take me in I will help buy the groceries and do my share of the chores around the house."

It was a pleasant ride to Minnesota. The snow had all melted, the countryside was turning green, and the trees were leafing out. Farmers were out in their fields tilling the land and preparing it for spring planting. The cows had been taken out of calving lots and turned onto green pastures with their newborn calves that all seemed to be playing, sleeping, or eagerly having lunch while their mothers licked their back ends. Everything looked new and fresh. Just like my life, thought Anna, a new and fresh start. Anna loved spring; it was her favorite time of the year. She was reminded that this was her first spring as an American, and she thanked the Lord for all the blessings she had received.

When they arrived at the train station, Gert looked around and saw her sister waiting for them. Gert introduced Anna to her younger sister Sarah. After introductions, Anna excused herself so that Gert could ask Sarah in private if she would mind having extra company for a while. Gert told her sister that Anna would help with chores around the house and help pay for her share of the groceries and that Anna needed a job to make some money to pay for her trip to Dakota.

"Where is Anna from?" inquired Sarah.

"Fresh from Norway and only a child out in this world alone," replied Gert dramatically. "Anna could sure use some friends here in Minneapolis, but she doesn't want to intrude and she wants it to be alright with you."

"She looks like a lovely young lady to me, Gert. Let's welcome her to our family for a while and see how it works out."

Gert was relieved as she had grown quite fond of Anna and didn't want to disappoint her. She went back around the corner and, seeing Anna, announced, "Welcome to the family, Anna!"

Sarah was quite nice to Anna, who wanted to know all about her family. "Well," said Sarah, "I married George Christman eleven years ago, and we have six busy and healthy children and two dogs. My husband is a doctor. He works in the clinic and hospital nearby. I do my best to keep all those kids under control and will be happy to have you and Gert here to help. They are spoiled enough already, so please don't be pampering them. We live on the west edge of town, almost in a cornfield. That way the dogs and kids have plenty of room to romp around and I can look outside and see something other than another house. I was a farm girl and it wasn't easy for me to move to the city. Like they say, 'you can take the girl off the farm, but you can't take the farm out of the girl.' Anyway I've gotten used to it and love my family. George is a good doctor and a good husband, and I joke that he gets lots of doctoring practice on these rowdy kids of mine. Someone is always bruised or sick or has something broken. What about you, Anna?"

Anna smiled and replied, "Well, if you exclude my heart, I don't think I've ever broken anything!"

They lived in a big, white farmhouse with many small rooms and creaky wood floors. Thomas Crapper had recently invented the toilet, and George had converted a large closet into a luxurious indoor bathroom. The kitchen was sufficient to serve large families and perfect for Sarah's always hungry crew. Sarah wasn't joking when she said it was right on the edge of a field, which was just being plowed in preparation for the spring planting. Hundreds of birds dotted the furrows in search of worms, and the air was alive with their songs. It was one of those rare sunny days in Minnesota, where it rained more often than not and could be quite gloomy. Sarah led them to Gert's empty room on the second level and showed them in. "If you two don't want to sleep together, I can put Anna on a cot in the sewing room."

Anna noticed that the bed was pretty small so she volunteered, "If it isn't too much work, I would gladly use the cot. That way I won't be a bother to Gert, and she can have this room to herself."

"Perfect," said Sarah. "Let's dig out that old cot and make you two feel at home. George will be here soon, and I have a huge kettle of soup on the stove ready to be warmed up. He will be glad to have two more women in the house to pick on. He knows Gert is coming, but Anna will be a surprise. Now brace yourself, Anna, and I'll introduce you to the kids. There are only six, but I swear some days it seems like sixty! Don't worry if you get them mixed up or forget a name. Darned if I don't even do that myself sometimes."

Anna immediately took a liking to Sarah, who seemed as good and as down to earth as her sister, Gert. She said another of her silent prayers thanking God for having met this wonderful family and for having found new friends to stay with in Minneapolis.

George (Dr. Christman) was home a little late as there had been a bit of a crisis in the clinic. "Hey Gert, how are you doing?" he said with a big smile while giving her a welcome hug. "And who might this pretty young lady be? Is this a friend of yours, Gert?"

"I found her lost and confused on the train and had to help the poor thing find the connection from Chicago to Minneapolis." She giggled at Anna, who giggled back. "Her name is Anna and she is going out into that wilderness west of us to tame mustangs and hunt wild game, or whatever those adventurous types do. Maybe we can help her find a job so she can fill her pockets with some Minnesota money before she gets back on the train. She fancies South Dakota and intends to own a ranch out there some day."

"Wow," replied George and then said to Anna, "you sure aren't the normal girl your age. The ones I know walk around giggling while making eyes at the boys and flirting with them. I hope some of you will rub off on my two daughters."

Anna smiled back at George and said, "Thanks, I'm sure your daughters will turn out wonderful."

After supper each of the Christman kids took turns on Anna's lap while the dogs napped nearby. They had never met or seen a genuine Norwegian or a world traveler. They all wanted to hear just one more story about Norway or the ocean or New York. "Mercy sakes," announced Sarah. "You kids are going to wear this already travel-weary girl out. It's almost bedtime anyway, so let's give her a break."

"Ah Ma," said John the oldest, "we just enjoy hearing them stories. Couldn't we stay up late tonight?"

"Don't worry," said Anna, "We'll have lots of time and lots of adventures this spring. I'll tell you every story I know in time."

After getting the kids to bed, George, Sarah, and Gert sat down with Anna so they could get better acquainted with her. George promised to introduce her around tomorrow since it was Sunday. "Maybe one of the neighbors knows of a good job?" Sarah asked if Anna would like to go to church with them, which delighted Anna. She hadn't been to church in quite some time and she missed it. They visited into the night and finally went off to bed, but not before Anna had Gert show her around the kitchen again. They didn't know it yet, but the Christman family was going to have some of Anna's famous pancakes and fresh baked bread in the morning.

George woke up and followed his nose down to the kitchen, where Anna handed him a steaming cup of coffee. "My lands almighty," he said, "I haven't been treated like this for years. I wonder if Sarah would let me have another wife? Is that fresh bread I smell?"

"Sure is, it's the least I can do to repay your hospitality. Are you ready for some hotcakes or do you want to wait for the rest of the family?"

"Don't mind if I do," replied George. "The only way I get anything to eat around here is to beat that raft of kids of mine to the table!"

It wasn't long before that raft of kids and Sarah and Gert smelled what was going on downstairs. "Pancakes! Our favorite!" happily shouted the children in unison.

"I think we need to say the blessing," interrupted Sarah, "before those chow hounds of mine eat us out of house and home. It smells great, Anna. Where have you been all of my life?"

After the blessing, Anna started dishing out pancakes. "I see that you have lots of eggs, Sarah. Can I fry some of them up, too?"

"Do these pancakes have apples in them?" asked Gert. "This is as good as having apple pie for breakfast. I think these are the best cakes I've ever eaten. I've had to come all the way to Minnesota to finally taste one of those famous New York pancakes."

After cleaning up the dishes (Anna insisted on doing it herself, but Molly and Carol, the two daughters, begged to help, so she let them), everyone got ready for church. The community's Lutheran church was only a few blocks away. Anna was amazed that some of the hymns had the same tunes as those at her old church in Norway. She joined in with the singing, but it was hard not to mix in some Norwegian words with her English words. Sitting there, praying and singing in that church and looking at the Christman family, Anna decided that this was the best thing that anyone could get out of life. She prayed to have a family of her own some day, just like this one.

After church and after shaking hands with the pastor, most of the families went downstairs for coffee and cake, served by the church ladies. George proudly took Anna around to most of the tables and introduced her to all of his friends, bragging about her pancakes and homemade bread. This didn't escape Herbert Brown, who happened to own the local City Café.

"Hey George," he said, "Would you mind loaning her to me for a few weeks? My cook is pregnant, and I'm hurting for some help."

George replied, "I don't think she is looking for work, Herb." He turned and winked at Anna. "But if the wages are good enough, she might possibly consider it. I can tell you this much, if she makes everything as tasty as she made my breakfast this morning, you will need to add on to that old hash house of yours 'cause it will be overflowing with customers."

Later that afternoon, Herb drove to the Christman house and knocked on the door. "Mind if I have a few words with that young lady you got visiting?" He asked Anna if she could possibly help him out for a while, and she said that she'd give it a try. Pleased with finding a job so quickly, Anna said that she would stop by in the morning and get the feel of the place and then start work on Tuesday.

Herb was surprised when he showed Anna around and she seemed to know all about the restaurant business. "Have you by any chance done this before, Anna?"

She just smiled and said, "Yes, I've been a cook, a dishwasher, a waitress, a till operator and even the manager. But I'm guessing that a cook is what you need most of all, Herb."

"You sure got that right, Anna. I think I've just gotten lucky and found myself a new cook."

"I'll be here bright and early tomorrow morning. I would like to have only the best ingredients for my recipes. I want the cream to be thick and fresh. I like large eggs laid within a day or two of when I use them. Same with the meat and milk and flour. Do you have daily specials or a set menu? Let's show these Minnesotans what real cooking is all about. How about chicken and dumplings for dinner tomorrow and pancakes and ham for breakfast? And of course fresh apple pie if you can find me some good tart pie apples. And I need blueberries for the pancakes please."

"Wow, I need a secretary to keep up with you, Anna."

"See you in the morning Boss. Is four too early? What time does the breakfast crowd start coming in?"

Anna arrived a bit early and had to wait for her new boss to unlock the doors (he soon would give Anna the keys so she wouldn't have to wait for him). She went right in and took over, getting bread and pies ready for the oven. After she got the baking started, she whipped up her famous pancake batter and liberally sprinkled blueberries into it. Then she sliced lots of ham, got the eggs ready to be fried, and tested the grill. About an hour rolled by before anyone came in. Although she didn't have to take the orders, Anna paid close attention to the customers. Instead of having the waitress deliver the meals, Anna did it herself when she could, giving the customers her big smile and thanking them for stopping by. When she had time, she even came back to their tables and asked how everything tasted. The standard answer was "Where are we at? This surely can't be the same City Café that we ate at last week? Those are the best pancakes we've ever eaten."

Herb smiled and said "This here lady is from New York where she was a fancy chef and famous for her cooking. Come back for dinner if you think breakfast was good."

Within a few weeks, George's forecast had already come true. The City Café was crowded and had a waiting line to get in. It seemed all of Minneapolis wanted to come and see the famous chef from New York and sample her food. Herb's City Café was on the map, and he was wondering what to do with all the extra cash and where to seat all the customers. He was overheard saying to someone that going to church that day when he met Anna was the luckiest day of his life and that he was never going to miss another church service for fear that God might take her away.

One day an old farmer in bib overalls came in for coffee. "Been hearing about that apple pie you serve here and thought I'd try it for myself," he said. "Maybe it will perk me up a mite."

Anna wasn't real busy, so she served it herself, asking if he wanted some fresh cream on it.

"Don't mind iffin I do young lady. What's your name?"

"I'm Anna. What do you go by?"

"Obert."

He seemed a bit down in the dumps, so Anna decided to visit with him a while and see if she could help. She found out that he had a small farm down the road from George's house and that he had been recently widowed. The old man really missed his wife of forty-five years, and they never had children. "It's awful lonely out on the farm nowadays," he told Anna. "Wish I had some company out there. By the way, this pie is even better than what Martha, bless her soul, used to make me. I can see what all the fuss has been about."

"Tell you what, Obert," Anna said, "George gives me Wednesday afternoons off so that I can have a little peace and quiet and rest my soul a bit. How about showing me that farm of yours if you don't have too much on your schedule Wednesday afternoon?"

Obert lit up like a Sunday sunrise. "You would do that for me? I'd be honored to show you around the ol' place, Miss Anna!" It was the first time Obert had smiled since Martha had died.

Wednesday afternoon, Anna walked down the road to Obert's farm. Anna smiled to herself thinking that if Obert had lived in Norway and he and Martha had sons, his sons could possibly be named Obertsons. Obert was on the porch waiting. "Can't believe you actually came over, Miss Anna. Nobody's visited me since Martha died."

"Well there's a first time for everything, Obert," Anna smiled. "I like your farm already, and I'm ready for that tour you promised me."

"Sure thing, Anna." He took Anna around to every old farm building. They were showing their age and hadn't had much attention. Most needed a good painting, and like their owner their backs were sagging a little. Shingles were missing and doors were left open, some of them off of their hinges. Weeds were growing in the corrals and the garden was overrun with them. They stopped at the chicken coop.

"Are your hens laying good?" Anna asked.

"Sure are, but the egg market isn't any good, so I just throw out what I don't eat."

"Oh no. Good fresh farm eggs are hard to come by, Obert. Why don't you bring them by George's house two or three times a week, and I'll take them to the café and feed them to that hungry crowd over there. Maybe I can get the owner to give you a little over market for them?"

"That would be grand Anna! I haven't shown you all my livestock yet; would you like to see my horse?"

Sure enough, back behind the barn was a good looking blue roan gelding.

"He looks smart," Anna told Obert. "Do you ride him much?"

"Hardly any nowadays, but he can run like the wind, and he likes to get out in the woods and snoop around. I don't have a pasture big enough for him to get proper exercise."

"You know," said Anna, "I'm going out to Dakota later this summer. It sure would be nice to know how to saddle a horse and get the hang of riding. I've never ridden a horse, and I've heard that in Dakota unless you want to walk wherever you go you need a good horse. Would you mind giving me riding lessons? Maybe in trade I could bring you a pie or some fresh bread?"

"Why Miss Anna, I'd be more than proud to teach you. Don't need nothing in return. I'd just be glad of the company. How about we saddle Blue right now and get started with them lessons? One thing you'll need, Miss Anna, is a good pair of riding pants rather than those fancy dresses. Blue might get scared and run off seeing that dress flapping around, especially on a windy day."

"Maybe we should start the lessons next week, Obert. I'd be mighty embarrassed if that happened. That will give me time to find a pair of riding pants."

The City Café was doing so well that Herb, just like Tom, had to add on and buy more tables and chairs. "You're sure costing me a lot of money, Anna," he kidded. "And all of these extra mouths to feed. I didn't know there were this many restaurant eaters in all of Minnesota. It seems like you already know half the town. How do you do it? You greet them customers like they've been lifelong friends of yours. And those young bucks are all just itching to take you out on a date. I think that most of the eligible young men in Minneapolis are coming through my doors just to get a look at you, let alone have a piece of your pie."

"Don't you go and make me blush, Herbert. You know darned well that it is our fancy dining atmosphere that keeps them coming."

Anna's boss about fell off his chair laughing. "One thing I know for sure, Anna, it ain't the atmosphere."

Anna made several trips out to visit Obert and to see Blue. Her riding lessons with Obert were going well, and she and Blue got along great. After a few lessons she was racing around the countryside on him like a wild cowgirl. She had been a bit scared at first, but once she got the hang of it, riding Blue felt like the freedom she had longed for, galloping through the fields with her hair flying in the wind and her eyes watering as the landscape blurred by. This was all a new and exhilarating experience for Anna and she loved it. She had also grown to love the horse and the smell of leather and horse sweat. She decided then and there that if it was ever possible her ranch would have lots of horses and that she would ride through the countryside every day if she possibly could. She had always envied the birds, being able to fly off to wherever they wanted. Riding Blue had to be a close second. She told Obert, "If Blue was for sale and if I could afford to buy him and if it wasn't so far, I'd forget the train and ride this horse all the way to Dakota."

One day she was having pie with Obert at his table and noticed a rifle in the corner. "Say, Obert, I've always wanted to learn how to shoot one of those. I'll be wanting one of my own when I get to Dakota. And if I heard right, I'll need to know how to use it. Now that you've got me riding, how about a few shooting lessons? I already know how to skin and gut most critters, so if you teach me to shoot I can get us some fresh squirrels or rabbits for supper."

Obert quickly got the .22 out and found the shells. "This is a Winchester 1876 twenty-two lever action rifle—the perfect squirrel, rabbit, skunk, and assorted critter gun. And it's a good rifle to learn on. Let's go put up some cans and bottles behind the house and see what you can do."

Anna took to the rifle like fleas to a hound (in Obert's words) and was ready to go hunting that afternoon. "Them squirrels are hard to hit, Anna, and they don't sit still long for you to get a bead. You have to spot them before they spot you, and you have to be quick. If you can hit squirrels, you can get most anything." Within a mile's walk, Anna had shot four squirrels and a cottontail. "I'll be darned," said Obert, "I got me a hunter here."

"Let's get these guys skinned and cleaned and in the pan," said Anna. "This hunting is hungry work, Obert. These squirrels are a little different than the ones my dad used to bring home in Norway, and I can't wait to see if they are as tasty."

It wasn't long before Anna had the squirrels and the rabbit in the frying pan. "You are really something, Anna," said Obert. "I think you went from learning to shoot to putting game into the frying pan in less than four hours. Hope Martha doesn't hear this, but I think I got a crush on you," he joked. It was good to see him laugh; his heart was on the mend.

Over the next weeks, the old man and Anna got to be the best of friends, and he showed up at the City Café almost every day for dinner. Herb knew that Anna had been helping Obert and could see the change in him. "Don't know what you're doing for that old timer, Anna, but it's like night and day the difference in him lately."

"He's helping me more than I'm helping him," she replied. "What he is teaching me could very well save my life some day out in the Dakota wilderness. I'll be forever grateful to that old timer."

Anna knew that her time in Minnesota needed to come to an end. She had been told that winters on the plains could be tough, and she figured that she either needed to stay in Minnesota all through this fall and winter until next spring or get going as soon as possible. Thanks to the generous hospitality of the Christman family, Anna had already saved up more than enough for the trip and a horse, saddle, and rifle when she arrived in South Dakota. She still had part of what Rasmus had left her in New York, too. In fact, Anna had more money than she ever dreamt possible. As much as she loved it here with the Christman family and Obert and her work family at the café, she knew that staying longer would make it even harder to leave. Her goal had been South Dakota, which is where she wanted to be, at least until she knew whether or not it would be home for her.

She made a few excuses and left work early Saturday afternoon and walked to the train station. Once there she learned that the train to Hettinger, ND ran twice a week. The Milwaukee line to Hettinger had just been built. A few years earlier she would have had to go to either Bismarck or Dickinson, North Dakota, which would have added another fifty or more miles to her destination in South Dakota. If she left in two weeks she should be there by the end of June. She figured that would leave her enough summer and fall to find the Larson family, a place to live, and to see if she truly belonged there. She wrote three letters and mailed them before returning to the Christmans.

Dear Nils and family,

I am praying that Tove and Heidi have safely arrived by now and that you are a complete family again. How I would love to see you all together.

My time has gone well. I am in Minneapolis staying with the wonderful Christman family. I have met so many nice people here. I have a great job at a café, and a farmer friend who has taught me to ride and rope as well as to shoot straight and hunt. Before you get to thinking he's my boyfriend, I'll add that he's old enough to be my grandfather. I will have to leave here soon since I already have train tickets purchased from Minneapolis to Hettinger, North Dakota. I should arrive there on June 17th, about the middle of the day. I will write to the Larson family, using the address that you gave me, and let them know of my plans. If they can't meet me in Hettinger, I will buy a horse there and ride to their home. I think that I can find it with the map that they sent to you, the one that I copied.

Enough about me. Please write to me using the Larsons's address and let me know how your family is doing. And please give everyone my love and a hug.

Yours truly,
Anna

Dear Mr. and Mrs. Larson,

Nils has told me so much about you that I feel like I already know you. I am so anxious to meet you in person and to see your home in South Dakota. It sounds wonderful there, so wild and free. I pray that I am strong enough to fit in.

My train will arrive in Hettinger around the middle of the day June 17th. Nils said that you might be able to meet me there, but if you are busy, or if it is an inconvenient time, please don't bother. I have a copy of the map that you sent to Nils and I think I can find you. I will buy a good broke horse in Hettinger and that time of year the weather should be nice enough to stay overnight under the stars for a night or two.

Thank you so much for taking me in until I find a home of my own. I will do my best to hold up my end of the work at your ranch and not be in the way. I can cook and clean and I can ride and hunt. I don't know much about cattle, but I want to learn. God bless you for your help.

Yours truly,
Anna Ingevich

Dear Donna,

I only have time for a note, but I want to let you know that I am ready to leave Minnesota and will arrive in Dakota June 17th. I am pretty nervous but at the same time pretty excited. I have somewhere to stay when I get there and will be looking for a place of my own.

Are you still working at the boarding house? I miss it and you so much! If my South Dakota dream works out,

maybe you can come and visit me? If it doesn't I'll either
come back to Minnesota or to New York.
God Bless you, I pray that you are well.

Love,
Anna

From the post office, Anna walked back to the Christmans, not at all eager to tell them the news. Leaving Minneapolis was going to be just as hard as or maybe even harder than it was to leave New York. She would let the Christmans know first, then everyone at work, and then Obert. Gert was getting ready to leave, too, so Sarah would be on her own again to cook and clean for her household. At least George made a lot of money and they could afford some help if Sarah needed it. When Anna got back to the house, she decided that now was as good as anytime.

It was past supper time and almost the time of night when she would either read to the children or tell them stories. Tonight she announced that it would be a story, and she asked all of the family to gather round to hear it. It was a story about a young girl who had been lost but luckily had found the most wonderful family in the world. They had taken this young girl in and had loved her as their own. They had helped her get along in a strange new world in a distant state and in a distant country. The young girl truly loved all of them and would have a very hard time leaving them but knew that it was what she had to do. She would hope to come back and visit them some day, and she would forever hold them in her heart. She would have to leave in two weeks in order to complete her journey before winter came again.

About half way through, the audience realized this was not a story but Anna's way of telling them that she was leaving. Every eye in the Christman home had tears that night. After they had all gone to bed, Gert came sneaking into Anna's room and sat on the edge of her cot. "You know Anna," she whispered, "You really are a member of this family now. If things don't go right for you in Dakota, my sister and her family are only a train ride away, and you'd be welcome here again in a Minnesota minute. I visit here every spring, and I'd sure love to have you come back and see us at the same time that I'm here. It would be like a family reunion for the Christman tribe."

Anna gave Gert a long hug. Then they sat there in silence for a while until Gert got up to leave. "God bless you," said Anna as Gert left.

"Sweet dreams."

Since she had already broken the news to the Christmans, Anna decided that she needed to tell her boss right away, too. Two weeks wasn't long, but it would give him some time to replace her and keep his business going. After all, he had started the little cafe on his own, so he should be able to keep it going on his own, especially now that Anna had built up its customer base and reputation.

Herb and Anna were both at work early, as usual, and Anna asked him if he would have a cup of coffee with her. She said she needed to tell him something.

"I suppose you want a raise, Miss Anna. Can't say that I blame you since you are running the place almost by yourself. You know I wouldn't let you do so much, but I figure to just get out of that gal's way and let her run while I sit back for the ride. How much you wanting? The cash is flowing in Anna, even though I have spent a lot on remodeling and adding another room to the building."

"It isn't that at all," she replied. "I don't know how to do anything without giving it my best, and I think that you have been fair with me. I wouldn't feel right if I worked any less hard. I'm not looking for a raise or for any praise, but I need to let you know that I have to be moving on to South Dakota in two weeks. This job and this place were never meant to be permanent, and I just wanted to do my best and to help you out while I was here. Remember when your cook quit? I said I would help out, but I never said that I could stay for long."

Herb's face fell. He could pout as authentically as her boss in New York had when Anna left. "You can't do this to me, Anna. It'll ruin the business. Everything will go right down the drain without you.

My customers will all leave me, and I'll go to the poor house. Please reconsider, Anna. How about a partnership? I'll gladly give you half of the business. We can rename the old joint and call it Anna's Place or something. Please Anna, please?"

Anna held her ground. "I love it here, Herb. I love this cafe and I've even grown quite fond of you. I would never rename this place, and I would never coerce you into giving me half of it. I have to follow my dream. I thought about staying until next spring, but it would just make leaving harder. Here is what we need to do to keep this place going. I've had my eye on Liz. She's pretty straightforward and steady. I went through this same process in New York, and from what I hear that place is still doing just fine. Let me have the reins with the employees, and within two weeks I'll have you a team in place that can keep this business growing. I'll train Liz to run it, and I'll work with Harry on my recipes in the kitchen. You can take over as our greeter and make sure the customers are happy and feel welcome. This is their home away from home, right? We don't want a poor meal to ever be served to anyone in the City Café, right? Now let's get busy."

He was still pouting, but Herb knew that she was right, and he knew that if Anna said it could be done it could be done.

Wednesday afternoon came too soon for Anna. Obert was sitting on the porch waiting for her. He had washed his bib overalls and was shaving again. He had even made some lemonade, and lemons were hard to come by that time of the year. "Good afternoon, young lady. I've been sitting here almost all day waiting for our weekly visit. I even skipped dinner at the café so I could shave up and sweep the house out. Come and see. It looks almost as good as when Martha was here. What's the matter kiddo, cat got your tongue today? Is that a tear, my dear Anna? Is anything the matter? That boss of yours didn't do something did he?"

Then Obert realized what was up. Anna had told him that she was going to go to South Dakota some day. She had wanted shooting, riding, and hunting lessons to prepare her for that trip. Now she was leaving. "It is way too soon, Anna. I was hoping you'd be here all year. It's my own fault. I should have dragged out them riding and hunting lessons as long as I could. I should have had a plan to keep you here longer."

Obert was trying his best to help her out. He could see that she was having difficulty speaking. "Don't let this old goat and his ramblings bother you, Miss Anna. I guess I knew it had to happen sometime, just didn't think it would be so soon. Time sorta flies by for me when you're around, and here I am being selfish and only thinking of myself. You need to do what you need to do dear. You've pretty much turned my life around and taught me that I can live without Martha. I even enjoy going to the café and giving that boss of yours a bad time. But Anna, I'm gonna miss you so much."

"Oh Obert," said Anna, "thank you so much for helping make this a little easier for me. Of all the wonderful people I've met in America, you are the one I have grown to love the most and the person that it will be the hardest to say good bye to. And being the gentleman that you are you are doing most of it for me. I will miss you too, more than you could ever imagine, and when I come back to Minnesota I'll be looking you up and making sure that you've kept Martha's house clean and Blue fed well. I'll have one more afternoon with you next week, then my train leaves on the 17th. I can't thank you enough for teaching me to hunt and ride and shoot and just be a country girl. Would you mind if I took old Blue out for a ride today? I need to feel the wind blowing through my hair and dry my tears. We'll have some of that lemonade when I get back, and sit here on the porch so I can enjoy your company and this beautiful farm of yours."

The next few days went by quickly. Anna was so busy preparing the café for her departure that she hardly had time for anything else. She wanted to do something special for the Christman family and Obert before she left, and she also needed to get packed. This time she would actually have enough clothes and other items to fill that trunk of hers. Her boss at the cafe had fallen into line and was helping her as much as he could. Anna was trying to say good-bye to all of the customers that she had gotten to know personally, which was most of them. Many of the young men in the area had stopped in hoping for a date, but Anna had made it clear that she wasn't in the market quite yet. "Maybe in time," she had said to them.

Three days before her departure her boss sat down with her. "Why don't you take these last couple of days off, Anna? I think you've gotten Liz up to speed, and I can see she is excited about trying her hand at running the place. I've gotten myself cleaned up and think I can look and act like a proper owner and greeter. Harry's pancakes were almost as good as yours this morning. I actually think that this joint might make it without you, but just barely. I've prepared a little gift for you. I know I don't show enough appreciation. He got out an envelope and gave it to her. This here's your wages up to date and also for the next two months as a bonus. If you ever decide that Dakota isn't for you, I'll expect you to come back and see me, and I'll hold open my offer on a partnership if you'll have me. It'd be pretty lopsided with me getting the best of the bargain, but there's nothing I would like better."

"There's nothing I would like better either, Herb! We'll see if this Dakota dream of mine turns out as planned or if I come crawling back to Minnesota begging for my job."

"That would be the day, Anna," Herb laughed. "And I doubt Dakota will ever be the same after you get through with it."

The 17th came too soon. Anna hadn't had time to do all that she had wanted to, but the train wasn't about to change its schedule for her. It was leaving mid-morning. George and Sarah and the whole family packed into the 1905 Model C Ford that he had recently purchased and were ready to drive Anna to the train station. They all wanted to see her off and wish her well. When they arrived, they were greeted by signs that read "Good-bye Anna" and a cheering crowd. It looked like the entire neighborhood was there to see her off. Anna was overwhelmed and went around hugging her friends and thanking them for coming. It was hard not to think of Norway, where she left with nobody to say good-bye to.

Obert was there with his Winchester model 1876. "I want you to have this, Anna, to remind you of me. I can scare the skunks off with my old shotgun, and I think you'd have a lot more use of this than me. It'll make me proud to give it to you and these here two boxes of shells to go with it."

Anna gave him a hug and a kiss and shed a few more tears. "This is the best gift anyone has ever given me, Obert. I'd sure be proud to own it and to think of you every time I use it. You've taken care of me much better than my own father did, so I hope you don't mind if I think of you as my American grandfather."

"It would be my honor, Miss Anna."

More good-byes were said, more hugs were given, and more tears had fallen. Passengers were boarding, so Anna got in line and found a window seat. Her friends stood there, waving good-bye until the train left Minneapolis heading for Minnesota farming country and the prairies of Dakota. It was the dawning of a new day and a new life for Anna. She was excited as well as sad. She was thrilled yet a bit scared. She was on her own again and heading for a date with her dreams.

Anna watched the countryside go by as she munched on one of the tasty ham sandwiches Sarah had packed, along with some of the leftover lefsa they had made. It was Anna's mother's Norwegian recipe and had come to be a Christman family favorite. The city turned into country and the woodlands were slowly turning into the rich and fertile farm ground of western Minnesota. The whole world seemed to be a brilliant green. The corn in the fields was growing like a new born colt and was almost four feet high in most places already. Water sat in pools and along the rail tracks everywhere as there had just been a shower. The resulting rainbow was still gracing the horizon, and the air coming in Anna's window smelled sweet and pure. As they traveled farther west, the flat Minnesota farm ground was becoming slightly hilly and the streams were thinning out to thirty to forty miles between them. Anna figured that by now she might actually be in Dakota but wasn't sure if it was North Dakota or South Dakota. She was pretty sure, but not positive, that when the train reached Dakota it ran mostly on the North Dakota side of the border.

Day gave way to night, and Anna stared out the window into seemingly nothingness. It was the darkest she had ever seen, and the big bright stars in the sky seemed to be beaming down at her. Did anyone at all live out here? This country was wide open, large, and intimidating. All those stories about train robbers and wild Indian raiding parties came to her mind. She wished that she hadn't had the porter put her rifle away for the trip.

Early the next morning the train, which pretty much did parallel the border between North and South Dakota, slowed up for the stop at the border town of Lemmon, South Dakota. Most of Lemmon was on the SD side of the tracks so it was a SD town. The train tracks angle a little to the north after leaving Lemmon and Hettinger is located entirely in ND. It is about 45 miles west of Lemmon so it was also about that much closer to Anna's final destination of Reva, SD.

Anna's heart started beating a little faster. She knew she was probably less than two hours from her final train stop at Hettinger. Would the Larsons be there to meet her, or would she be on her own to find them? Did they let women homestead on 160 free acres? Were there still Indians and thieves to worry about? How bad were the wolves? Would they have horses for sale, or would she have to walk? So many things ran through her mind that she finally just shut her eyes and tried to take a nap. Sleeping would be the fastest way to get there, but on the other hand she didn't want to miss anything and she wanted to study the countryside here closely. She compromised and took a short nap while they were stopped in Lemmon, then got a cup of coffee and again watched the tall grass go by as the train worked its way through the countryside. She guessed that it was pretty windy as the grass was waving and swaying back and forth. She didn't see any deer, but the horizon was speckled with antelope and a large jackrabbit bounced by every now and then looking like it could run circles around the train. They were the most graceful rabbits Anna had ever seen. Above them in an eerily blue and cloudless sky an eagle circled, probably wishing that it could have the rabbit for lunch.

Anna jumped when the train conductor announced "Hettinger North Dakota folks." This was it; she was almost to her final destination after a steamship journey across the ocean and a train trip across America. She couldn't wait to get off and see what Hettinger was like—and to see if the Larsons were there waiting. Nils had told her that they were a few years older than she was but they had only recently been married, and that they were a handsome couple. Anna couldn't wait to meet them.

Before she went to get her trunk, Ben, the same train employee that had helped her in New York, came by and said he had something for her. By now Anna had become friends with him, and she strained her mind to remember what she might have forgotten. "Follow me please Anna," he said. "We have to go to the livestock car." They walked up a loading ramp, and Ben unlatched the sliding door and opened it up.

"Oh my goodness!" Anna shrieked. "It's Blue!" There was a short note for her on Obert's saddle which was sitting on the stall railing.

Dear Anna,

I am getting too old to take care of Blue. He whinnerd to me that he wanted to go with you and I decided you should have him. You can take better care of him than I can. Would be a shame to break the two of you up. I even found my old rifle scabbard and put it on the saddle. Your Winchester will fit it perfect. Blue's ticket is paid for. I miss you so much.

Your friend and grampa,
Obert

Anna hugged Blue as he whinnied at her. She put his saddle and bridle on and asked Ben if he could retrieve her .22 so she could put it in the scabbard.

"Of course. Least I could do for such a nice young lady. I was told strictly to keep this a surprise. I hope you enjoyed it."

"You'll never know how much, Ben. I was scared to death at the thought of trying to buy a good saddle horse here."

She walked Blue down the ramp and jumped on him, looking around the station and the settlement. The station was almost deserted except for a buggy with one bay horse hitched to it. Just then a pretty lady dressed in work clothes came out of the station and walked over to Ben and asked, "Do you know anyone named Anna Ingevich? She's probably some fancy-dressed lady looking a little outta place and lost. She was supposed to arrive on this train."

Ben smiled at her, "Do you mean that Anna Ingevich?" He pointed at Anna, "The one sitting on top of the big blue roan filling her rifle with shells?"

11

Destiny

Reidun ran over to Anna, and Anna jumped off Blue. "I've been so anxious to meet you, Reidun," Anna shouted. "I can't believe you took the time to come all the way to town to meet me. I'm so excited to be here!"

"You sure aren't what we were expecting, Anna! So nice to finally meet you, too! Nils has said so much about you that we feel like we're already friends. Odd couldn't come as he is tending to the cattle, so he sends his apologies. We figured that you would need all the help you could get, but it looks like you came prepared to do it all on your own. Where did you find that beautiful blue roan?"

"This horse was a complete surprise, Reidun. I'll explain all of it to you on our way back to the ranch. I can't tell you how much I appreciate that you came to town to help me."

"It was no trouble, Anna. We needed some supplies anyway, and I was bursting at the seams to meet you. Odd isn't always the best of company and having another female around for a while will suit me fine. It gets kind of lonely out there sometimes. Come on; let's go see the new general store. We can hitch your horse behind the buggy and let him tag along."

Anna and Reidun went to the store after loading Anna's trunk and tying Blue to the wagon. Hettinger wasn't much more than a store, a few houses, a railroad station, and some corrals with a blacksmith shop all connected with dirt paths. If it hadn't been for the railroad, it wouldn't even be here, Anna thought. Reidun mostly needed groceries, which Anna offered to buy. Reidun was surprised and thankful. "Our account is getting behind here and I didn't know if they'd extend our credit, so I'm mighty grateful, Anna. Where did you come across that much money? I heard that you even helped Nils and his family with Tove's ticket."

"I get along as good as I can," Anna replied, "And I am glad to help out. It's the least I can do for you guys. I would probably never have made this trip if it hadn't been for your hospitality and generous offer to keep me until I can get my feet on the ground and find my own place."

"You're something, Anna. A pretty young girl like you striking out on her own and traveling across the world. Most girls would be trying to trap a big rancher or some rich doctor or lawyer rather than making their own way. Let's head south toward the ranch while we still have daylight."

As they traveled along, Anna remarked, "It is beautiful here, Reidun. It looks like the prairie stretches into forever. You could run a million head of cows here, and they would all be fat as butter. I don't think that all this grass could ever run out."

"Wait until you see one of our bison herds. They go through a swath of grass and leave it bare as a baby's butt. Sometimes it takes a couple of years for it to grow back. We'll travel as far as the north fork of the Grand River and camp there for the night. If we don't sleep in too long, we can get into the ranch early tomorrow afternoon."

"The Grand River?" asked Anna. "How will we get across it? Is there a ferry?"

Reidun laughed, "You'll see."

Anna did laugh when she saw the "Grand River," which was only a couple of feet deep and about thirty feet wide where they camped. The water was moving lazily downstream, nothing like the torrents of gushing water Anna was used to in the rivers of Norway. "You call this a river, Reidun? And a "grand" one at that? Are you sure that herd of bison you told me about didn't just pee in the gully around the corner and create this?"

The girls laughed. "You and me are gonna get along just fine, Anna. I love your sense of humor, and although our rivers may not be so 'grand,' your smile sure is. We actually have two of these Grand Rivers, a north branch and a south branch."

They made a small camp and had a long visit. Anna had so many questions about the area, the people—were there any that lived here?—the animals, the weather, how the people made a living, were there really Indians and wolves, and on and on that Reidun thought they were never going to end. When she finally got a chance to say something she asked Anna about Blue.

"You told me he was a surprise?"

"I became really good friends with an old retired farmer from Minneapolis. He had a run down place and this beautiful blue roan horse. That old man did more for me than anyone I have ever met. He taught me to ride, shoot, hunt, and take care of myself. He became closer to me than my own family, and I love him and called him my grampa. To make a very long story short, he secretly put Blue on the train as a surprise gift for me, paid his passage, and the porter gave me the shock of my life when we got to Hettinger."

They finally drifted off to sleep, which didn't seem to last nearly long enough. Reidun was up early and already had a little campfire going when Anna awoke.

"I'm not used to being the last one out of the sack," she said. "What can I do to help?"

"Not much," said Reidun. "We'll just have a quick cup of coffee and then hit the trail."

"Ok. I'll take Blue and your buggy horse down to the stream for a drink."

The coffee tasted good and was hot. They sat and enjoyed it a few extra minutes and then hitched the bay to the buggy and tied Blue back behind again. "I'm guessing we'll be there mid afternoon," Reidun went on. "Looks like a little weather brewing in the west today. With any luck we might get a good rain tonight, and with a little more good luck we'll beat the storm home. Rain is always welcome here; seems we never get enough of it."

"What is that?" Anna interrupted.

A big red fox was ignoring them, ready to pounce on something in the grass. All at once he leaped into the air, coming down on a mound of dirt. When his head popped up he had a big fat mole in his mouth.

"A red fox. They are beautiful and harmless creatures. I would love to have a fox coat someday. Anyway, as I was saying, we always need more rain and the river even shrivels up more for lack of water in the fall. Our first year here was really dry with only a few inches of rain and not much snow. We had lots of snow this past winter though, which is a mixed blessing."

"Why?"

"Makes it hard to winter the livestock and keep the chores done, but the extra snow also makes for good spring runoff when it melts and the soaked up prairie means early grass. So we don't know what to pray for and just leave it up to God. The grass and the crops look good so far if the hot weather doesn't hit too early in the year."

Reidun's thoughts mirrored her prayers. They needed some big crops and a lot of hay this year, along with good cattle prices if they were going to pay the bills.

"The cattle are already putting on fat, and we only lost a couple of calves in a late spring blizzard, so it should be a good year if the cattle prices hold up. You ever done any gardening, Anna? I got all kinds of seeds, and my garden has a good start this year. I can loan you some of them seeds next spring if you want. I have my garden close to the river, so if it doesn't rain I can irrigate it."

It was Reidun's turn to ramble on and on as Anna listened in amazement. Most of what Reidun said needed time to sink in, but just listening to Reidun put a smile on Anna's face. So far so good. This truly did look like paradise.

"I can't wait to meet Odd," Anna interrupted.

"He's been looking forward to it too, Anna. 'Bout the only other girls he sees is the cows, and they aren't much for conversation. It isn't all bad though. I always figure I'm better looking than the cows, so I don't worry about him wandering off with another woman."

Anna laughed, "I'll wait and see how handsome Odd is, but I know this: You would have had most of them Minnesota boys camping on your doorstep, Reidun."

"Oh, by the way, Anna, did I mention that I have a little neighborhood get together planned for Saturday afternoon at the Reva hall? Maybe even a little music and dancing if Joe brings his guitar."

"I don't know how to dance," Anna admitted. "But I do enjoy any good music."

Anna had never been to a party, and was intimidated by the thought that she was the reason for this one. She worried about being accepted by the Dakotans and what to wear. Her wedding dress had been used and needed to be washed and ironed.

As if to pile on to Anna's stress, Reidun added, "There are a few bachelors in the area just dying to meet the new girl in town. Well, not exactly "town" as we don't have one of them yet. But we do have the little meeting hall over at Reva and a postal stop. You are a gorgeous young woman, and you will be a lot more than they expect. I can just see their jaws dropping. Just want you to have a little fair warning."

Anna didn't think that she was pretty and never did realize how beautiful she was. She was somewhat blinded by her practical side, and vanity wasn't in her character. Although she thought of herself as plain, those around her saw the beauty.

"But there is one of them that I can think of that wouldn't be a bad catch," Reidun continued. "About your age, too, and a genuine Norwegian. Iver Olson, or is it Tenold? There's some funny story associated with his name. He came over on a ship just like you did, and he was pretty young when he first got here. If I remember right he rode the rails from New York just like you, but Hettinger wasn't here yet when he came so he must have had to ride horseback farther, maybe from Dickinson, North Dakota. You probably followed about the same trail that he did, only he came a few years earlier. Iver lives a few miles from our place over by the Slim Buttes with his uncle. They are south of the river a ways, but it is a beautiful spot just the same. Our place is just over that hill. Do you see that horse loping for us? Odd must have spotted us coming."

Odd pulled his horse up beside the wagon. "Hey you two beautiful gals! Are you lost? Race you home, Reidun." He was off in a flash.

"He's such a show off, Anna. Guess it's one of the things I love about him." She urged the bay into a faster trot, and they headed down the hill toward their homestead.

It was a rather barren homestead with a little sod house that had a bit of a porch and a lean-to on one side. There was a small barn, a chicken coop, and two corrals. None of the buildings were painted, but they were straight and functional. Several horses were in one of the corrals, and two cows were in the other. Chickens loitered about the yard everywhere. A cat peeked around the corner of the barn, and a black and white border collie ran out to greet them. Reidun explained that they had dug a well but watered the stock mostly from the stream.

They pulled up in front of the house, and Odd ran over with the dog trailing him. He already had his horse unsaddled and in the corral. "So, this must be the famous Anna Ingevich that I've heard so much about. I'm Odd. Well not really odd, but that's my name." He grinned. "Nice to meet you, Anna," he said as he reached out and gave Anna a friendly western handshake. The collie greeted her with some sniffing.

"It's so nice to meet you too, Odd. I've heard so much about you and your homestead that I feel like I already know you. It was so nice of you to let Reidun come to town to meet me."

"No problem," he replied. "I couldn't have kept her home if there'd been a prairie fire between here and Hettinger. Besides, we were a bit worried about a New York city- slicker like you getting lost in the wilderness out here. Looks like we had you figured wrong. Appears to me like you're a genuine cowgirl already. Where'd ya get that big blue roan from? He looks like a dandy."

"I've already told Reidun the story, but he was a gift from a dear friend."

"You got supper ready, Odd," Reidun interrupted.

"Well…er…of course I was gonna make supper, but I had some trouble with that south border fence. And the cows…."

"Sure, sure," Reidun interrupted again. "Let's head in and see what we can round up. Heaven knows you'd starve on your cooking, Odd."

"I don't need food, I'm living on love," Odd grinned.

Anna liked him immediately. He and Reidun were quite the pair, and it was easy to tell that they were head over heels in love with each other. "You guys like pancakes?" Anna chimed in. "If you have fresh cream, some eggs and sugar and flour, I'll whip some up. It'd be a fast and easy supper."

"Why that's the best offer this gal has had all week," said Reidun. "Pancakes it will be. Where did you learn to cook?"

"Mostly at home from my mom, but I practiced all the way from New York to South Dakota."

It was a glorious western sunset, and Anna asked if they could eat out on the porch so she could enjoy it and study the landscape. "The skyline here is like the prairie," Anna remarked. "They both seem to go on forever. The sky seems bigger than the sky at home, but I guess that's impossible since it's the same sky. Look, there's a doe and her two fawns drinking out of the river."

"Lots of them around here," Odd replied. "One thing we got is plenty of wild game. Mostly we eat deer, antelope, grouse, and prairie chickens. Occasionally I go over to the slim buttes and get a few turkeys. And I shoot cottontails or jacks sometimes. We eat fresh meat all spring and summer and fall, then start drying it for the winter when the only fresh meat we usually have is cottontails or deer. We get a few cats out of the river, but they get sorta muddy tasting in the summer."

"Cats?" asked Anna.

"Catfish," replied Reidun. "They have long whiskers just like a house cat."

"Oh, how soon can we go fishing?" asked Anna. "I love fishing. I used to go out on the North Sea with my dad when he would let me. I made some of the money for my ocean passage cleaning fish on the docks of Bergen. The fishermen were so good to me, and so much fun to be around. I had almost forgotten. It seems a lifetime away."

"It's good to remember something that brings a smile to your face," Odd said. "You can go fishing anytime you please, now that I know that you can clean them yourself." Odd's laugh was contagious and they all joined in. "Please tell us about the North Sea and Bergen sometime?"

"I'd be happy to. Got any jobs for me tomorrow?" asked Anna changing the subject. "I'm ready to go to work, you know."

"I'm changing pastures for the cows, and you can help me move them if you want. Or you can just hang around here and keep Reidun out of trouble for me."

"Ha," Reidun replied. "I think I'll send Anna out with you to keep YOU out of trouble."

"Ok, ok," said Anna. "Just so I'M no trouble. I'll help anywhere I'm needed."

Morning came earlier on a ranch than in town, or so it seemed. It depended on the time of year, but the sun was up early in the summer and so were the ranchers. They just seemed to follow the sun. Fortunately their horses didn't come with headlights so they could quit when the sun went down. Odd figured he might have to wake up Anna to help him move the cows, but when he came out the next morning, ahead of the sun, Anna already had the coffee going.

"Darn," said Odd, "I wanted to beat you out of bed so I could tease you about sleeping in. You went and ruined my fun, Anna."

"Maybe I'll let you saddle your horse faster than I saddle mine if it'll make you feel better," she smiled.

"What you two yammering about?" Reidun joined them in the kitchen. "Boy that coffee smells good. I see that you beat Odd outta the sack Anna; he's such a slacker, you know."

"Are you two gonna gang up against me again," whined Odd. "What's a man gotta do to get some respect around here?"

"Making me breakfast in bed would be a good start, Odd." Reidun winked at Anna.

"I know when I'm licked. Think I'll saddle up ahead of Anna so she doesn't rub that in too."

It was a beautiful sunrise, and the air was crisp and clear. The flies weren't so thick yet, so it was the perfect time of the year for the cows: No bugs, the grass still green, the water still fresh, and the baby calves not big enough yet to bang their mother's bags with their heads so hard. Anna enjoyed watching them so much that Odd had a difficult time getting her to help him start the round up.

"Look at them, Odd," she said. "They're just like children. Their Moms want to give them a little love and a kiss and say hi, but they just detour around her efforts and head for her lunch end without even saying thanks. Poor mom has to lick their back ends while they get a nice hot breakfast."

"Aren't you happy you're not a cow, Anna? Now let's get them started before it gets hot out. They'll move a lot easier while the morning air is still fresh and cool."

Anna moved her horse around the cows like she'd been doing it all her life. Not too close to them, not too far. She was in that perfect zone where the cows moved along without noticing that they were being moved. "Nice work," commented Odd. "That's a good cow pony you got there."

"Sure, give my horse all the credit."

"I just can't win," complained Odd.

"Why are we moving these cows anyway?" asked Anna.

"It's almost breeding time, and I want them on a smaller, fresher pasture so my bull doesn't have to walk his legs off trying to keep these cows happy. Poor fella, he'll have 38 of them to take care of."

"I betcha he won't do any complaining," quipped Anna. "This is a nice pasture. Lots of trees for shade when it gets hotter out and plenty of water."

"You figure things out fast, Anna." "Shade and good water, along with a lot of grass, are the main ingredients to get the cattle through the summer and make big, heavy calves to sell in the fall."

It wasn't even noon yet and they had moved the cow/calf pairs to their new home on the range for the next couple of months. Anna was searching the wildflowers in the new pasture when her sharp eye caught some movement. She spotted the wolf first, circling around behind the herd. Odd pulled out his rifle. "Hold on to your horse," Anna, this gun shoots pretty loud, and it might set him off."

Anna dismounted and held both of their horses tight while Odd took a bead on the wolf. He kicked up a puff of dust right in front of the wolf, and it was gone before he could get another shot off. "Darn critters," said Odd. "I think the calves are big enough that I don't have to worry about wolves getting them, but you never know. Them wolves are the smartest critters I ever run across. I've watched them stalk a bison for days, like they were making friends with the beast. Then when the old animal gets used to them being there and least expects it, they'll have it for dinner. It isn't easy to watch, but that's the way nature works."

"I guess that they are just another piece of nature's puzzle," Anna replied. She didn't know it at the time, but sometime in the distant future a wolf attack would disrupt her life in a major and severe way. "What about the coyotes?"

"Oh, they're pesky but not much of a problem. They get a chicken now and then, and they worry me at calving time, but mostly they just clean up the cows' afterbirths. I think they have plenty of ready made lunch around here without bothering us ranchers too much. I actually sorta enjoy listening to them talking and yipping in the evening. They're as much a part of the prairie as the grass is."

"Me too," chimed in Anna. "I have only been here a couple of days, and I already listen for them singing their songs at night. Is that a fox? We had lots of them in Norway."

"Yup, a red one, the most common out here. Some say they're the smartest critter of them all. The pelts are beautiful in the winter. Reidun would like a fox coat to keep her warm, and I'd love to have enough pelts to make her one."

"She has already mentioned that to me."

"Maybe I'll run a trap line this winter and see if I can get enough for her coat. Their fur is all rubbed out and flea bitten now, but it is beautiful in the winter when it's prime. Let's make one more ride around the cows to make sure they're all paired up. Last year I left them too soon, and a couple of the cows went back to the old pasture looking for their calves. Had a heck of a time getting them back. Took twice as long as the original move. I won't make that mistake again."

Sure enough, one of the cows was already heading back toward her old pasture, so Odd and Anna turned her around and moved her back into the herd. "That brat of yours is right here somewhere, old girl," Odd said to the cow. "Probably that one over there bellering like he's lost." Sure enough, it was. There was a happy reunion and the calf immediately found a handle to suck on.

"They truly amaze me," Anna commented. "Those 'kids' all look the same to me, but these Moms can pick theirs out of the crowd."

"Cows have an amazing sense of smell. One sniff and they know if it's theirs. Sometimes when one of them loses their calf in the spring, I keep the dead calf and skin it. Then if I get a set of twins, I take one of the twins and tie the dead calf's hide over it. The mother of the dead calf takes a whiff of the old hide and thinks it's her calf, risen from the dead. Otherwise I'd have to fight her for days to get her to take a new calf, and even then it sometimes doesn't work."

Anna was trying to imagine a little calf walking around with the hide of another dead calf on it, and she smiled at the thought.

"Well, it looks to me like they've all paired up and are pretty content," Odd observed. "Let's get home and see what Reidun's up to. Probably fussing over that party she's throwing for you. You women are always trying to play matchmaker and get us poor unsuspecting guys hitched up."

"Yup, you guys sure have it tough," Anna agreed, "having to put up with us poor defenseless and helpless females."

Odd laughed. "Beat you home!" He galloped off whooping and hollering.

Anna just took her time on the way back, trying to take in all the new sights and sounds and smells that the prairie was serving up.

One of her favorite sounds was the meadowlark, a large bird with a yellow belly. Their song was so unique, and they seemed to show up every time she stopped. The jackrabbits amazed her too. So long and lanky and tall, hopping along like they had springs built into their hind legs. They were gray now, and Anna would be surprised to see them turn snow white for their winter camouflage. The wildflowers were beautiful and she wanted to stop and pick some of them but decided to start home instead.

In the shade of a big cottonwood tree, she finally saw her first rattlesnake. It saw her, too, and since she was so close it immediately coiled up and started rattling its tail. "Ok, old man," she said, "that's one sound I'll never forget. I think this is where most ranchers would get their .22 out of the scabbard and have some target practice, but you were here before I was, so let's just part company and call it a truce, ok partner?" The snake apparently didn't believe her and rattled a little faster. "Ok, ok, I'm leaving." She started off but turned to look back. The snake was already gone, disappeared into the grass. "Thank you," Anna hollered back at him. "Nice meeting you too!" Blue looked unconcerned and just plodded along toward the Larson ranch.

Odd popped over the hill. "Just checking up—thought the greenhorn might've got herself lost or something."

"Thanks, Odd. I'm just taking my time and enjoying your ranch. Is there anything better, Odd?"

"Better than what?"

"Owning your own land and caring for it and having it care for you and provide for your family."

"Guess I never thought of it that way, but you sure are right. It makes a person feel pretty proud and at the same time pretty humble to own and be the caretaker of a chunk of God's earth."

"Well said," Anna replied. "It's only ours for a spell, but it's always God's."

They rode home slowly and thoughtfully. Odd seemed to be a little quieter, like he was soaking up Anna's words. They were in sight of the farmyard.

"What are you two up to now?" Reidun hollered. "Dinner is getting cold, so why don't you two cowpunchers belly up to the table and get some grub?"

"I'm starving," Anna hollered back. "Be there as soon as I get Blue unsaddled."

It was a typical cowboy dinner—beans with a little bacon stirred in and hot biscuits with butter and wild buffalo-berry jam. "Mighty fine dinner," Anna told Reidun.

"It'll fill your belly," she said.

"And maybe make you sing a bit later," Odd grinned.

"Will you ever grow up, Odd Larson?" Reidun teased.

After dinner Odd went out to work with the gelding he was breaking while Anna asked Reidun to sit down. "You made the dinner, now I'll do the dishes."

"Thank you, Anna. How was the round up?"

"It was amazing, and I learned so much about cattle and the land. That husband of yours even had some words of wisdom."

"About time," Reidun chimed in. "Maybe this will speed his growing up process?" She patted her tummy and looked at Anna with a gleam in her eye.

"Oh Reidun! I thought you had a little extra glow. How long have you known?"

"I started suspecting a few weeks ago. I figure it'll be coming about December. It's a little scary being my first. I'm sure glad to have you here to share this with, Anna."

"I'll do all I can. You and Odd will be the best parents in South Dakota. Have you told him?"

"Nope, been waiting for you to grow him up and I wanted to be positive I was pregnant. I suspect the party will be a good time to tell him."

"I'm so excited, Reidun! This is the best news ever."

"I'm excited, too, but to tell you the truth I'm a little worried. The closest doctor is down in the Black Hills somewhere, maybe Belle Fourche. You seem so good at everything, Anna. Have you delivered any babies?"

"I helped our dog back in Norway. Does that count?"

"Sorry I asked," Reidun laughed.

Saturday afternoon came quickly. They finished chores up early and made a day out of getting ready for the party for Anna. She did her part by making a cake and two pies, and Reidun whipped up another batch of beans. "I love it when we get together with the neighbors," Reidun reflected. "These potluck suppers are my favorite. We have some good cooks in the neighborhood, but I'm guessing your pies will be the most popular dish. I think I'll skip the beans and go straight to dessert to make sure I don't get left out."

"I think the best part of the day will be seeing the expression on Odd's face when you break the news to him."

Odd came in. "I got the wagon hitched. Let's get those goodies loaded and head over to the meeting hall. I can't wait to brag about my calf crop and that gelding I'm working with."

"I can't wait to show off Anna," replied Reidun.

"Yeah I know," Odd sulked. "She'll be the life of the party, and I won't get any attention at all."

"So much for growing him up," Reidun winked at Anna.

They were the last to arrive. "I thought we'd be the first," said Reidun. "I guess you're the most excitement this community's had for a long spell, Anna."

"It's sort of embarrassing, Reidun. Do I look ok?" Anna blushed.

"Just like New York came to SD, my dear. You'll knock their socks off."

Anna blushed a little more. They unloaded their items for the potluck onto the table, which was filled with all sorts of good looking and smelling dishes. The neighbors were already visiting and having a good time. The three eligible bachelors were grinning shyly at the edge of the crowd, and after introducing Anna to everyone else Reidun finally got around to taking Anna over to them.

"About time," the one that Anna had already noticed said. "We've been waiting all spring for this. My name is Iver Tenold, Miss Anna, and I reckon you're about the prettiest thing this prairie has seen for years. Except you of course, Reidun."

Anna blushed again.

"I didn't know you were such a ladies man, Iver Tenold," replied Reidun. "Anna, this is Billy Iverson, and this other handsome bachelor is James Freeman. Why don't you three boys quit your drooling and get acquainted with Anna? That is if Iver here will let you two get a word in." Reidun left the four of them to help organize lunch and visit with her other friends.

Anna hadn't come looking for someone to replace Rasmus; she just came looking for a place to call home and something to settle that empty feeling she often had. It had been easy for her to turn down all of the men that had tried courting her back in New York and Minneapolis because she just wasn't ready yet. But something about this Iver Tenold had caught her eye, maybe even her heart. He wasn't that handsome, and he was only an inch or two taller than she was. He wasn't the big, broad shouldered type some women fell for. But there was definitely something about him that held her attention.

They had only visited a few minutes, and Anna had already decided that Iver was intelligent and confident and knew how to work. Reidun had told her some of his story already, and it was nearly identical to Anna's. He had left Norway as a boy and had come to America on his own, possibly on the same ship but a few years earlier. He had gone through Ellis Island and New York and Chicago and Minneapolis and had gotten off the railroad somewhere in North Dakota. He had purchased a horse there and had made his way to Reva by himself. He was a self-made man with the air of someone who could take care of himself and everyone around him. Anna was intrigued. Iver was smitten.

Before the night was over he had asked her to dance with him. She explained that she didn't know how, and he confessed that he didn't either. They both laughed and went on visiting about their plans and hopes and dreams. Iver asked Anna if he might be able to come over to the Larson ranch and see her again. Maybe they could go on a picnic or something?

"This is all so new to me, Iver, and I've just gotten here. Could you give me a few days to think this over?"

"I'll give you all year if you'll consider it. But the sooner the better 'cause I won't get anything done over at the ranch just thinking about you. I'll be plumb worthless." He laughed again and so did Anna. She liked a sense of humor in a man.

The other two bachelors had bashfully tried to interrupt a time or two, but they finally just gave up. They were no competition for Iver.

Reidun had finally told Odd the news that he was going to be a father. After standing there dumbfounded for a minute or two, he jumped on the picnic table and hollered at the top of his lungs. "We're pregnant! I'm gonna be a daddy!" He looked at Reidun and said, "Reidun, you've made me the happiest man on earth." He jumped down and gave her another hug. "The drinks are on me folks!"

"What drinks?" asked Iver.

"Well the lemonade, of course. Unless your uncle Chris has some of that homemade wine of his around?"

"Only for special occasions," Chris replied. "And this is about as special as they get. I'll break out a couple gallons of my latest batch and we'll all have some of my buffalo berry wine and celebrate the start of a new generation of Norwegian South Dakotans. I'll head over to the ranch and get some of it right now."

Anna tried the wine and had to admit that it was pretty tasty. Odd wouldn't let Reidun have any. "We gotta start watching what we eat and drink," he said.

"You mean *I* have to," Reidun responded.

"If it makes you feel any better, I could drink a glass for you."

"Ok you two love birds," said Anna. "The bay has been standing there patiently all day. I think he'd like to head for the corral and have some hay."

"You're right," said Odd. "Hasn't it been an amazing afternoon though? I still have to pinch myself. Isn't that Reidun something?"

"Next you'll be offering to do my chores for me, Odd," Reidun added.

"Well, I heard that a little work is good for pregnant women," he laughed. They all smiled. It had indeed been the best of days, especially for Anna. She had something new to think about and to dream about tonight.

12

A Date With Destiny

Iver came riding over the very next day. "We're missing some steers," he lied.

"Sure you are," Odd grinned. "You sure that's what you're missing?"

"Are you going to ask me in for some coffee or do I have to invite myself? Is Anna around? I don't want her to forget what I look like."

"I'm in here," Anna said through the door, "and the coffee is on. Maybe I should go look for them steers for you while you and Odd have a cup or two?" she offered.

"Oh, uh, well I think I might have just remembered where they are, er might be, so why don't you stay and have coffee with us?"

"Ok, but how're you gonna drink coffee with your foot in your mouth?"

"Done it many times," Iver laughed. They all did. "By the way Anna, have you done any thinking on what I asked?"

"Yes, I have, and the answer is still the same. Give me another day or two. But why don't you stop by the day after tomorrow about noon and we'll see."

"Yipee," yelled Iver. "Sounds like a date to me."

"Now that you've drank all our coffee and Anna's said that she

MIGHT see you Tuesday, why don't you go see if you can find something constructive to do, Iver?"

"Ok, ok. I know when I'm not wanted. Reidun, could I come over Monday night and camp on your porch, just to make sure Anna doesn't sneak out on me or change her mind?"

"Would you get home, Iver Tenold, before I put you to work myself?"

"Yes ma'am." He tipped his hat to Reidun and Anna. "I'll see if Prairie can lead me back to Chris's place."

"Don't forget to look for them steers," Odd laughed.

Reidun and Anna giggled after Iver left. "I think that one might be just as bad as Odd," said Reidun. "You'd think they were brothers."

"Or just as good?" added Anna. "Why don't you and that soon to be born baby of yours take a nap while I do some work around the house? Then if he's ok with it, I want Odd to teach me how to break horses to ride. It looks like that's an important skill to have around here."

"It sure is. And I happen to know that Iver Tenold loves his horses and that he wants to fill a ranch with his own herd."

"I could live with a horse herd of my own, Reidun."

Anna had to admit that Monday was moving slowly and that she was looking forward to Tuesday. Odd picked out a two year old filly and put her in the round corral for Anna to work with. He explained how he broke them, first gentling them down, then teaching them to get used to a halter by dragging the halter rope behind them for a day or two, then tying them to a fence until they didn't fight it anymore. "Once they are at that stage," he explained, "it is up to you to get them used to your voice and actions. Use that horse brush on their entire body until they get used to you touching and feeling them. Soon they will look forward to it, especially the brushing and your voice. Then move to their legs and work with them until you can pick up all four and work on their hooves. That's about the most important part of a horse—if their hooves go bad and they get lame, you are out of a horse and on foot."

"I can see the wisdom in that Odd. Like a wagon without its wheels."

"The next step is called sacking them out. I throw a blanket or two on their backs and let them walk around the corral with them until they get used to the feel. When they are ready, I slowly put the saddle on and sometimes a bridle. If they are gentle enough I try riding them with the halter and no bridle-bit in their mouth at all. I first walk them around the corral a few times without a rider to get them used to it, or even just tie them up for a few hours with the saddle on."

Anna could see it in her mind. She was absorbing every word. She had already grown to love horses and was thinking of how great it would be to tame a wild horse.

"Then when I think they are ready, I ease onto them and hope for the best, which would be no bucking and a nice walk around the corral with me hardly hanging on to the saddle. If the worst happens and they start bucking, I try not to let them have their head so they don't learn to buck hard enough to throw me off. Once they learn that they can get rid of you, they're apt to do it again every chance they get, especially if you get caught in a tight spot. Now she's yours to break Anna, let's see what you got."

"I hope I can remember all of this, Odd. Will you be around to remind me and help?"

"Sure, but sometimes it's best to learn your own way. Horses are mostly just common sense. Treat them the way you'd want to be treated, and they'll take good care of you."

"Thanks so much for helping me. How long does it take?"

"Sometimes a week, sometimes a month, sometimes several months, sometimes never. Once they are broke to ride the training begins. Starts and stops, reining, working cows, roping, taking the right leads, crossing water. You name it. Once you got a good broke horse, you'll love it and it'll love you, just like me and my horse or you and Blue, I suspect."

"You're right" said Anna. "Nothing like it in the world. You got a name for this filly?"

"Nope. Why don't you name her?"

Anna worked with the filly, which she named Star of the West (she had a nice star on her forehead), until late afternoon when she went in to help start supper. Reidun was up but still had telltale bedspread marks on her cheek from the nap.

"That felt so good, Anna. I don't know who needed it the most— me or junior in there."

"It's good for you, Reidun. You need to let us pamper you a little. To prove my point I insist that you move to the porch and have a cool drink of water while I start supper. Did you have anything in mind?"

"Let's eat up as much of that leftover antelope as we can and then we'll strip the rest to make jerky. The meat spoils fast in this warm weather."

"Leave it me," Anna replied.

After supper, Odd went out to the porch. "Just checking," he laughed, "to make sure Iver isn't camped out on it. I wouldn't put it past that rascal."

The next day Anna was anxiously waiting for Iver to arrive, but she tried not to show it. She swept the porch twice, then went to the corral and watched the horses. Iver showed up exactly at noon. It was a bit cloudy and looked like showers might build up. He jumped off of Prairie and handed Anna a bouquet of summer flowers that he had picked along the way. "Not much compared to you, Anna, but they were all I could find," he said.

"Thanks, Iver. They are so pretty. I love flowers. I'd like to have my own roses someday, maybe even a lilac bush in front of my house." (She would later find that her comment hadn't gone unnoticed.) "You mentioned a picnic, and I think it's a fine day for one. Reidun helped me get a couple of sandwiches put together, and Odd offered the wagon and the bay. I have a jug of cool well water, and I threw a couple of cane fishing poles in the wagon in case we want to try our luck. Let's go up the road a spell and have our picnic under that big cottonwood by the river if it suits you."

"Does it ever," said Iver. Thanks so much, Odd and Reidun."

"Have her back early," Odd scolded.

"I will, sir, I promise," Iver saluted.

Off they went in the wagon, picnic and all. Iver had the biggest grin that Odd and Reidun had ever seen on his face.

Iver broke the ice by asking Anna what she thought of South Dakota so far.

"It is so different from home in Norway that I really don't know what to think yet. You've been here, what, five years now? I should be asking you."

"Well, I think it's what you make of it. In Norway I had no chance of owning my own land. My brother John was the oldest and he was destined to inherit the farm and that was that. I love land and farming and livestock more than most anything, and it's pretty much what brought me to America. Land and livestock are my dream, and my dream took me here, to South Dakota. It isn't perfect by any means. Sometimes too dry, sometimes too wet. Sometimes too hot, sometimes too cold. Sometimes it lures you to sleep with its kindness and beauty and then wakes you with a fury and anger hard to comprehend. But here is where the land is, as far as you can see. I wake up every morning thinking that I'm dreaming and that this isn't possible, but it is. I'm guessing that you had the same dream as I did? What are you looking for, Anna?"

She thought for a moment and then just said, "Yes, we had the same dream."

Iver pulled the wagon as close under the tree as he could. "Speaking of dreams, if I could have dreamt the most perfect dream ever, this would have been it, Anna Ingevich. I'll pull this lap robe off of the buggy and spread it on the other side of the tree, closest to the water. Then we can put our picnic on it and just enjoy each other, the sky, the water, the land…I don't think there is anything I wouldn't enjoy if you were part of it, Anna."

Iver was too engrossed with Anna to realize that he forgot to tie the bay to the tree. "You've only known me for three days, Iver. Don't you think that you should get to know me better before you start saying things like that? I'm not nearly as perfect as you're making me out to be."

"I feel like I've known you all my life," Iver replied, and there wasn't a smile on his face. He was serious. "I think that I knew you before I met you, if that makes any sense. I don't believe in coincidences but the same thing, the same dream brought the two of us here to this spot in the middle of the world a million miles from our homes in Norway. I aim to see to it that the same thing that brought us here keeps the two of us together. I can be as stubborn as a mule, Anna, and this is what I want, more than I ever wanted anything. Even more than I wanted a ranch in South Dakota. I think that my being with you was meant to be."

Anna wasn't ready to be that serious yet. "I guess we'll just see what happens." She smiled at him.

"My, these are good sandwiches. Just like I like them. You can't put too much butter on good fresh bread. Did you bake this bread? If you tell me that you can cook, too, you'll never get me out of Larson's yard. I'll camp there until you're an old woman, or I'm dead of exhaustion."

"Reidun made it," Anna ignored Iver's comment and lied. After dinner they lay back on the buggy robe and watched the clouds build in the western horizon.

"I'm guessing it'll rain later on," said Iver. "But we have lots of time. The grass sure could use some rain and the crops too. Chris and I planted some wheat this year. Took lots of money for the seed, but if a good crop comes in we could make it big. I've already got three quarters of land of my own Anna. Not what you would call a ranch but a good start I figure. Chris has promised to help me buy the old Robbins place when I get a little more ahead. Then I'll have a real spread."

They didn't notice that the bay had walked off with the wagon and was already going over the hill, headed for home. They were too engrossed in each other to notice anything else. A while later the clouds started building more quickly and a low rumble moaned in the west, finally getting their attention.

"Looks like that storm is coming faster than I thought." He

looked back to see the horse and wagon gone. "What the heck, where's the…? What's going on here?"

Anna jumped up. "Oh my goodness!" She grabbed the blanket and the picnic basket. "We'd better start hiking fast, Iver. It looks like we could get drenched." They were about half way back to the house when it hit, first as a few gusts of wind and then as a full blown rain pounding them, coming down in almost horizontal sheets. They covered as best they could with the blanket and just kept plodding along as there wasn't any protection from the storm. Anna laughed at their predicament, even though the lightning was popping all around them. They were soaked and their shoes were blobs of mud, making it hard to walk.

About the time it was over, Odd popped into view with the wagon. "I'm never going to hear the end of this," Iver remarked. "The wagon going home without us and here we come carrying the blanket."

"Great first date," Anna laughed.

Odd pulled up. "And to think I trusted you, Iver Tenold." He was wearing his "Odd" grin. They jumped up on the wagon with him, and he turned back for the Larson ranch. "Why, Iver, you don't seem to be saying much."

Iver and Odd put the wagon away and led the bay into the corral. Anna headed for the house with the soaking wet blanket and Reidun met her at the door already laughing. "Don't look at me," Anna laughed with her, "that EXPERT horseman you introduced me to forgot to tie up the wagon."

"Do you suppose it was on purpose?" Reidun kidded. "Maybe he planned to get left there with you?"

Anna blushed and went into the bedroom to dry off and change clothes. Odd and Iver came in, and Reidun offered Iver some supper before he had to head home.

"That would be great," Iver allowed. "A muddy walk in the rain with a pretty girl gives a guy a big appetite."

"Heard that you had a little trouble with the bay, Iver," Reidun smiled.

"Not at all," he smiled back. "Everything was going just the way I planned until that doggone storm came up."

He glanced at Anna who was frowning and thinking to herself that maybe Reidun was on to something?

"I'm just kidding," Iver quickly added.

Iver saddled Prairie up and headed south right after supper, but not before asking Anna if he could come again, maybe tomorrow. Anna told him not until Saturday.

"That's a long time, Anna."

"Don't you have any work over there?" Odd asked.

"Nothing this important," Iver replied. "See you Saturday, Anna." He headed down the trail singing an old Norwegian song as Anna watched him leave.

"What are you thinking, Anna?" Reidun asked.

"With that one, I'm not sure what to think, but he's certainly got my attention."

"He aims to have more than that, but you're right to go slow. Tell me all about your date. Did he propose yet?"

"I know you are just teasing, Reidun, but in a way he actually did. What he said made an awful lot of sense, and he wasn't joking around with me. I didn't come here looking for a man. In fact, it was just the opposite. I was running from one. Finding someone like Iver was the furthest thing from my mind, as far as Norway is from South Dakota, but I guess I found one. Now I'm not sure what to do with him, but I can't just ignore this and I can't just ignore the way I feel around him. He can be funny one minute and dead serious the next. He keeps me on my toes and I like that. Tell me again how you met him and everything you know about him and his family. I don't want to miss anything, Reidun. I couldn't take another broken heart, that's for sure. And if I let this get serious, I'll need to tell him about Rasmus, not that it should matter to Iver, but I like to have all the lutefisk on the table if you know what I mean."

The next day, Anna started working with the filly after breakfast and doing a few of the barnyard chores. Among other tasks, she had learned how to milk the cow, which had been Reidun's job. Anna actually enjoyed milking, which no one else seemed to like. There were three farm cats that always followed her into the barn, begging to have their bowl filled with some fresh milk. Just for the fun of it Anna squirted one of the cats in the face one morning, thinking that the cat would jump up and take off. Instead, it held its ground and gobbled the milk as fast as Anna squirted it into its face. This became a game, and all three cats got a few squirts every day.

Odd caught her one morning and scolded her good naturedly. "Those lazy cats are supposed to be keeping the mice down around here, Anna. Now you've gone and put them in the soup line."

"I'm just bribing them, Odd. They promised to catch more mice if I'd treat them to a little milk once in a while. Besides, I think the big tabby is pregnant. You wouldn't make an expectant mother go out and chase mice would you?"

"Just leave some milk for me, I like my butter and cream."

The filly that Odd had let Anna start working with was a challenge for sure. She had a lot of fire in her and wasn't about to give up her freedom easily. Anna sensed that there was to be no hurrying the job with her; it had to be slow and easy or not at all. With that filly, trust was essential. Anna had to work her way into the horse's heart before anything else would happen. The filly had big wild eyes and she trembled when Anna tried to touch her, but she had softened some by the end of the week.

When Iver arrived Saturday, she asked him if he would help her with Star, so he went over to the corral with her to take a look. Star was in the round corral with a halter and a halter rope which she was dragging around.

Iver remarked, "I think Odd showed me this filly a while back. If I remember right he said that he had worked with her, but he was going to put her off until last because she was a real challenge. Now that sly old dog has you working with her. Guess he figures if you can handle her you can handle anything."

"I like a challenge," Anna grinned. "I'll show Odd who the best horse handler around here is."

"I know a trick or two. If you'll let me, I'll help you and we'll make good old Odd look like an amateur."

Together they worked with the filly the rest of the day. Iver promised Anna that he wouldn't tell Odd that he had been helping her with the filly. That night Odd showed up and asked them what they'd been up to.

"Oh, we went fishing for a while," Iver fibbed. "And then we hiked over to that big grassy butte to look around." Iver happened to have an arrowhead in his pocket that he was going to give Anna anyway, so he pulled it out. "Anna found this arrowhead up on top and gave it to me to keep in my pocket. Here Anna, you should take it now or I might forget it and leave it there."

"Thanks, Iver. It is beautiful isn't it?"

"Can I come back tomorrow? It is Sunday you know."

"I heard there's a Lutheran pastor in the area and that they are having a genuine Sunday church service in the Reva hall tomorrow afternoon. If you'll take me to church, Iver, I'll go with you."

"I love church," Iver fibbed again. "I'll come a little early and we can work on our joint project for a while, and then ride to church in the afternoon."

Iver did have a way with horses. It was almost uncanny the way that little filly responded to him so quickly Sunday morning. Of course Anna had been working with her daily, but Iver's presence made a big difference. "I think we have something else in common," Iver told Anna. "We both seem to love horses. I've got something I'd like to show you next week but it will be a fairly long ride. You up for it?"

"Depends on what it is, Iver."

"I can't tell you or it wouldn't be a surprise. I've been keeping it a secret and you'll be the first to see it."

"Ok," she answered. "Let's figure out which day to go and see your secret on our ride home from church this afternoon. You didn't forget about church, did you?"

"Of course not. It's been the only thing on my mind all morning."

"You shouldn't be telling tales on Sunday, Iver."

"Let's get a saddle on this Star of the West of yours and whisper some sweet talk into her ear, see what she has to say?"

"Don't you think it's too soon?"

"She looks ready to me. See those big brown eyes of hers, soft as a kitten now. They used to look as wild as a polecat. We'll just slide the saddle on and off a few times, maybe tighten the cinch a little and lead her around the corral with it on. That should be enough for today. We'll let her think on everything overnight, and then if I can get over tomorrow we'll get back to business."

"Do I recall saying you could come over tomorrow?"

"Well, uh, I just figured that since we had this project going together you'd want me to..."

"I'm just having fun, Iver. Of course you can."

"How about this. I'll come over tomorrow and we'll work on the filly. Then you can ride over to our outfit and help me do some branding Tuesday. Chris had some late calvers, and we need to brand their calves before taking them out to the breeding pasture with the rest of the herd. Chris has promised me that I could buy all of his heifer calves this fall and start my own herd with them. My uncle has taken me in like his own son. Even said he'd let me buy them on credit and for half price. As soon as you say 'yes' we can call it OUR herd. Chris has some of the best Herefords in the country."

"Is this a proposal I'm hearing, Iver, or a bribe?"

"Well, I'm not ready to get turned down, so I'm trying to sweeten the pot a bit. There is no doubt in my mind, Anna, and as soon as you say 'yes' I'll be the happiest Norwegian in America."

"I'm a slow thinker, Iver, but you might just have me coming around. We have that long ride and the 'surprise' you've been telling me about. How about we take that whole day for me to figure out what I'm going to do with you?"

"Can we just skip today and take that ride right now?"

"Did you already forget about church again?"

"Of course not," he said half serious.

"Ok, we're working with the filly Monday and branding on

Tuesday. If the sun is shining Wednesday, let's saddle up and see that surprise of yours."

"I know what I'm praying for in church today," he smiled. "Let's get to heading for church so I can start praying."

"You may be able to sweet talk me, Iver Tenold, but God can see right through you."

"Well, I'm sure he won't blame a man for trying. Look here Anna, I even brought my suit coat to wear over my shirt so I could look all proper for church today."

"Well aren't you a dandy. Let's see if you can impress both God AND me today."

Off they went, laughing and visiting.

Reidun reported to Odd, "I think they're just as good as hitched. Looks like we're going to have us a wedding."

"Another good man bites the dust," Odd added with that big, good natured grin of his, just to make sure that Reidun didn't scold him. She did anyway.

It was a good old country fire-and-brimstone sermon that seemed to last as long as the entire calving season to Iver. Anna on the other hand took in every word and even sat there a while afterwards with her eyes shut, contemplating the sermon and saying a prayer. Anna was praying for guidance and at the same time thanking her creator for bringing her here and for all the opportunities that this land had to offer. Later that day, Iver asked her how to pray. He was serious. "You seem so good at it," he said.

"I don't think there is a proper way, Iver. I just start talking with Him like I do with you. I don't always hear His answers, I just visit with Him. One thing, Iver—don't always be asking for this and for that. Take as much or more time thanking Him for what you've got as you do asking Him for more."

"Thanks, Anna. That helps a lot. You probably know what I was praying for today. I guess begging for is more like it. Tonight I'll say another prayer with the thankful part. After all, He did bring you here."

It was a fun afternoon after the church service. By now Anna knew most of the neighbors and they all knew her. Her pie had been the talk of the previous gathering, at least with everyone who was lucky enough to get a piece. She even visited easily with the other two bachelors who had hoped she might look their way with something other than visiting on her mind. She had a way of saying no in a way that made them feel good about it and themselves. If she couldn't be their girlfriend, she could still be a good friend. Iver really appreciated that, since they were his neighbors and they did a lot of work together. Brandings, roundups, cattle shipments, and other ranch work was often a community effort with each rancher taking turns helping the other. Life out here was hard, and these community efforts were part of the glue that held their lives together. A rancher was independent, but at the same time he was dependent on his neighbors and his family. Anna would find out the true meaning of this a few years later.

Chris asked Iver what he was up to Monday morning.

"I know I've been pretty worthless and a total slacker around here ever since Anna came to the country. Please forgive me. Look at it like an investment if you can? If she ever says yes to my proposals, she'll be moving here, and you'll be getting homemade bread and pie mostly every day."

"Plus the view will be better," Chris chuckled. "You young'uns take all the time you need. I got along without you before you were here, and I can get along a while again. Just don't take all year if you can help it. You have big ranching ambitions; dreams like that take a lot of work and sweat. They don't just happen, Iver. By the way, I'm thinking of changing my name too. There are a LOT of Olson's in the country, most of them not even related to us. That Ole must've been a busy feller. You're the only Tenold that I know of, and I sorta like that."

"Chris Tenold it is," Iver chimed in. "And Chris, I'm slow in telling you this, but you're the best uncle a man could ever have. Without you I wouldn't be here, so if it hadn't been for you I never would have met Anna. Without your help I wouldn't have three quarters of land and a start on my own cowherd. I guess that I'd practically be nothing and have nothing if it weren't for you Chris."

A tear came to Chris's eye. "You sure know how to make an old man happy, Iver."

Iver saddled up and headed north to help Anna with Star of the West. They were making sure that Odd didn't catch them working together with her. Anna had a trick in mind, and Iver thought it was an awesome idea. The filly was fully cooperating with their plan. As soon as Odd was gone, they saddled her again and resumed breaking her. Iver silently slipped on top of her back before she knew what was happening, while Anna held the halter rope. The filly barely flinched.

"Hand me the halter rope now," Iver said to Anna.

She did, and Iver walked the filly around the corral. Star didn't even offer to hump up. She trusted both Anna and Iver. Anna was smiling her huge smile; this was an amazing moment for her. Star had gone from a wild, almost untamable horse to a trusting friend, which was what needed to happen. Both the horse and the rider depended on each other, and they had to know and trust each other equally. After Iver got off, he asked Anna if she wanted a try.

"Of course I do! It's what I've been dreaming of since Odd first showed her to me."

Iver held the halter rope while Anna got on. Star acted like it had happened a million times.

"She's a natural," Iver said. "Sometimes the horses that are the meanest to start with turn out to be the best and the most loyal. I can tell that you and Star are a pair meant to be together."

Odd came riding in later that afternoon. Iver and Anna already had Star back in with the rest of the horse herd. Iver started setting Odd up while Anna snuck back to get Star. "Say Odd, I been thinking that was a pretty nasty joke that you're playing on Anna."

"Whadya mean?"

"I mean setting her up with that wild-eyed, nasty filly of yours. I think you meant it as a joke because you know that no one will ever tame that beast. Anna could get hurt."

Odd slouched a bit. "Yeah, guess I never thought of it that way. I just wanted to give her a challenge and teach her that all critters can't be tamed. I didn't mean any harm. She didn't get hurt did she?"

"No, not yet, but you should put her onto a nicer horse before she does."

"I will, right away. I sure feel bad, Iver. What do you think I can do to make it up to her?"

"Well, the filly will never be worth much, but I guess she might still make a brood mare someday. Even though she'll never be a riding horse, I guess you could still give her to Anna as an apology. As much as Anna loves horses even a worthless one would seem like a great gift to her."

"Least I could do," said Odd. "She's all hers."

Anna was behind the wall listening. This was her cue. She came around the corner riding Star. Anna and Iver burst out laughing. Reidun too. They had let her in on their joke. Odd just stood there looking disgusted, and then he too finally started laughing. "You dirty dogs sure got the best of me. Guess I deserved it though. And by the way, Anna, you really can keep her. Looks to me like she suits you pretty well. She would sorta be your wedding present if you ever say 'yes' to this barnyard pest of ours. I think it's the only way we'll ever get him off our porch."

"Supper is almost ready, so come and get it," Reidun changed the subject. She didn't need to say it twice.

"I'll be just a minute, but don't wait for me," said Anna. "I have to unsaddle this wild and unbreakable filly of mine."

13

Secrets

In the morning Anna rode Blue over to Chris's place to help with the branding. She had done a little roping but wasn't good enough to catch a calf, so Iver gave her a few quick roping lessons on a fence post, showing her how to make a nice loop and throw it without letting go of the rope and losing control of it, then taking back the slack when it went around the post. "A calf is no different, except he's usually moving." After throwing a few more loops Anna decided that she wasn't ready to be a roper yet.

"Why don't you do the branding," Iver said. "The fire is going good enough to keep the branding irons hot. Chris and I can rope the calves and drag them to the fire, and you can brand them while Chris and I hold them down."

Anna did her best, but she didn't like the smell of the burning flesh and hair. She especially hated the anguish and pain it was putting the calves through. "Do you really have to do this to them?"

"Believe it or not we still have rustlers that like to steal unbranded cattle. As soon as they take them, rustlers will put their own brand on and then the cattle are as good as theirs. It's kinder to brand them at this age than to wait until they're older."

There were only about twenty-three of the late calves to brand, so they finished fairly quickly. After giving the calves an hour's rest they moved the herd out of the corral and started them off for the breeding pasture.

"Sure you two love birds don't need help moving them?" Chris offered.

"Naw, I don't think Anna needs any help, but I'll tag along anyway just to keep her company," Iver added.

Off they went, tired from roping and dragging and branding but feeling young and carefree. "These sure are nice cattle," Anna told Iver. "Did Chris really mean it when he told you that the heifer crop was yours for half price?"

"He sure did, darling." Iver looked over to see if "darling" registered with Anna. "The only condition was that I had to get married. I think he's getting tired of feeding me."

"So if I don't marry you, I'm responsible for you losing your herd?"

"Looks that way, Anna. Would be mighty cruel of you." He put a pout on his face.

"Men." declared Anna. "You have a million ways of trying to trick us ladies."

They reached the pasture and opened the gate to let the pairs in. Since the main herd was already there and this was a small bunch, it was easier to make sure they were all paired up. "Let's ride the whole pasture," Iver suggested. "Make sure nothing is lame or sick. If they eat too much green grass too fast the cows can get sick and die. It's called grass tetany. Makes you sick to see a healthy critter just up and die, but it's a part of ranching. Between the start of calving season and now is the worst time of the year for losses, it seems. Cows can get milk fever when their calves can't eat all of their milk. Lots of other things can go wrong too. Calves can get scours or pneumonia if it's too wet and cold."

"What is scours?" Anna asked.

"It is a stomach and intestinal disease. I'm not really sure what causes it, but the poor calves that get it basically poop themselves to death. They can't get enough liquid, and their little eyes just sink into their heads as they get more and more dehydrated."

"It sounds terrible."

"It is, but from this age on, they seem to really do well. We had two cows struck by lightning last summer. Guess it comes with the rain, the bad with the good. I see a hole in the fence that needs mending. I always carry a bit of wire and a pair of pliers in my saddlebag. It'll only take me a minute or two. By the way, would you like to just stay at our ranch tonight so we could get an earlier start on your surprise tomorrow?"

"Iver Tenold, you know that wouldn't look good. What would the neighbors say and what would Odd and Reidun think?"

"Sorry. I was just anxious for us to get an early start tomorrow. I think you are going to love my surprise."

"If nothing else, it should be a beautiful ride, Iver. I've never been to the Slim Buttes. They sure look pretty from here."

"Wait until you see those huge rock formations close up. They sure are something."

"Is that the surprise?"

"I'm not saying any more."

Anna started packing the night before. Odd loaned her his saddlebags so she could fill them. She took water, jerky, sandwiches, bread and jelly, and an extra shirt and jacket in case they got caught in the rain. It didn't look or feel like it was going to be rainy though or she wouldn't even have wanted to go. It would be a long day for her since she planned to be in the saddle before day break. The moon was still shining when she left for the Tenold ranch.

Anna and Blue covered the first mile at a fast walk. Then when it started getting light out and she could see the ground better, they lit out on a good solid trot. Iver had a pot of coffee for them when she arrived, and they sat with Chris for a few minutes drinking coffee and visiting. Chris was just as excited about Anna as Iver was, and he let it show. "You two have fun today. There's an old cabin up by Moonshine that you can use for shelter if it rains, but it looks like it's gonna be a hot and dry one to me."

"What's moonshine?" asked Anna

"Some of those early gold prospectors didn't strike it rich in the Black Hills and came out here looking for gold. When they couldn't find any gold they started making liquor, which is also called moonshine, for a living. They built a little cabin in the woods that we call Moonshine. Anyway, I'll be looking for you to be home by dark, so don't loiter too long up there. That country is so pretty that it's easy to lose track of time just trying to take it all in. If you don't get back here by dark, I'll be fretting."

"Don't worry about us," Anna said. "We'll be fine and we'll make sure to head for home a few hours before dark. We both have good saddle horses, and I don't have to worry about Iver forgetting to tie up the wagon on this trip."

Chris laughed. "See you two later. I'm just an old bachelor cook, but I'll have some beans ready for supper when you get back."

The sun was fully up when they left, but they had a good jump on the day. Iver said, "It's about four miles to the buttes, and then it might take another hour or two depending."

"Depending on what?"

"Depending on if I can find the surprise."

"Iver Tenold, this isn't just some trick to get me out riding in the buttes with you is it?"

"Nope, I promise you'll love it. If I can find it."

They rode to an area that Iver called The Gap. It split the rising formations called the Slim Buttes into a north grouping and a south grouping. The big ship-shaped rock formations were to their southeast, and it looked like the buttes ran for several miles in both directions. They weren't very wide, but they were many miles long. After riding around a couple of the ship formations, which Anna had to admit were magnificent, Iver said, "let's head over the top and then off to the southwest along the rim for a spell, then head back into the heart of the buttes."

It was an amazing vista from the top of the Slim Buttes. Anna could see almost forever to the west and to the east. The buttes were like a spine running along the back of a giant landmass. From here she spotted herds of antelope, some deer, and even a small herd of bison. The grass was dotted with coveys of grouse, partridge, and prairie chickens which often flew up almost under their horses. The sky was crystal blue with a few fluffy clouds loitering lazily across it, and there was only a slight breeze from the northwest, which was the typical wind direction in South Dakota. Iver kept thinking to himself that if Anna says yes today it will be the best day of my life. If she doesn't say anything it will still be the best day of my life. "I just pray that she doesn't say 'no,'".

There was a homestead off to the west, but other than that there was no sign of civilization except for a few man made holes dug by the gold-seekers. Iver had been telling Anna about The Battle of the Slim Buttes, which had been waged on the eastern slopes of the Slim Buttes, not far from where they were riding, back in the fall of 1876. "It was the army's first victory after the Battle of the Little Bighorn in June when Custer and all his men were killed. The only survivor of that battle was a horse named Comanche. In the battle of the Slim Buttes a Captain Mills of the 3rd Cavalry surrounded an Indian village and in a surprise attack killed most of them. Chief American Horse survived but was mortally wounded and died later."

"It must have been terrible, especially for the children."

"I can only imagine, Anna. I still find old arrowheads, shell casings, and stuff when I ride through the area. If we get time on our way back we can go look for some. It won't be much out of our way."

They made great time, following a well-used deer trail through the timber until they got to the west edge of the rim. Then they continued for a couple miles further south, where they entered another canyon and rode back to the east again. On the edge of a rim, tucked on top of a hill, Iver got off his horse and motioned for Anna to stop and be very quiet and to stay there. He crawled up to the top and peeked over, then crawled back to Anna. He whispered to her, "Let's tie our horses up here, and you can follow me to the top. We need to be extra cautious not to make any noise."

Anna didn't even answer, but tip-toed behind him to almost the top, where they got down and crawled on their elbows and stomach the rest of the way. Anna almost yelled out loud when she saw Iver's "surprise." About forty-five wild horses were grazing right below them, many with foals. What appeared to be the stallion was off to their right about a hundred yards watching the herd. They were mixed colors, looking as colorful as a rainbow. Bays, blacks, sorrels, paints, grays, whites, and even a buckskin or two. Anna smiled in amazement. They just laid there for a few minutes in wonder, and then they slid back down to their side of the ridge so that they wouldn't be detected.

Iver again whispered to Anna, "I found them about three months ago, and they just took my breath away. Must be some leftover Spanish horses along with some Indian ponies mixed in. They probably moved here from the Rocky Mountains in Montana. I couldn't believe my eyes when I first spotted them. No one in the neighborhood has mentioned seeing wild horses, so I think we might be the only ones to know about them. I've been checking on the herd weekly, and they seem to like this valley the best, but they'll move on when it gets grazed out. I'm so happy they were still here Anna. I would've felt like a fool if they hadn't been, and you would have thought I was just up to no good."

"Oh, Iver, I'm so glad they're still here. It's one of the most amazing sights I've ever seen. They are just plain magnificent."

The two worked their way back to their horses and silently rode back along the trail they had come on. When they were far enough away, Iver started talking again. "Those horses are up for grabs, Anna. If you agree, I think that we should try to round them up and take care of them. Out here they have no protection and are fair game for wolves, cougars, and ranchers that might shoot them if they get on their range. We could let them run virtually wild, but take the yearlings each year and break them for saddle horses. They would bring a premium as everyone knows how tough and reliable these mustangs are. We could even do a little control breeding by bringing in another stallion." He paused. "What do you think, Anna? I've never been so excited, but there might be something I'm not thinking of. I do know this, Anna. I love you and I love horses."

"Let's find some shade to stop and rest in. We need to break for lunch anyway."

They sat up their picnic on a soft area of grass surrounded by trees and Anna began: "Those horses are beautiful, Iver. I don't know if I've ever seen anything so breathtaking as that herd. Whether or not you decide to try to round them up and start your own horse herd with them is entirely up to you. I can see pros and cons each way, but if it'll make you happy that's the way I'd lean. They aren't really what I need to talk about though. It's us. You and me. I've been dragging my feet a long time, but I've had my reasons. There is something that I need to tell you about. It might change the way you feel about me, I don't know. I do know this though; I would never start a relationship that wasn't based entirely on honesty and trust. It's no different than with you and your horse Prairie. Without honesty and trust, things fall apart."

"What are you trying to tell me, Anna? I love you, and that could never change."

"Maybe, maybe not, Iver. Please hear me out. A few months over a year ago I was running away from my home in Norway. My only thought was to find a new life in America. On the voyage over, I met a man and fell in love with him. I dreamed of being with him and starting a new life with him. He said that he loved me and asked me to marry him. I said yes. We planned to get married as soon as we got to America and could find a preacher. When we got to Ellis Island, he was told he had a telegram waiting for him. The telegram contained the worst possible news for the two of us. He hadn't told me, but he was engaged to be married in Norway. His fiancée refused to go to America with him, so they broke up and he left for America without her. Her parents didn't know of this at the time, and when they found out they were so ashamed that they put the girl on the next ship for America. It seems they may have liked their future son-in-law better than their daughter, or maybe it was just a matter of pride for them."

Anna paused to let this sink in, and Iver was intently listening.

"At any rate, my fiancée suddenly found himself engaged to two girls and had to decide between us. I honestly think that he loved me the most, but his honor and the fact that he didn't think that the other lady could survive alone in America without him pushed him toward her. I didn't know what to do, but I ended up telling him that the best thing for everyone would be for me to leave and for him to meet his other fiancée when she arrived. He didn't say much, I think that he was too emotional to talk, but he agreed. I was heartbroken and left all alone in an unknown world. I had been alone for most of my life, but this was the first time I had felt so lonely and when the reality of how alone I actually was hit me."

Iver didn't say anything so Anna went on:

"From New York, I worked my way to Chicago, Minneapolis, and then to SD and to you. I haven't been able to answer you yet because I wanted to make sure that I was really in love with you rather than just trying to forget my old fiancée, Rasmus. And I wanted to make sure my heart was never broken again. I've loved every minute that I've spent with you, Iver, and I think that I've proven to myself that I truly do love you and that you truly love me. So my answer to your proposal is yes, but only if these facts haven't changed your mind."

Iver didn't even stop to think. "You've made me the happiest man on God's earth, Anna. I couldn't care less if you'd already loved a thousand men. I just want to be the LAST man you'll ever love."

On their way back they talked about setting a date for their wedding. "I'd like to do this tomorrow, Anna, but in fairness to you I have to get a home ready for us first."

"It needn't be anything much," Anna interrupted. "If we are going to build the ranch of our dreams, we need to think of it first. I have some money saved up and so do you. Everything we have should go into land and cattle, and maybe that horse herd you're dreaming of. Anything else at this point is just a waste of money. Maybe someday we can have a proper house, but not now. We need to build a ranch first."

"You're the smartest and wisest woman I've ever met, Anna, not to mention the prettiest. I was thinking the same but was afraid to say it. Now you've done it for me. When should we get married?"

"How about after most of the fall work is done but before winter sets in? That will give us time for a proper engagement period, and it will give you time to work on our home and whatever else we need to do to get ready."

"There's that little dugout home out west of Chris's place. Maybe we could get that ready? It could work for a while anyway."

"We can make it do, Iver. Don't worry. I'll let Odd and Reidun know of our plans tomorrow. I think they will be happy to know that they are going to get their house back to themselves, especially now that they are adding on to the family. This is going so fast, Iver."

"Oh my. In all of my worrying about whether you'd have me or not, I've plumb forgot to have an engagement ring ready in case you said yes."

"You'll never guess what my last engagement ring was. Please don't worry about frivolous things like rings Iver."

"Oh Anna, just one more thing before we mount up. Even though I don't have a ring to make it proper, I've dreamt about our first kiss since I first saw you, and I don't think I can hold out any longer."

She leaned over and put her arms around him. "I would like that, Iver."

They got back to the ranch before dark as promised, thanks to finding the wild horses right away. It had been too late in the day to explore the battleground when they went by, but Iver promised her that they would go back sometime and spend a day there. Chris was waiting at the door, and he could tell by the grin on Iver's face that there was good news. "You guys ready for supper?"

"Thanks, Chris," Anna replied, "but I'd better stay mounted and get going or Odd might have to come looking. We had plenty of lunch with us and we've been munching on our way back. Thanks so much for everything. I'm sure Iver will fill you in on what happened today."

"Will I ever," Iver said, still grinning. "Chris, you're looking at my future bride and your future daughter-in-law."

"I'm not your Dad, Iver."

"You might as well be, Chris—closest thing I got to it."

"I'd be honored to call you Dad," Anna chimed in as she started to leave.

"Nothing would make me more proud than that, Anna. Can I give my future daughter a hug before she leaves?"

"Of course." Anna dismounted and gave Chris a big hug. Iver stood in line waiting so he got one too.

Back at the Larsons', Odd and Reidun were overjoyed at the news. "Iver is the best friend a man could have," Odd told Anna. "I hope that I can be the best man at your wedding."

"I'm sure that Iver wouldn't have anyone else, Odd. We'd be honored to have you stand up with us. And Reidun, I love you like a sister. Would you do me the honor of being my maid of honor?"

They hugged and Reidun said of course. Odd just stood there waiting.

"How about me, do I get a hug too?"

"Oh you poor abused husband," Anna laughed. "Of course you can have a hug too."

"I don't know what I'm going to do without you here, Anna," Reidun confided. "You've gotten me so spoiled that I've probably forgotten how to cook and clean."

"Well, I intend to keep spoiling you as long as I can, and I'm hoping that baby of yours arrives before I am married. If it doesn't I'll stay here anyway, even if I have to postpone our honeymoon, which probably won't be more than a trip to Reva for church or the buttes for a picnic." The two ladies laughed. Then Anna continued, "I'll hate to leave this house. It's a palace compared to what we're planning. We intend to put everything we've got into a ranch and maybe build a home later if and when we can."

"That's smart thinking, Anna," they both said. "Whatever you and Iver are in will become a home. That's the important thing."

The summer and fall days and weeks slipped by quickly. Anna's main job was to ride the pastures and look for sick or lame cattle and to take the tally, meaning that she needed to count them and make sure everything was in the pasture. Odd had a couple of cows that seemed to think that the grass was greener on the other side of the fence, and almost as often as not Anna would find one or both of them where they weren't supposed to be. At first it was just them, but Anna found that they were training their calves to do the same thing.

In the beginning she was patient with them and put them back in where they were supposed to be nice and easy, but after a few more of their escapes she got irritated. It got to the point that if they were out and saw Anna coming they headed back to the fence and crawled in before she could get to them. "I'd like to fix them smart alecs," she told Odd one night. "One of them has a heifer calf, and I'll bet that if you keep it for a replacement heifer she'll continue the tradition her mother has started."

"I'll make sure I don't keep her," he smiled. "Maybe sell her to Iver for your herd."

Later that week Anna noticed that Reidun looked a little weary and maybe a bit pale. "You ok," she asked?

"I think so, but I've been having a little more pain in my lower back, and I've been spotting blood a little."

"Where did you say the closest doctor was?"

"I'm not sure. Maybe Belle Fourche in the Black Hills. It's about 100 miles south."

When Odd came home, Anna was direct with him. "You need to take Reidun to a doctor. She's been more tired than she should be, and I'm worried. Do you know where there is a doctor?"

He agreed that Belle Fourche was the closest. "It'll take me four or five days to go there and back, Anna. We'd have to take the bay and the wagon. I wouldn't want Reidun riding a horse that far."

"Me neither. You two get ready to go. I want you leaving in the morning."

"What about the herd, the milk cow, the chores, and the horses I'm breaking in the round corral?"

"Don't worry. I think I can handle it. If anything major goes wrong while you're gone I'll go and get Iver or Chris to help out. Iver is coming over tomorrow night anyway, so that is one day for sure you don't have to worry about. I won't take no for an answer, Odd. Even if nothing is wrong, Reidun should have a checkup by a good doctor."

They started packing. The next morning when they got up Anna had coffee and some breakfast ready. "Eat up, you two. I should say three. You have a long ride today."

"Maybe I'll go hitch the bay first," said Odd.

"He's already hitched up, and I've packed a couple loaves of bread, some meat, some cold pancakes and two gallons of water. Just in case, I also loaded a couple extra blankets. Did you take a change of clothes, Reidun?"

"Sure did. Thanks so much, Anna."

"I love you guys," Anna replied. "Be safe and I'll be praying that everything is ok with Reidun and the baby."

"Your prayers mean a lot, Anna."

"We should be home by Sunday," Odd guessed.

"Did you remember your rifle, Odd?" Anna added at the last minute.

They were off, and Anna was on the ranch by herself. Anna didn't know it at the time, but the experience of running the ranch by herself would later prove very useful. She ate the leftover breakfast, gulped another cup of coffee, and headed for the corral to check the horses. She sorted off the two geldings Odd was working with, and then did the other chores, including the dreaded chicken coop chores. She actually didn't mind gathering the eggs, but the chicken dust still bothered her and reminded her of having to clean coops in Norway.

With chores over, Anna worked the geldings a while. She saddled each of them but didn't take them out of the round corral. It would be a bad day for a wreck, she thought to herself, not wanting to take any needless chances by riding them out in the open. She was trading Star and Blue off every other day for the pasture ride, and it was Star's turn today. So Anna saddled Star and headed down the trail to the summer pasture. One of the usual fence crawlers was out in the neighbor's pasture, and as always when she saw Anna coming she headed for the fence and crawled back into the right pasture. "I'll get you one of these days!" Anna yelled after her. Star perked up her ears and nickered as if to add reinforcement to Anna's warning. Other than that all was well on the pasture front, so Anna headed back to work with the horses some more. On her way by the corral, she noticed one mare's face was severely swollen up and the horse was having trouble breathing. Anna was really worried, and although Iver was coming over later she figured the mare might not last that long, so she galloped full throttle over to the Tenold place. Iver was in the corral working horses too. Anna pulled up and slid Star to a stop by the corral. "We got a mare that's gasping for air, Iver. Her face is all swollen and she can't seem to get her breath."

"Were there any marks on her nose?"

"I don't know. I didn't really notice. But I didn't look that close either. Why?"

"I'll explain later." He got Prairie out of the corral and threw a saddle on. Then he grabbed a piece of hose and jumped on.

"What's the hose for?" Anna asked.

"I'll show you when we get there." He galloped off and Anna followed.

The mare was really gasping when they arrived and looked like she could barely stand up. "Horses can't breathe out of their mouths," he explained as he slowly pushed the hose up her nose. "If their nasal passages get too much pressure on them and the air is totally restricted, they suffocate and die."

"What in the world would you guess caused her head to swell up like this?"

"I don't have to guess," he said. "Look at these two little holes about an inch apart on the end of her nose. Rattlesnake bite. A cow would've been fine, maybe a little sick, but this often kills horses when they get bit on the end of the nose, and that's where they usually get bit, especially the young dumb ones. They're just too inquisitive for their own good, and when they stick their nose down to see what's rattling the snake strikes them right in the nose."

"Goodness. There's something new to learn every day."

"How come Odd isn't helping you? Where's he?"

"That's another story, Iver. They left this morning for Belle Fourche to get Reidun a check up with the doctor there. Probably won't be back until Sunday. I would've lost this mare if it hadn't been for you."

The mare was getting used to having the hose up her nose and was breathing much easier. "The swelling will eventually go down, and when it does you can slowly pull the hose out."

"Can I reward your good deed by inviting you to stay for supper? We could fire up the stove and fry that grouse I got with my .22 coming home from the pasture check."

"Sounds mighty delicious, Anna. I suppose that since you're here all alone you'll want me to stay overnight for protection and company. A lady might get scared out here all by herself. I heard there's a band of rogue Indians raiding ranches in the area. And there are usually some rustlers sneaking about."

"Iver Tenold, you are the devil in disguise. I'll be booting you outta here right after supper. Maybe I should saddle up too, and help you find your way home in the dark."

"Yeah, good thinking," Iver added, "It's pretty scary out there. You could hold my hand and protect me all the way home."

Iver came over again the next day to check on how Anna was doing. He had been in the hayfield more than usual this year since he was cutting Odd's field too. Odd's old mower had worn out, so Iver and Chris offered to do his mowing if Odd would help them with their stacking.

"How is the haying going, Iver? I'd like to help with the stacking too if I could," Anna said.

"That's where I draw the line, Anna dear. Stacking is hard and dirty work and it can be dangerous. I've even had rattlesnakes come in with the bucker piles when they are dumped on the stack. And for some reason it's always extra hot and extra dry and dusty when we're stacking hay. No future wife of mine is going to do that kind of work. And for sure I wouldn't want those pretty long legs of yours all scratched up from the sticks and stems and hay needles."

"How is the hay crop?" Anna asked.

"Sort of light, but I'm sure not complaining. Any year that you have enough grass to make hay is a good year. I'd like to keep Chris out of the hayfield too. I worry about him working so hard."

"You know that you couldn't keep him out of the hayfield if you tied him to the barn, Iver."

"Yeah, I know, but it still bothers me. I'd like to put up as much hay as we can. If the winter gets hard, we'll need lots of hay to feed those heifers we're buying. We want them in good shape next spring for breeding. Then we'll be off to having our own herd. Once we get our first calf crop, we'll have some money coming in. Would you like to ride with me and check the wheat field? It's starting to head out, and I'm so excited. I get one-third of the crop, so I'm praying for a good, high yield. And I'm remembering to be thankful when I pray too, just like you taught me. Anyway you might help me in the praying department, since you have more pull with Him than I do. We could really use a good rain to keep the crops and the pastures going. It's starting to get mighty hot and dry."

When Iver saddled up to go home that night, there was a bank of clouds and lightning filled the western sky. "See what I mean, Anna? He seems to like you a lot."

"He loves each and every one of us equally, Iver."

Iver left and when he woke up the next morning the rain gauge had the usual assortment of flies in it, along with almost an inch of rainwater. "Well I'll be darned," he said out loud to Chris before catching himself. "I mean thank you, Lord!"

"Isn't it glorious after a rain?" Chris added. "The air is so crisp and clean, and the dust is washed off of everything. I bet the prairie feels just like I do when I get me a bath. It even looks happy, don't you think? I think those prairie flowers are smiling at us."

"Yeah, Chris, it really is something. I feel like a hundred bucks. Think I'll go look at the wheat again. I suppose we'll be checking cows and fixing fence today until it dries out enough to get in the hayfield again."

"I suspect you got that right, Iver. How many days till the wedding now? I'm looking forward to having fresh bread and pie around here."

"Little under two months now. I can't wait either. I know I joke about it some, but I worry about it a lot too. Anna is the finest thing to ever come my way, and I want to do everything just right. I don't want to ever do anything that won't make her proud of me. I hope that being a good husband will come natural 'cause I sure don't have any idea how it's done."

Chris thought for a while, and then told Iver, "You won't have any problems, Iver. I've watched you with the cattle and horses, and you are very kind and good hearted, even when the critters are trying your patience. I've also watched lots of other men. Those that treat their animals bad treat other folks bad sometimes, even their families. They try to hide it from others, but it shows. Your nature is to be kind and thoughtful, so being that way with Anna will come natural to you."

"Thanks Chris. That makes me feel better, but just the same I'm going to work mighty hard at it."

"I know you will, Iver. That's the way you approach everything. Why don't you ride the range while I get the fencing gear ready? I'll start on the summer pasture and meet you there."

"Yes sir, and thanks again, Chris. I hope I'm half as wise as you some day."

"The problem with wisdom is that I had to get old to find it, and I'm afraid that I may have gotten more old than wise."

Odd and Reidun were back the next afternoon, as anticipated. They had been able to see Dr. Townsend in Belle Fourche despite all the activity there. Belle Fourche South Dakota had become a major cattle-shipping point, and in its peak season it was the largest in the world, often shipping as many as 2500 carloads of cattle per month.

After a full check, Dr. Townsend had said that he thought the baby was fine and so was Reidun. He figured the problems had been caused by too much work, worry, and activity. He made Reidun promise to take a long nap every day and get a good night's sleep every night. "No hard house work and no working in the hayfield. The baby is due in a couple of months, and from now on no horse riding would be the best. If you got thrown hard, he warned, the baby could die." He asked her if she had a place to stay in Belle when the baby was close.

"I don't know anyone here," she said, "and we're a bit short on cash now, so I don't think the boarding house would work either. I think we can get by on our own," she said weakly.

Dr. Townsend scolded them both and then said, "I expect you to be here at least a week before this baby comes. It is your first, and the first can be trouble. Minnie and I have three extra bedrooms for cases like you. You'll be welcome to stay with us free of charge until that baby is safely in this world."

Odd hadn't known what to say, so he just thanked the doctor over and over and promised to get Reidun back to Belle Fourche as soon as they thought the baby might be close.

"Sooner," Dr Townsend had added, "if you think there's a problem."

After finding out that Reidun and the baby were ok, Anna wanted to know all about their trip. Reidun didn't get to reply as Odd tried to change the subject.

"How are the cows doing?" he asked.

"I won't tell you a thing until you're done telling me everything about Belle Fourche."

"Ok, Ok," he smiled. "Belle is getting to be a big city, and it's full of cowpunchers. So many folks there we thought we might not get to see the doc. I can tell you this; there is no way that we could have found a nicer doctor between here and Mexico. He even wants Reidun to come and stay in *his* house before the baby comes."

"The stockyards have tripled in size since I last saw them. There's a fancy hotel with a saloon and dining room. Fella by the name of Bullock is buying up all the proved up claims along the Belle Fourche River thinking he's gonna get rich. Might even be related to those Bullocks we got here in Reva. I heard he bribed the railroad to put their station on his land."

"Sounds sort of greedy to me," Iver said.

"I was glad to get outta that town. Too many ways to get into trouble there. We were told that the trail through Buffalo and then east to Reva was a lot smoother than the trail through the south end of the buttes, so we took it on the way home. It was longer but didn't take any more time. I gotta be real careful with this cargo you know." He looked at Reidun.

"Anything new in Buffalo?" Iver asked.

"Not much. Still working on a church. Saloon is doing pretty good, I think."

"Of course," said Anna. "The Devil's work always does good, it seems. Many a good person has been ruined by drinking too much."

Iver made a note to himself. "No more whiskey, especially around Anna." Then he finally told Odd that the cowherd and everything at the ranch were just fine. Your hard working hand, my future wife, has taken good care of everything for you."

With haying season about over, harvest was upon them. There was only one threshing machine in the neighborhood so it was an event. There had only been a few more showers that summer and fall, so the harvest wasn't big. But Chris and Iver had the best wheat field in the area (or so they said) and claimed that it ran twenty bushels to the acre. Anna hoped they weren't stretching it because more bushels meant more money for their ranch. Iver and Chris had been working on a house for the newlyweds in their spare time, but Iver had to admit it wasn't much. "I sure hope Anna meant what she said," he told Chris. "This old dugout is a pretty poor excuse for a house."

"Why don't you bring her over this afternoon and see what she thinks? After all, the wedding is only two weeks off."

Iver took Chris's advice and rode over to get Anna. Reidun asked Iver to stay for dinner.

Iver asked them if the mare had recovered from the snakebite, and Odd said, "You'd never know it happened. She's just fine, thanks to your quick thinking. I never would have come up with that trick and would have probably watched her die. Thanks again, she's one of the best mares I've got."

"Speaking of mares," Iver grinned at Reidun, "how's that baby coming?"

"Feel for yourself," she said.

Iver looked over bashfully at Anna. "It's ok, but I don't want you feeling all the pregnant women you see."

"Wow, tight as a drum. Poor kid doesn't have much room in there to play. About time for him, or her, to take a peek at the outside. Whoa. I think there's a mule in there, Reidun. Did you feel that kick?"

"I sure did! I think we should load up for Belle Fourche any day now. Can't be much longer."

"I really hope that the baby comes before our wedding," said Anna, "or we might have to put it off. I don't want to leave you alone for a minute until you are either safe in Belle at Dr. Townsend's or back here with a bundle of baby. Of course if that is the case I still might not want to leave. Oh Reidun, it'll be so precious. I truly can't wait."

"What if it turns out like Odd?" Iver chimed in, winking at Reidun.

"Iver Tenold," Anna scolded him, "let's go see that palace you've been working on."

"It's so grand, Anna. I'm thinking we'll need a couple of maids just to take care of the place. If you three get to feeling cramped here," he looked at Reidun, "you can move in with us. So many bedrooms we wouldn't even notice you."

Of course Iver was joking. There was one bedroom, and it was tiny. There was also a very small kitchen/stove/everything else room. "What do you think, Anna?" Iver asked cautiously.

"I think it'll do just fine. What else could we need? This is just what we talked about, and I wasn't expecting any more. It will be wonderful, and best of all it will be ours. I wouldn't mind a little lean-to porch so I have a place for a rocking chair though, if we get time some day."

"That sounds wonderful, Anna, only I'd like two of them rocking chairs so I can sit with you."

"We can watch sunsets together."

"Only thing I'll be watching is you. You put those sunsets to shame."

"I've already said yes, Iver. You can quit laying it on so thick now."

"Yeah, but we ain't hitched yet, so I'm not taking any chances."

Reidun had some small cramps the next morning. Anna fetched Odd, and they had a little conference. "I think I'm hitching up the bay this morning," he announced.

"Are we going for a ride?" asked Reidun.

"You betcha, all the way to Belle Fourche. Weather is good today. Anna has proven that she is capable of caring for the stock, and you're making the both of us a little nervous. We ain't taking any chances, so we're off to see Dr. Townsend."

"Don't you say a word, Reidun," Anna added. "You just lay back and relax for a spell while I load the wagon with some food and water. I'll put on three blankets plus the wagon robe so you'll be as comfy as possible."

They were off to Belle in less than an hour. Iver met them on the road and found out what was going on. "What about the calves?" he asked Odd.

"They'll just have to wait. Don't know how I could do it now, Iver."

Iver and Odd had planned to wean their calves and trail them to market that week. The prices were still pretty good, and the market always seemed to drop in December.

"You two be careful," Iver said. "Got your rifle, Odd?"

"Yeah. Anna asked me the same thing before we left."

"Ok, I'm expecting to see my new neighbor when you get back."

Iver continued on to the Larson's ranch to visit with Anna. "This sorta messes up our plans, Anna. Odd and I were gonna wean the calves this week and then take them to market. I sure wanted that out of the way before our wedding day, and I'm a bit worried the market will go down if we wait any longer. Usually does this time of the year."

After a few minutes of thought, Anna spoke up. "Let's do this, Iver, if you agree that it will work. Why don't you ride over to the Bullocks and see if that kid of theirs would help us for a few days? Between him, you, Chris, and myself we'll get the weaning done at both ranches. Then you three men can take the calves to market. I'll stay back with the stock and take care of both ranches until you're home."

"That's too much to ask, Anna, too much responsibility."

"Not at all, Iver. I can leave the horses to fend for themselves for a few days. The training can wait, and it might do the horses some good to have a vacation. That'll just leave me with chores and cow checking. I've handled this ranch by myself before, so what's another one?"

"Have you ever been around cows at weaning time? They like to go crazy looking for their calves. It's noisy with all their bellerin' and they're hard to keep put."

"Thanks for the warning, Iver, but I think that I can handle it. You just bring a big fat check back from the buyers in Belle Fourche. And don't you dare sell any of those heifer calves of Chris's. That's our future herd."

"Yes, ma'm. We'll have to pick Odd's replacement heifers for him too. I know that he wants to keep about twenty-five. Chris has the best eye in the country for good cattle, so we'll let him do the choosing. Having Chris do his picking for him will really please Odd."

The next two days were as busy as any they'd had all spring and summer, but they finally had the calves that they wanted to sell sorted off from both herds, and the three men started herding them toward the Belle Fourche market. They had left all of Chris's heifer calves and twenty-five of Odd's with the cowherds for Anna to watch. Anna rode through the cattle twice a day to make sure none of the cows ran off looking for their calves. Having many of the heifer calves still with their mothers helped to keep all of the cows a little more content. She went around the Larson herd early, then rode over to the Tenold ranch and rode around that herd. Then she did the chores there and checked the horses. After that she rode around the Tenold herd once again before riding back to the Larson place and going around that herd again. She ended the day by doing the Larson chores and going to bed, usually without supper and exhausted.

When the men finally got back from market four days later, she had to admit that she was ready for a break. "You look like you lost some weight, Anna," Iver said as he ran over to her and gave her a hug. "How did it go?"

"It went fine, Iver, easy as pie."

"Yeah, I'll bet," he replied. "Doing what you did on one ranch would've been hard. Doing it on two would've made most seasoned cowhands quit."

"I can't quit," Anna smiled, "cause I'm the boss!"

"It's starting already," Iver smiled back. "Suppose you want to know what YOUR calves brought?"

"I sure do!"

Odd and Reidun arrived three days later with their brand new son whom they had named James. "What a girl." Odd bragged about Reidun. "Popped him out in record time. And just look at him. Almost as handsome as his Dad, huh? I was sure worried, but there was nothing to it, Iver."

"Easy for you to say," said Reidun.

Anna was already holding the baby. "I think I want one of these for myself some day. Your timing was perfect, Reidun. Now I can quit worrying about you and get myself ready for my wedding, not that it will take much. I already have a wedding dress, well used, but this will be its first wedding. Iver here wants to take me to New York for our honeymoon, but I'm thinking maybe somewhere more exotic. Where did you guys go?"

"What's a honeymoon?" they chorused.

"Say Iver," Odd asked, "you have any trouble getting your marriage license?"

"My what?"

"You gotta have a license you know. Get them over in Buffalo at the court house."

"Oh my goodness, I'd better saddle up and ride hard. Anna, why don't you show Odd that little surprise we have for him and Reidun?"

Anna retrieved the calf check out of the kitchen drawer and gave it to them. "What the heck is this?" Odd asked.

"Just a little surprise from your neighbors," Anna smiled. "We got your calves weaned, Chris picked your replacement heifers, and Chris, Iver and the Bullock kid took your calves to market. We heard the price has already dropped, so we got them sold just in the nick of time."

"Holy cow," said Odd. "I've been worrying about how I'd get that job done all week, really all month. I figured it'd take me all winter to get them marketed being this far behind. Thought I'd lose a ton of money hitting the poor market later on. You guys are unbelievable! Who took care of the ranches while you were taking the calves to market Iver? There's no way that Anna could have done it all by herself, is there?"

14

Anna And Iver

Anna and Iver's wedding day had arrived. Iver rode all day and all night to get back from Buffalo, which was the county seat of Harding County. They had their first snow of the year, and he rode in a partial blizzard all the way back and came in looking like he was nearly frozen. Chris helped him clean up and change, and they met Odd, Reidun, and baby James at the new, partially finished, Lutheran Church. Anna was hidden in the back of the church. Most of the neighbors were already there, but the preacher was a bit late for the wedding. He didn't seem too worried.

"They've never had one without me yet." he quipped.

Reidun had worked on Anna's hair all morning. Iver had never seen her look more beautiful, and when she came out he gasped and smiled wide. "I can't believe that this is really happening," he whispered to Odd. Iver had secretly gotten wedding bands, which Odd held in his pocket, producing them when the preacher asked for them.

James started crying toward the end of the wedding service, so the maid of honor had to leave the ceremony to take care of him. "I think someone is hungry and in a hurry to get this over," proclaimed the minister. "And since most of you have to get home for chores and the weather doesn't look very good, the groom may now kiss the bride!"

The church erupted in cheering, and all the cowboy hats were tossed in the air. Iver and Anna took time for a long, serious kiss, not just a peck on the cheek. Iver felt like he had died and went to heaven. Anna was overjoyed. A million thoughts and dreams had been racing through her mind since leaving Norway, and this is where they had taken her. Mrs. Iver Tenold. It must have been meant to be. God must have arranged it. She closed her eyes and said a short prayer, and then she and Iver kissed again. "Where have you been all my life?" she asked him.

"With you, Anna. I think I've loved you since the day I was born."

Anna had made her own wedding cake. It was delicious but certainly not a bit fancy. After their small reception, everyone started heading back home. The first snow of the year was turning into a two-day affair, and it was mounting up. People were ready to get home to their fires and put their horses away for the day. Iver and Anna were anxious to have their first night together. After thanking everyone for coming and giving the Pastor a present, they loaded up and headed for the ranch. They had borrowed Chris's buggy for the occasion, and of course the tricksters in the community had tied tin cans to the back and posted a "just married" sign on it. Iver took it all down. "I hate to ruin their fun but it might spook the horse. I don't want a runaway buggy today."

When they got back to the ranch Iver put the horse and buggy away and headed to their new "house," where Anna had a fire going already. Iver had stacked enough firewood for the winter, and in a few months they were going to be glad of it.

"One thing nice about a small house, Iver, is that it heats up a lot faster."

"I don't think I'll ever need another fire in my life, Anna. Just one look at you and my temperature goes up forty degrees." They snuggled in front of the small stove, truly enjoying the feel of each other for the first time. "I still feel like I'm dreaming, Anna. Please don't wake me up. I want this to last forever."

"I feel exactly the same, Iver. I'd like this night to last forever too. Let's try to make every hour and every day of the rest of our lives feel this way. I want to hold you all night."

In the morning the air was still crisp, but the sun was out melting the year's first snow. "It looks like a field of diamonds and lace," Anna said, "all sparkling in one giant land of enchantment. Look, the wind isn't even blowing. What a beautiful day for the first day of our life together. I think God made it just for us. Can we skip work today and just enjoy it?"

"As a matter of fact, Chris has offered to do all the chores today and tomorrow. He wants us to do whatever we please. I have an idea too."

"As if I can't guess what it is?" Anna smiled at her new husband. "I'm betting that it might just include a ride to the slim buttes to check on a certain wild horse herd."

"Brilliant idea Anna, I never would have thought of that! Let's make a picnic and get going. We'll take the wagon. Don't forget to throw the blankets in. It's warming up fast but we still might need them."

"For what?" She smiled back at him.

After loading up enough supplies for the day, they set off to find the wild mustangs. They went a little different route this time so that Iver could show Anna more of the 1876 "Battle of the Slim Buttes" battleground. "This was the main ravine that the Indians holed up in I think. The battle went up and down along these draws. The berry thickets and trees gave the Indians lots of cover, but they never really had a chance to win since they were outnumbered, surrounded, and surprised."

"I'm trying to close my eyes and imagine how it all happened, Iver. It must have been terrifying, especially for the women and children."

"Yes, I can't imagine the horror of fighting for my family's lives." Iver looked at Anna for a long moment. "But they were somewhat accustomed to it I guess. The Black Hills and these buttes have changed ownership many times, all among Indian tribes until white people won the last war in the progression. It seems that warring with other tribes was their way of life, and the Black Hills and the prairie was a prize worth fighting and dying for to them. The Sioux were the last group of Indians to conquer this area, pushing out the Kiowa, the Arikara, the Crow and the Cheyenne. The US conquered it last, even though we lost the Battle of the Little Bighorn, and now settlers like us are on prairie land once occupied only by Indians. It is harsh, but not much different than the past history when you think about it."

"Let's go to the Black Hills some day, Iver. I hear it's beautiful there too. Why is it called Black Hills?"

"It's from an Indian word, Paha Sapa, which means hills black. When you look at those mountains from a distance they appear black in color."

"Maybe we can find some of those gold nuggets."

"I don't want to discourage you, but I had a friend do that for a spell. After giving up he said he figured the old timers that came through in the gold rush days had scoured every inch of the surface and had found all of the nuggets, but that there was still a lot of gold underground for the real miners. Our gold is here on our ranch."

"I couldn't agree more."

When they reached the place that they had last viewed the mustangs they crawled slowly over the rim rock to look for them, but the horse herd was gone. "My guess is that they moved to the southeast with the wind. They've been working their way that direction since spring. We've got a good breeze from the northwest so let's move about three valleys east of here and try to find them. We'll have to come in downwind from them so that they don't detect us. If we try from this direction they'll smell us for sure and be gone as fast as I can say I love you."

Iver was right; they were two valleys to the southeast. "I think they would take my breath away every time I see them, Iver, even if it was ten times a day."

"I certainly know the feeling. Can you imagine how excited I was when I first found them?"

"Have you decided what you are going to do with them?"

"I think so, but I'm not sure how to do it. I'd love to have them be a part of our ranch somehow, but I want to move them there in a way that doesn't make them feel captured. Wouldn't it be something to preserve their bloodlines, their hardiness and courage? Just think of all they've survived just to be here."

"You truly love horses don't you?"

"I like cattle. But I love horses."

"Me too, Iver, we'll figure something out. Now let's do something we might not get another chance to do for a long time. Let's find a nice spot out of the wind and in the sun, spread our blankets in the back of the wagon, have some lunch, and just lie together and enjoy each other and dream our dreams."

Iver was excited all the way back to the ranch, going through different ways that he might get the wild horse herd moved. He didn't know it at the time, but the hard winter that was quickly coming on them would be his ally in this endeavor. Anna didn't offer much; she figured that the herd was Iver's discovery and that she wouldn't interfere. This would be his challenge, and he seemed to love any challenge.

They were late getting back, but they had figured it would be when they left. "I'll take care of the wagon and horse, Anna, if you'll get us a bite. I've been chasing wild horses all the way home in my thoughts and it's really made me hungry."

"Ya Iver, it might be a long winter, and I'd better start fattening my man up for it. We have one more day of honeymooning tomorrow. Got any ideas?"

"I've been too busy thinking about tonight!"

"Just hold your "horses", Mr. Tenold. Let's get that wagon taken care of and light the fire."

"Mine is already lit, Mrs. Tenold."

"I meant the stove."

"Who needs a stove?"

The next day was sunny, and it had warmed up into the sixties again. "I hope this is the start of an Indian summer and that it doesn't snow again for a month or two. That would sure help stretch the hay further."

"What's an Indian summer?" Anna asked.

It is a long extended fall, with the weather remaining nice going into what normally would be winter months. It made life a lot easier for the Indians, as it does for us."

"If we get those horses moved here, Anna, we'll need more pasture. If we get the Robinson place bought, that will be plenty, but there's also a school section coming up for grabs. The rent on them is usually dirt cheap; it almost costs less than owning the land. I'm going to do my best to get the lease on it, but it sorta depends on whether any of the neighbors want it too and run the price up at the lease auction. Should be plenty of room there to run our horse herd year 'round if we get it. What would you like to do today, Anna?"

"Let's ride out and look over our Hereford herd. I sure wish they were a couple years older."

"They'll get there. We need to be thinking of where we can get a good heifer bull for them next spring. I'll feed them really good this winter so that they grow out nice. Conception is a lot better when they're in good shape at breeding time, and we'll need that first calf crop, probably more than any future ones."

"I hate debt," Anna added. "The faster we pay it off the better."

With the two-day honeymoon over, Anna and Iver settled into married life easily. Their circumstances had been so similar and they had so much in common that they were as much like old friends and business partners as they were marriage partners. The evenings went by with energetic conversations about Norway, the ship, Ellis Island, and their journey through America. They usually drifted to sleep talking about the horse herd or the ranch or their family. Anna let Chris know that he was always welcome in their house and he made it a habit of showing up for dinner, but he didn't come over for supper unless it was a special occasion or unless Anna made it a point to ask him.

"I figure them two need their time and space," he told Odd one day. "But it looks to me like they're getting along like bread and butter."

Anna rode over to check on Reidun and James every chance she could. Odd complained that she just ignored him and went straight to the baby.

"I can't help it, Odd, he's so much cuter than you are," she kidded. "You two look so happy. You've made this house a home, and now you're a family. What more could anyone ask of life?"

"A husband who got some work done rather than wanting to hang around the house all day playing with the baby?" Reidun smiled.

"Ok, ok, I know when I'm not wanted," Odd pretended to sulk off, but he had no more than left when he poked his head back in the door. "How about bringing over a pie next time, Anna? I sure miss your cooking." He finally left, and the two girls had some time to themselves.

They were virtually sisters now and loved each other as such. "I'll whip up some fresh bread before I leave, Reidun. Anything else you need? I think James has grown an inch since Tuesday. Your milk must pack a pretty good punch."

"I just wish I didn't have so much of it. The bed is soaked sometimes. At the rate James is growing, he'll take it all soon… and want a steak on the side. Have you had any news from Nils and Tove?"

"No, but you just reminded me that I need to send them a letter to brag about my new home and husband. Matter of fact, I need to write several letters."

Dear Nils, Tove, and family,

I apologize for not writing sooner. So much has happened since we last saw each other and I've been so busy. That is no excuse though for not letting you know how I am doing. First, I want to thank you so much for getting me in touch with the Larsons. I don't think that I would have been able to make it here on my own without them. They are simply wonderful. Reidun is like a sister and Odd is like a brother. The best news of this letter will be that they now have a son! Little James was born a few weeks ago and is growing like a colt.

Here is some more good news. Reidun and Odd introduced me to Iver Tenold when I arrived here. We fell in love over the year and were married a few days ago. I now am Mrs. Anna Tenold. Iver is a perfect match for me. He is a Norwegian, and his path to America was much the same as mine. We have a home here, and I am now a rancher's wife. I love him, and without your help in getting me here I would never have met him.

Please write back when you can and let me know how everyone is doing. How do Tove and Heidi like being Americans? I hope this finds all of you well.

I love and miss you all,
Anna

Dear Donna,

I am sorry that I haven't written sooner or more often. I have made my way to South Dakota and am now married to a rancher here. I truly love him and the prairie. I miss you and the boarding house so much, but I really can't say that I miss New York. If you ever decide to take a vacation or want to see the west, please come visit us. I know it takes a long time to get here, but you might enjoy the train ride. I would meet you in Hettinger, North Dakota and we could ride to the ranch together in our wagon.

If you have any spare time, please write to me and let me know what is new in your life and how you are doing. Maybe you have found someone and are married now too?

Wouldn't it be something if we were both starting married life at the same time?

Please say hi to Tom and everyone at the diner for me. I miss them too, along with all the wonderful customers that we had there. May God bless you!

I love you,
Anna

Dear Obert,

I hope that my letter finds you well and staying out of trouble. Blue wanted me to say hello for him too; at least that is how I interpreted his last whinny. You couldn't have ever given me anything better, how I love that horse. I'll bet that you miss him, but please know that he is fat and sassy. He even lets me shoot your Winchester from his back. That rifle has given us many good meals of cottontails and grouse. By "us" I mean my new husband, Iver, and me. He is a rancher, so Blue has lots of other horses in the corral to keep him company. You would like Iver. He is a lot like you, Obert. He is a kind man and he loves animals and he loves the land.

I hope to get back to Minnesota to visit you some day soon. I miss you so much. I think of you every day, either riding Blue or using the rifle. Please say hi to everyone over at the café for me. I hope you are still eating dinner there.

God bless you, I love you,
Anna

Dear George and Sarah and family,

I am slow in writing to you and apologize. I sure miss you and all of the Christman tribe. You were so kind to me and you truly made me feel like a part of your family. I hope that this finds all of the kids well and as ornery as ever.

I do have a lot of news from South Dakota to share with you! I now have someone special in my life and am married as of last week. My husband is a rancher here, and I am now Mrs. Iver Tenold. I just pray that I can have a family as nice as yours some day. Iver and I have a lot in common as he is from Norway and immigrated here a few years before I did. We both love horses, cattle and our ranch. I hope and pray that he can meet all of you some day.

Would you please do me a favor, George? I worry about Obert, and if you could check in on him once in a while I would so appreciate it. He's out there all alone, and thanks to me he doesn't even have his horse there to keep him company. He's probably never had a doctor checkup in his life.

I wish that you could come and visit me sometime so I could show off my new husband, friends, and home. We even have a herd of Hereford cattle that I know you would like, George, as you often mentioned your dad's herd of Herefords.

Have you heard from Gert? I need to write to her too. Give her my best if you can.

I love and miss you all so much, please give all the kids a hug from me.

God's blessings,
Anna

The weather went from sixty-five degrees on Thursday to ten on Friday, then dropped below zero Saturday.

"I don't like this," Chris commented. "Hard on cattle. Wish it would even out. I saw four wolves this morning. Hope it isn't a bad omen."

It was. They had another six inches of snow the next night, and the cold air didn't move out like it normally did. Before Christmas they were tromping in snow everywhere, even in the open where the wind could hit it full force and move most of it to drifts. The cold winter days with all the feeding and extra chores kept the men worn out. Iver told Anna that it made everything twice as hard; having to shovel snow every day before the real work began. "I'm worried about the mustangs, Anna. If it clears up enough tomorrow would you like to go over with me and check on them?"

"Of course, I feel like a bird in a cage here. Would be good to get out to the buttes and breathe some fresh air, even if it is a little too fresh."

The wind was down the next morning, so they saddled up and headed off to where they had last seen the herd. The horses had moved into another canyon with better protection, but it was plain to see that they were suffering. "They've lost weight, Anna, especially the mares. Those colts are still trying to nurse. I can't blame them, they must be starving. If this weather doesn't break soon these horses will really be suffering. They've been trying to paw through the snow for grass, but it's too deep most places. Looks like they have mostly been eating leaves and pine needles. I wish there was something we could do to help them."

"I have an idea, Iver, if we can handle it. If the weather is decent again tomorrow let's put some hay on the wagon and bring it over for them. We'll get up early and do the hard chores and let Chris finish so we can head this way. The path through the gap is still open enough for the wagon. Do you think we could do it?"

"That's a great idea! It won't be easy but we'll give it a shot. This horse herd needs nourishment bad. I'm sure glad we have extra hay this year."

The following morning was extremely cold, with the temperature still well below zero. It hadn't quit snowing but the snow that was falling was more like frost so it didn't pile up. It took Iver and Anna an hour to load enough hay to feed the wild horses and another several hours to get to where they were. The mustangs saw them pitching the hay off of the wagon but didn't even try to run away as they were already pretty weak. Iver and Anna were both soaked with sweat from the hard work of pitching the hay off. They pitched as fast as they could and left as soon as the wagon was empty, hoping that they hadn't disturbed the herd and hoping the horses would find the hay right away. On their way out they saw the bones of one of the colts, recently picked clean. "Wolves are here, Anna. Damn wolves. Sorry, but I can't stand the thought of them killing these horses."

"Damn wolves," Anna repeated to herself.

The next morning they made the same trip with more hay. Iver had come up with a plan. "If they get used to me feeding them, I might be able to use hay to lure them out of the Buttes and over to the ranch. What do you think, Anna?"

"It's perfect. They'll hardly notice us moving them. This hard, bitter winter may actually help us."

After a few days of getting fed, the mustangs got used to seeing the wagon, and they let Iver and Anna get pretty close to them. The herd was too weak to object anyway and slowly but surely they were being moved toward safety. There was even more snow, almost daily, and Iver felt an urgency to get them out of the buttes where he was afraid they'd get trapped and either starve to death or be killed by the wolf pack that was growing more ravenous daily.

Anna's .22 was useless, so he let her carry his rifle. It was Anna against the wolves, at least until the horses were safe. Iver couldn't get there every day, but every chance he had he took some hay, gradually luring the horses out of the buttes and onto the prairie. Once he got them that far, he was able to bring more hay since it was closer to the hay supply and easier for him to get back to where the horses were. That really helped as it allowed him to bring enough hay for a couple of days and he could also move the herd in larger increments since they could see so much farther.

They hungrily followed his hay trail closer and closer to the Tenold ranch. It took well into January, but the mustangs were finally on their ranch and in a pasture. In the process, Iver guessed that they had lost about seven colts and two mares and a yearling or two to the wolves, but the stallion and most of the herd were still intact. The best thing about it, Anna commented, is that "we got them here without them knowing our plan and we befriended them along the way. I think they've grown to trust us some."

"They're no different than me, Anna. You feed me every day and I'll stick around forever."

"Oh Iver, did you ever think this was even possible? This terrible winter has helped bring us our dream."

"I got to admit it has. I seriously doubt we'd have gotten those mustangs any other way. Now let's just hope they can survive the rest of the winter. Spring's a long way off yet, and all these extra mouths to feed have seriously jeopardized our hay supply."

The weather did give them a short reprieve when they had a "January thaw" the last week of the month. But during the second week of February the snow came again—another 30 inches with gale force winds and more bitter cold Canadian air sweeping down on them with it. Their hay was getting so low that they started rationing, but even with the short supply of feed the horses had gained some strength. These animals were used to going without, and their hardiness was showing. Even so, Iver and Anna didn't want them to go backward again. Some of the wolves had followed the horses all the way to the ranch, and Anna had the rifle blazing. Not one more of her horses or any of her heifers would be wolf food if she could help it.

One particularly cold morning she took the rifle out and checked the cows and the replacement heifers. Anna noticed some motion on the side of the hill, so she hid along the windbreak to wait and see what it was. A lone wolf was moving back and forth along the shadows, downwind of the calves. Slowly it made its way to within striking distance, but Anna was ready. Her finger was nearly frozen in the trigger guard, but she managed to squeeze a shot off and the wolf jumped up. She thought at first that she missed, but just as quickly as it had jumped up it slumped over and died. Anna went over to inspect it. She truly felt sorry for the skinny bag of wolf bones she saw. "Sorry buddy, I know you're one of God's creatures too, but I've sworn to protect these calves and these horses."

As if to prove that miracles still happen, spring came just as the last stack of their hay disappeared. Odd had been coming over to inspect the mustangs often and had already picked out a buttermilk-colored stud colt. "If you ever sell that one, I'd sure be proud to own him. Might even leave him a stud and breed a few of my mares to him. I love that color. He looks like a thousand bucks to me."

"Sold," grinned Iver. "I think that mare will have a full brother or sister to him later this spring; I hope she has another buttermilk or buckskin. I like those colors too. It looks like despite the hard winter most of the mares will foal this year. I was worried that some of them might abort their fetuses with all the stress. Anna and I are so excited. This will be our first colt crop, and it was practically given to us."

"I'd bet no one else in Dakota could have managed what you and Anna did, getting those horses here and saving them from starvation and the wolves. You both worked yourselves to the bone, day and night, to save that herd of mustangs. I doubt that anyone else would've even attempted it, let alone got it done. It was sorta like a miracle."

"My wife believes in miracles, Odd."

"I think I do too, Iver, when I think of how lucky us two Norwegians were to get wives like Reidun and Anna."

"Ya, I guess that would be another miracle for sure."

"Getting back to horses again, I'll need a pony for James before you know it, but don't know of anyone that has any of those little kids ponies."

"That Bullock boy that helped me move the calves to market had one when he was little. Maybe they would sell it?"

It was nearly dinnertime, so the two friends went to see what their wives had been cooking. Odd mentioned looking for a pony for James.

"Why do you have to have a pony?" Anna asked.

"I don't know. I guess they're just smaller so the kids don't have as far to the ground if they fall off. Folks probably figure that little people need little horses? But on the other hand ponies can be the orneriest critters on earth and they seem to know every trick in the book to get a kid off their back."

"I have an idea," Anna said. "How about Blue? He's getting too old for hard work, and he's never bucked a day in his life. A rattlesnake could buzz under his hooves and a flock of grouse could fly up in front of his nose at the same time and he wouldn't flinch. He's the most trustworthy horse ever born, and I'd put James on him before I'd ever let him ride one of those nasty ponies."

"Great point, Anna," Odd said. "I think he'd be the perfect horse for James when he gets old enough. What do you want for him?"

"I remember tricking you out of Star of the West a while back. This would make us even."

"You drive a hard bargain, Anna. Deal! But after Blue has trained James, if he still has enough left in him, I'll bring him back to train your young'uns."

"Jumping the gun, aren't you, Odd," Iver interjected.

"Them things just seem to happen. Believe me."

After Odd and Reidun left for their ranch, Anna and Iver resumed their conversation. "I'm sure glad the weather finally broke. Just in time."

"Me too, the hay is virtually all gone."

"Spring is my favorite season of the year, Iver. Especially after a winter like we just had," Anna smiled.

"One thing about a hard winter though, Anna, is there's enough snowmelt to fill all the creeks, rivers, dams and dugouts. If it doesn't keep freezing every night, the hay and grass will have a good start too."

"I sure hope we don't have one of those late freezes this year,"

Anna said. "The fruit trees sometimes get tricked into budding out too soon and a late frost ruins the berry crop."

"I forbid it to freeze," Iver said pointing to the heavens. "I want lots of pie and jam."

"Did you save enough wheat seed to plant this year's crop, Iver? That wheat check sure came in handy last fall, made a nice payment to Chris."

"Sure did, and I'm gonna try to break up anther ten acres to the west of the wheat field. Might put some flax in that though. Chris says flax does better than wheat in freshly broken soil."

"If you do I could add some flax seed to the wheat flour. I think that might be pretty tasty. I've never seen a field of flax either."

"Beautiful sight, Anna, having a whole field as blue as the sky when it blooms out."

"How are you going to find time to break more ground with all you have to do? Especially with having a new herd of mares that will be foaling later this spring and summer? I can keep up with the chores and the milking, and I can keep shooting enough critters with the Winchester to fill our bellies, maybe even break a few horses on my own. But goodness almighty, Iver, we are overrun with work around here. I wish Chris were a few years younger."

"Me too, Anna, but we'll get by. The old timers say you never get your work done for the year. Sooner or later it snows, and then you're forced to quit for the winter. Then you just start over again the next spring. I'll never be one to shirk a good day's work, but no matter how busy it gets I want to take time for you, Anna. A wife and a family are the most important use of a man's time. I know I'm jumping the gun with the family part, but it'll come. They're the reason a man works as I see it. I want you to have a nice house some day and some nice clothes and real furniture. Wouldn't it be great to sleep on a new bed?"

Just the thought of that made both of them smile. A nice, soft and comfortable bed with new sheets and pillows.

"I want all of the things for you that we don't have now and I'll work hard for them, but I'm pretty selfish and want to enjoy you and have you all to myself once in a while as I go about it."

"I think you have it right, Iver. You are the most important part of my life now too, and it would be a shame to work away our lives without enjoying each other and what we already have."

There was a special church service in Reva on the following Sunday morning and Iver and Anna invited Chris and the Larson family over for for dinner afterward. Odd, Chris, and Iver went out to see the mustangs, while Anna and Reidun saddled up Blue and took turns holding James riding around the corral. "He is growing much too fast for me," said Reidun. "Before we know it he'll be off to that new school I hear they're going to build up by Reva. If he's like his dad he'll be terrorizing the little girls, pulling their pigtails and chasing them with frogs."

"I didn't know Odd at that age, Reidun. Thank heavens! It sounds just like what he'd have been doing though. Guess it sounds a lot like he still is doing."

Reidun took a serious turn. "I think I may be pregnant again."

"Already? You two sure don't waste any time." Anna paused, looked down and back up at Reidun. "Please don't mention this to Iver or Odd, but I think I might be pregnant too. I didn't want to tell anyone until I was positive, but having you mention that you might be having another one made it irresistible."

"Oh Anna," Reidun gave her a big hug. "I hope so. We could share a pregnancy and be miserable together."

"You make it sound like so much fun, Reidun."

"Yup, it's about as fun as eating five gallons of watermelon and having to hold it in for nine months. But on the bright side we could go see Dr. Townsend and Belle Fourche together, maybe even go shopping in a new store."

Later that day, Reidun and Iver were talking out of earshot of Anna. Reidun scolded him about their house. "I know old bachelors who wouldn't live in your house, Iver Tenold. You should really start a proper new house for Anna and your family."

"What family? You know something I don't?"

"No," she hedged, "but I'm betting it will happen sooner or later. Anyway, a woman like Anna deserves a proper house."

"But it's what we planned, Reidun. Anna and I discussed this before we got married and we decided *together* that we didn't want to spend any money on a house. We decided to build the ranch first and then build a house when we could afford it. We got cattle and land to pay for."

"Men," Reidun groaned, "all you think of is horses and cattle and land. Give it some thought, Iver. My guess is that if you're like most ranchers you'll never be able to *afford* it."

"Ok, Reidun, I will. Did Anna put you up to this?"

"Iver Tenold, you know better than that. That girl doesn't have a selfish bone in her body, and helping herself is the last thing she would ever think about doing."

"Guess I know that by now too," said Iver. "She always gives me the biggest and best of everything and puts me ahead of herself. On the other hand I'm always being selfish and thinking of myself."

"I know that isn't true, Iver. You are one of the most generous men I've ever known."

Anna was indeed pregnant, and she finally broke the news to Iver when she was positive. He picked her up and swung her around a couple times, then let her down carefully like she had become a case of eggs all of a sudden. "Sorry, I couldn't help it Anna love. I'll be extra careful with you from now on. Oh my goodness, I'm going to be a daddy! Chris! Chris! You in the barn, Chris? You're gonna be a grampa! I'm gonna be a daddy!"

Chris came out of the barn running and gave Anna a careful hug. "I think the happiest day of my life was when Iver told me that you said yes, but this just might top it. Guess we don't have to tell the neighbors." He looked at Iver. "They could probably hear you whooping all the way to Belle Fourche. Let's do something to celebrate! How 'bout an afternoon of fishing? We haven't tried that hole over east of the Larsons' all year."

"Great idea, Chris," Anna said. "I found some worms in the

garden spot early this spring and relocated them to the corner of the house so I could find them for an occasion like this. I'll dig a few of them up while you and Iver get the poles."

The three of them loaded up and headed for Chris's favorite fishing spot, a nice deep hole where the river took a turn and a few cottonwood trees shaded the water enough for the fish to hide there. It was a picture perfect day, and the three of them enjoyed celebrating and basking in the good news of Anna's pregnancy. Days like this were rare in a rancher's life, so it would stand out in their memories for a long, long time.

Iver was like an overprotective watchdog all year. "You shouldn't be riding, Anna. You shouldn't be in the hayfield, Anna. You shouldn't be hauling water, Anna. You shouldn't be slaving over the stove, Anna. You shouldn't be working so hard, Anna. You should be taking more naps, Anna. You need to drink lots of milk, Anna. How about another steak, Anna? You're feeding two now, you know."

"Iver Tenold, if you tell me one more thing that I have to do or have to not do I think I'll go crazy!"

"Ok, but you shouldn't get so excited you know..."

"Iver!"

Their mustangs were adapting well. Even the stallion had settled down and seemed to like the new range and possibly the security on the Tenold ranch. Iver and Chris had been the top bidder at the school land lease auction, so they acquired another 640 acres to use. The school section lease had Gap Creek going through it and lots of trees, bushes, and embankments for protection, so it was ideal for the horses and for foaling. Iver built a small corral by the creek where the wild horses liked to hang out. He left the gate open at both ends, and when they got used to going through the corral he used it to trap a yearling every so often so that he could start working with it. Folks from Buffalo to Bison to Belle Fourche to Hettinger had come to see their now famous herd of mustangs, and all of the yearlings were already spoken for if Iver could get them tamed and green broke.

By June they already had three new colts. "This is better than any Easter egg hunt," Iver remarked. "I get so excited just thinking of coming out and finding a new colt sucking its mother. They could make us rich," he told Anna one night.

"I don't want to be rich, Iver, but I do want to get all of our debts paid. You know how I hate owing money to Chris and the store. To me being rich is having no debts and having a little money for the collection plate on Sunday for our Lord. It gives me such a good feeling to be able put something in the collection. They're having a fundraiser so they can add a little kitchen to the church. Wouldn't that be nice? We could make coffee there and sit with the neighbors after church and visit a while."

"You know me. I never turn down a good cup of coffee. Does it come with cookies?"

Early Tuesday morning one of the neighbors from Reva came riding into their yard all excited. He told Iver and Chris that the Sabo family had suffered a tragedy. They had been cutting hay, and Mr. Sabo—Frank—got his foot caught in the mower bar, nearly cutting it off. He didn't bleed to death, but the whole family had gone to the doctor in Belle Fourche and they didn't have anyone at home to watch things.

"Why don't I ride over and do their chores and check on the livestock?" volunteered Anna.

Iver spoke up. "If you can watch things here for a bit, Chris, I'll ride over to Larsons'. If Odd has time he can help me organize as many neighbors as we can find and maybe we can get together and finish Frank's haying for him. He'll never be able to do it now, and if we get another winter like the last one he could end up losing his ranch altogether."

"You're right, Iver," Chris added. "We could never let that happen."

Iver helped Anna saddle up, and she left for Sabos'. Then Iver saddled up and rode over to see Odd. When Iver explained the situation, Odd was eager to help. "Let's both ride out. You hit the neighbors to the south of the Reva trail, and I'll go to the ones north of the trail. If we can get four or five of them to help, we could finish the mowing in one or two days, then go back and work on our own mowing for a few days until Frank's hay is dry enough to stack. Then everyone who can get away again will go back and get it stacked for him."

"I think I'll ride over and help Anna," Reidun spoke up. "It's probably the only time of year we could leave the place for a day or two. I'll hold James in front of me, and we'll be there by noon. When you have rounded up a few neighbors, why don't you start mowing today if there's still daylight? Anna and I will have supper ready for everyone haying there tonight."

"You are a darling, Reidun," the men harmonized. "Please take it easy on the ride. Don't want anything happening to you and James, or the baby."

"I'll be extra careful. See you two this afternoon."

Anna was about done with the chores when Reidun and James rode in. "Thought you could use some help, Anna."

"Sure can. Everything takes twice as long when you don't know the place very well. I haven't gotten the separator going, but the milk's in the bucket ready to go. I think that's all that's left of chores, plus gathering the eggs and feeding the chickens. If you and James can work on that, I'll ride out and check their cows and calves. I should be back in a couple of hours."

"When I get the chores done, I'll start supper for the men. I'll leave the bread and baking for you, Anna. You're so much better at that than I am."

"Ok. I'll hurry as much as I can. Do you have any idea how many will show up to help?"

"No, but I'm betting it'll be more than we think. Let's make extra. If we have too much, we'll feed it to them tomorrow. It'll take at least two days to do the mowing, even if they get several neighbors. Frank had only made one round when he had the accident."

Anna rode off, and Reidun headed for the chicken coop. She left James there to play with the chickens while she finished everything else up. Then she carried him to the house so that she could start on supper for those who showed up to help.

After their hard ride, Iver and Odd rode back home to get their haying equipment. When they arrived with it back at the Sabo place, three other neighbors had already shown up. They added their two machines, so by sundown five mowers were working on the Sabo hayfield. "Isn't that a wonderful sight," remarked Anna. "What a blessing to have neighbors that are willing to help each other out in their time of need."

"Nothing like it," Reidun smiled. "It's what keeps these communities together. We can all be as independent as that lone wolf I saw on the ridge today, but at the same time we know that if we need it help is on the way."

The men worked until the last speck of daylight had disappeared from the sky. They had mowed a good chunk of the field and figured that if they were lucky they could be finished before dark the following day. Frank had done a good job of cleaning the rocks and obstacles out of his field, making it that much easier. Rocks and sickles didn't get along well and changing sickle sections took a lot of extra time.

When the sun disappeared, the men all got on a wagon and headed back to the house. They could smell the fresh bread from a quarter mile off.

"That bread smells better than a newly mowed hayfield," Odd said to Anna when the men came in for supper. They were all hungry and devoured absolutely everything on the table.

"We don't wanna be eating leftovers tomorrow," they apologized.

"Besides," one of them grinned at Anna, "not everyday we get to eat cooking from a famous New York chef!"

After taking care of the horses, some of them left for home for the night, but a couple of the others just found a tree to sleep under. "It'll save time tomorrow, they explained; we'll get an earlier start."

"Good idea," said Anna. "This New York chef will have bacon and beans ready for breakfast...and dinner."

"Gonna be windy tomorrow," Iver added. "Help dry the hay out."

By late morning, all five machines were going again, two of them since seven a.m. Anna had been up before anyone else and true to her promise had breakfast and coffee ready for the men who had stayed overnight.

After breakfast, Anna and Reidun worked together on the chores.

One of the men brought his daughter along to help them out, and Reidun had put her to babysitting James so she could work with Anna. "I hope we get finished with some daylight left," remarked Anna. "I'd sure like to go through the mares yet today."

"I'd sure like some daylight when we get home too," said Reidun. "You never know what is going to go wrong when you leave the ranch unattended. Seems there's always something that isn't right when you return."

They finished the chores and set to making dinner, which meant adding more beans and bacon to the pot Anna had made for breakfast, along with more fresh baked bread and butter and gallons of cool water from the Sabo well. And of course more coffee. Rather than have the men take time to walk back to the house for dinner, Anna and Reidun loaded it in the Larson wagon and took it to them. "Pretty good service around here," Iver remarked with a smile. "Or maybe these two slave drivers just don't want us to take any time off!"

"We'll give you some time off as soon as this field is mowed. Now get to eating and get back to work." Reidun grinned.

They did as they were told, and by mid afternoon they had finished the entire field. "I sure wish Frank could've been here to see this," Iver said.

"I would like to be here when he gets home and sees haystacks instead of a field of grass," added Odd. "Does a man's heart good to help others, huh Iver?"

"Sure does. Nothing better for the soul, I reckon. Let's help the girls clean up around the house and get home to see what's gone wrong there. Anna and I want to go through the mares before dark if we can."

"And Reidun and I need to check the calves and milk that poor milk cow of ours. She hasn't been milked for a day and a half, and her bag is probably about to burst. We'll be squirting buttermilk outta those handles."

After three days of sunshine, Iver and Odd went back to rake the Sabo field so that it would be ready for the stacking crews the next day. This time there were even more neighbors there to help. Anna,

Reidun, and three other ladies made dinner for the stacking crews, who were able to stack the entire field in one day. They ended up making eleven stacks.

"That's about as good as I've seen on this field," remarked one of the neighbor men. "Guess all that winter snow was good for something." Everyone went back home, way behind on their own work but feeling good to have helped a neighbor in need.

Frank and his wife returned home the next week and both of them cried when they saw the field. "I don't know how I'll ever repay them."

"They don't expect anything, Frank. You'd've done the same for them. That's what neighbors do."

Iver and Anna got home early enough to check the mares. By now, sixteen of them had foals at their sides, and Iver had several of the yearlings on their way to becoming good ranch horses. They were still too young to ride, but getting them tamed down, halter broke, and used to a saddle on their back was more than half the battle. A rancher from Buffalo had ridden all the way to Reva just to see the mustang herd. With most of the summer and fall work done ranchers like him turned their minds back to what they loved the most, horses and cattle. This rancher was also a rodeo contestant and he was looking for a new roping horse. Iver and Anna both took time out to show him their horse herd. "You two are getting quite the reputation," he told them. "Do you have any prospects that you think would make me a good roping horse?"

When they got back from looking at the mustang herd, Iver took him to the corral and showed him the yearlings he was starting. "I know it takes a few years to make a good roping horse, but look at the size and strength of this yearling in particular. He has what it takes to hold a steer or most anything else you could throw at him on your ranch or in the arena. Better than that, he has brains, Mark. These mustangs have had to use their heads all these years just to survive, while other horse herds domesticated for stock have been pampered and had everything done for them. It'll give these quite an edge when it comes to training and to working."

"If you know what you want for him, I'll make a down payment right now, but I'd want you to keep him another year for breaking and training. I hear you can do in one year what it would take me two or three years to accomplish. And I'd pay extra if Anna has time to ride him a little just to make sure he's safe for my wife if she ever needs to use him."

"It's a deal," Iver said. "And I'd appreciate it if you'd make sure everyone knows where he came from when you take him around the rodeo circuit. It would be good advertising for Anna and me."

"I don't know," Mark grinned. "If your horses get too popular, I won't be able to afford another one. Only kidding. I'll be proud to show off one of your mustangs. I'm sure that riding one of your horses will make me look good too."

15

Obert Tenold

"*It's* time to bring our herd bull back to the corral," Iver said to Anna one day. "Fall's already started. Do you hear it?"

The sound was unmistakable and Anna looked up at a flock of sandhill cranes going over their heads, floating through the low hanging and wispy cirrus clouds and making as much noise as a church full of women at the ladies' aid meeting. "I love that sight and that sound," Iver commented. "But at the same time it makes me a bit anxious. It signals the end of summer and the start of fall. Before you know it winter will be staring down at us. Those cranes look so wild and free. I wonder where they're going?"

"Maybe they're like we were a few years ago, leaving but not knowing for sure where they'll land, looking for the perfect place to make a family. I hope they have as much good fortune as we did."

"Speaking of families," Iver looked at Anna while patting her swollen tummy, "Don't you just wonder what's in there? It makes me swell up with pride, but at the same time shrink down with worry. I hope I'll be a good father and that I'll make the both of you proud."

"You already have, Iver. Just look around at this ranch you've started. It's complete with an already famous horse herd and a group of pregnant Hereford heifers. I can't wait to see those little

205

Hereford babies in the spring. It'll be almost as exciting as our first foal crop was."

"The best crop of all is right in here," Iver patted her tummy again. "I'm hoping for a little girl as pretty as her mom is."

Chris came out of the house with a cup of coffee. "Hey you three, what's going on?"

Thanksgiving was coming up fast, and the church ladies decided that they should have a community Thanksgiving dinner after church service. Iver was all for it. "Nothing I like better than a potluck. Just thinking of all those dishes on the table makes my mouth water like the spring up in the north pasture. How about making an extra pie just for me, Anna dear?"

"How come it's always 'Anna dear' when there's mention of pies?"

"Well, all those berries up in the draw this year—we wouldn't want them to go to waste."

"Ok, Iver. You pick the berries and I'll make the pies."

"Berry picking ain't no job for men, Anna."

"It is if you want those pies."

"Where's the berry buckets?"

The community dinner was a great Thanksgiving feast. Iver and Odd went to the buttes and found a flock of turkeys and supplied a real turkey dinner for everyone. Frank was getting around pretty good as his foot had healed up enough so that he could walk on it a little and his family was able to attend. He said to everyone that Dr. Townsend had told him that it was a miracle that he hadn't had to amputate it. Frank's wife Betty had advised Dr. Townsend before they left Belle that they had two pregnant women in the community and he could expect to be seeing them sometime in December.

"I think we should take you two to Belle next week if it's nice," said Odd. "Winter will be here before we know it so maybe we should get a jump on things."

"I don't think we can leave too soon," said Reidun. "I'm guessing this one is coming sooner than we thought."

"I don't know what to think," added Anna. "But this being pregnant is sure miserable and I wouldn't mind getting it over with."

The sky was clear the next morning even though it had snowed a little overnight, so Odd and Iver loaded their wives into the wagon and were off to Belle Fourche to see Dr. Townsend. The preacher and his wife had offered to keep James rather than have him make the cold wagon ride to Belle, so Odd had taken him to their house the night before. The men decided that even though it was longer they would go around by Buffalo rather than through the buttes. There was a new café there, and they could stop there for a little rest and dinner and hot coffee.

They were going through the Reva gap in the buttes by eight a.m., and Anna spotted two wolves in the tree line. Odd thought he'd like to take a shot, but Iver just kept going. "I don't want to risk getting the new team of horses excited, Odd. They aren't very used to working together anyway. Let's play it safe."

"I agree," said Reidun.

"Look," Anna's sharp eyes had spotted another critter, a red fox. Both girls reminded their husbands that they were still waiting for their pretty fox coats to keep them warm this winter.

The antelope had herded together on the west side of the buttes already. "I hope that ain't a sign of a hard winter. We don't need another one of them," Iver said.

They arrived in Buffalo a little before noon and stopped at the café. "Boy does this bring back memories," Anna told them. "Those waitressing days were about as much work as ranching, but it taught me a lot. It taught me how good folks can be and that hard work can pay off. I'd like you to go back with me some day and visit the spots I worked in, Iver. Wouldn't it be something to retrace our steps back to Ellis Island and show each other all the places we've been and visit some of the folks that helped us get to South Dakota? I need to write another letter to Obert and see how he's doing. I owe him so much. He taught me to ride and rope and shoot and gave me his Winchester, his horse, his saddle, and his scabbard. When I think about it he gave me almost everything that was dear to him. That old man means so much to me."

"Why don't you write him from Belle tonight, dear? The letter'll go faster from there than from Reva so he'll get it sooner."

Anna did write to him that night.

Dear Obert,

So much has happened since I wrote to you last. Would you believe that I'm in Belle Fourche, South Dakota tonight writing this letter, and that the reason I am here is because I'm pregnant. Iver and I are so happy. If we have a boy, I'd like to name him after you. Iver agrees and sends you his best wishes. I hope that the two of you will get to meet each other some day soon. Iver is just like you. I can't wait to show him off to you, and of course Obert Iver too, if I have a son.

Blue is showing his age but still doing well. He is training our little neighbor boy, James, to ride, and if he's still up to it our first child will learn to ride on his back too. The Winchester still works fine. I think fondly of you every time I use it. I even let Iver borrow it once in a while but not often. I don't want it getting all scratched up. We saw a couple of wolves on our way to Belle but they were way out of range, especially for a .22, and we didn't want to spook the new team anyway.

I miss you so much, Obert. If you get tired of that farm of yours, why don't you come to Dakota and live with us? It would be so special to have you here, and it would mean so much to me.

Please greet the Christmans for me, and everyone at the café. God bless you!

Our love,
Anna and Iver

Later in December Anna received a letter from Sarah and George. Obert had passed away earlier that month. The letters had probably crossed paths in the mail, and Anna would always wonder if Obert had gotten her letter before he died. She prayed that he had. Having her son named after him would have made him feel good.

After they reached Belle Fourche, Iver pulled the team into a little hotel where the boarding house had been, and luckily they had two rooms left. It was late, so they decided to call it a day without looking for supper. "Let's just have a snack from the lunch bag we brought along and call it good. It'll save us a couple dollars." The girls both agreed, especially Reidun who had been having some cramps and just wanted to get out and stretch her legs and then lay down on a bed. After walking around a while, they all said good night and went to their rooms. It had been a long day and all of them needed a good night's sleep. Iver and Anna were so weary that they fell asleep on the bed without even taking off their clothes.

In the morning they ate the last of the food they had packed for the trip and then the four of them went to the doctor's office to find out if they could get in to see Dr. Townsend. His nurse told them to wait in the office until she could check with him about his schedule. After visiting with the doctor the nurse came back and told them that Dr. Townsend was busy all day but that he would skip his hour off at noon and try to see both of them during that time. "If you come back about 11:45 that should be just right."

"Thank you so much," they all replied together. "Please tell Dr. Townsend thanks and that we'll be back."

They had a few hours to kill and Anna wanted to do a little shopping, but Reidun wasn't feeling up to it. Her cramps seemed to be getting worse.

"Why don't the three of you go shopping together? I think I'll just head back to the hotel and lay down again."

"You don't think that the baby could be coming already," asked a worried Anna.

"I don't think so, Anna. I'm not really due for another two weeks."

They all agreed that Reidun had a good idea and decided to go back to their rooms and rest and then meet back at the doctor's office at 11:45 for their noon appointments.

They had only waited a few minutes when Dr. Townsend arrived. He seemed really happy to see Reidun and greeted her with a hug. "How's that boy of yours doing that I delivered a year ago—James, right? How have you been Odd?"

They caught him up on how James was doing and how the ranch was, and then introduced him to Anna and Iver.

"I've heard all about you two," he told them. "Your horse herd is putting you on the map. Anna, you could be Reidun's younger sister. Iver, your horsemanship has almost made you a legend around here."

"Thank you Dr. Townsend," they both replied. "Reidun has told us so much about you that we feel like we already know you. You have a reputation as a kind person and a great doctor, and we've also heard how kind and thoughtful your wife Minnie is."

Dr. Townsend looked at the time and decided they had better skip any more conversation and get on with the check ups. "Who wants to be first?"

"I think that Reidun might be closer than she thinks," replied Anna. "She's been having a few problems so why don't you see her first. She's had some cramping and has been feeling pretty tired."

"That doesn't sound too good, Reidun." Once in the examining room it didn't take Dr. Townsend long to diagnose Reidun. He took time to explain it to her then told her to send Anna in.

"That was a lot faster than I thought it would be," said a concerned Anna. "What did Dr. Townsend say?"

"He said that we got here just in time and that he wouldn't be surprised to see another Larson before tomorrow morning. He doesn't think that we have anything to worry about and that everything appeared normal, just a little sooner than we thought. He's ready to see you before his next appointment arrives."

Odd and Iver were relieved too, and both of them sighed and smiled at the same time.

"Really, Reidun? Maybe tonight?"

Anna's appointment took longer, but Dr. Townsend pronounced

her and the baby healthy. "I listened to a strong heartbeat and I think it even sounded Norwegian," he smiled at Anna and Iver. He looked at Anna and Reidun and said, "I really don't know which of you two ladies is the prettiest. Are you certain you aren't sisters? How did you two sodbusters find such pretty ladies?" he asked Odd and Iver.

"Oh they were tripping over their feet and doing all kinds of tricks to get us landed," Iver smiled. "If we hadn't said yes they'd probably still be crying and we'd have broken their tender little hearts. We had all kinds of women chasing us, right Odd?"

"Likely story, Iver. They have a tall tale contest going over at the hotel. I think you should go enter it, you'd win for sure," the Doctor laughed.

After their visit and appointments with Dr. Townsend, the four of them went for a stroll along Main Street, and since Reidun was feeling better they did some shopping in the General Store. Odd and Iver went straight to the gun rack and the girls found the dress rack. Iver did need a new rifle as the old used one he had bought in Dickinson was about wore out but he decided that if they spent any money it should be on Anna, not him. Odd felt the same way about Reidun. They told the clerk they would think on some purchases but didn't want to make any today.

"Let's find a nice little café and have some supper," suggested Reidun.

"Sounds great to us," the rest of them chimed in. After supper they all went back to the hotel for the night, waiting to see how long Reidun could hold out.

About midnight she woke Odd up. "I think the baby is on its way. The water just broke."

"What should I do?!"

"You can *calmly* walk over to doc's house and ask him if he wants the honors or if we should get the midwife he told us about."

Odd came running back to their room a few minutes later. "Dr. Townsend said to come over to his office, and he'd be ready for you. He already figured this was going to happen. Should I carry you?"

"I can walk on my own just fine."

Four hours later, Odd had a little daughter, and an exhausted but happy Reidun was showing her off. Iver and Anna had heard the commotion and were both there for the delivery.

"Thanks for showing me how it's done, Reidun."

"This was piece of pie compared to James. Oh Odd, we have a family of four now."

"You sure are something, Reidun. You made it look so easy and I know it isn't. You didn't even whimper. I'd have been screaming my head off."

"Congratulations to both of you," Anna and Iver chimed in.

Four very happy Norwegians went to bed that night. Reidun's new little girl had already nursed and was demanding to be noticed. Odd admired his wife and daughter all night, too happy to sleep.

The next morning they debated about what to do about Anna. Dr. Townsend had said that he thought she wasn't more than a couple of weeks off—Christmas at the very latest. If they wanted, they could all go home and Iver and Anna could come back in a week or two. Otherwise, Odd and Reidun and their baby could go back and leave both Iver and Anna there until the baby came.

After an hour of back and forth deliberation, Anna spoke up. "I've made up my mind," she stated positively. "The four of you will go back, and I will stay. I don't want to go all the way back to Reva and take the risk of not being able to get back here again. Since this is my first delivery I don't want to take any chances. Too many things could go wrong. We could have a blizzard and get snowed in, the wagon could break down, someone could get sick, or I could deliver too early. You name it and it could go wrong."

They were all intently listening to her rationale. Reidun was nodding her head in agreement.

"Iver, you need to be at home to tend to the stock in case a bad storm hits. Chris needs watching too. I can manage just fine here by myself. It will be the best for everyone. You should all leave as soon as possible today so you will get back home before it's too late. Either that or stay over tonight and get an early start tomorrow morning. Your choice."

After some deliberation they all decided to stay over one more night and get an early start in the morning in case something went wrong on the way back. It would give the new mother and her baby a little more time to prepare for the trip.

"Good idea," Anna agreed. "It's better to travel in daylight, and we don't want to take any chances with you or that new baby of yours, Reidun. Have you two decided on her name? I know you've been going back and forth."

"We wanted to name her either after my Mom, Esther, or you Anna. I think we've settled on Esther Anna Larson."

"That really makes me feel proud and happy," said an elated Anna. It is such an honor to have you name your little girl after me. Can I be her aunt?"

"Only if I can be her uncle!" Iver added. "Let's take Reidun and Ester Anna back to the room and leave them alone so they can get a nap and relax. The rest of us can look for supplies to take back home."

After taking Reidun and Ester Anna to the room, the others went to the general store and bought supplies so they could load the wagon with food and water for the early morning departure and the long trip back home. Iver and Odd both needed more ammunition for the winter and some other ranch necessities. They looked at some new horse tack but decided it was too expensive. "I'm gonna have to make my own saddles," Odd remarked, "if they get any more expensive. You'd think we were getting a fortune for our cowhides as much as leather goods cost, but we practically give them away."

Anna looked at the clothes. "I think I'll buy a new flannel nightgown for the stay here in Belle if it's ok with you, Iver, and maybe some new socks. What about you? I'd like to see you get a new shirt for Sundays."

"I'll get by, Anna".

"Smell this store soap," she added. "Wonder what they put in it to make it smell that good. Must be some sort of perfume. Wouldn't a bar of that look fancy in your kitchen, Odd? You should buy Reidun something special."

"Would you help me please? Us men aren't so good at picking things out for you ladies."

"Of course I will, I know a lot of things that she would love and needs."

"Why don't we buy a little extra summer sausage and some cheese and some of this store sliced bread and have a sandwich for supper in our room when we get back," suggested Iver.

"That sounds fun to me," Odd added.

After selecting a beautiful shawl and a new blouse for Reidun and finishing with their supplies, they loaded everything in the wagon and went to see how mother and baby were doing and have an early supper. Reidun had just nursed Esther Anna, who was taking a nap with her recently filled tummy. Anna got the sandwich material out and set in on the dresser. Iver offered to slice the sausage with his jackknife.

"You keep that in your pocket," Anna stopped him. "Last I saw it used you were skinning a rattlesnake with it."

"I wiped it off on my pants."

"Let's ask the hotel if they'll slice it for us," Reidun suggested. "I don't trust Iver's jackknife either."

After supper Iver opened the door to check the weather. "Brrrr, it's gonna freeze hard again tonight. I sure hope it doesn't snow. We had enough last year to last me a lifetime. Maybe we should all get to bed early and get as much rest as we can. Tomorrow will be a long day."

Their room wasn't very warm so Anna and Iver went straight to bed so they could snuggle and warm each other up. "I feel bad leaving you all by yourself, Anna. It isn't the way I planned this at all."

"I know how you feel Iver, and I sure wish you could stay here with me. But I'll manage, and we'd never forgive ourselves if something happened to Chris or the mustangs while we were here."

"Or if anything happened to you," Iver looked concerned. "As always you are right, honey. I love you so much. Just think, in a few days we'll be a family."

"It's what we've both dreamed of, Iver. Don't forget to pray for the baby and me tonight, and I'll pray for you."

They were up early and the hotel already had coffee on, so they gulped a couple of cups before hitching up the team. Reidun kept Esther in the room by the stove until the last minute. Then she and Anna bundled little Esther Anna up in a blanket that they had warmed by the fire, leaving only a tiny peephole for her to get fresh air. "This isn't gonna be easy," Reidun said. "She nurses every couple of hours."

Anna told Odd to make sure to put several blankets over the girls, especially while Reidun nursed Esther, and to "make darn sure they don't get cold."

Anna and Iver had another couple of hugs. "I love you so much, Anna, and I feel so bad that I won't be here with you."

"You will, Iver. You always are, right here in my heart. I'll get word to you when the baby is here, or if I know anything else sooner. Check with Reva on mail days 'cause I'll send a note with the mailman. He comes in every Monday and Thursday."

"I will darling, and I'll be praying for you and the baby just like you taught me."

"You guys get going now before I start crying or something. I'm lonesome already."

The wagon left and Anna walked back to the hotel and took a cup of coffee to her room. It had a rocking chair, her favorite kind, so she sat in it and rocked back and forth. At one point, Rasmus entered her mind as he still did sometimes, but not as often now. It was getting easier to force him out. She pushed the intruder away and focused on Iver and their horse herd and her baby to be. The thought of them always brought a smile to her face and warmth to her heart.

Anna spirited herself up from her daydream and went back out into the chilly December air. She walked over to Dr. Townsend's office and told his nurse that she was staying in Belle at the hotel until the baby came. The secretary asked Anna if she had anyone staying with her in case she needed help. "I'll be fine, Anna told her. I've just watched my friend Reidun deliver her little girl, and I've been through it with dozens of cows and mares. I'll know when its time and will come over to your office."

"Let me show you where Dr. Townsend lives, just in case it happens in the middle of the night. He'll want you to let him know right away. Since you're staying here in Belle, why don't you come in again Friday afternoon and we'll see how you've progressed."

Anna spent the next couple of days reading her bible and walking around town. She stopped by the café Friday, which was extra busy, so she asked for an apron and started helping out until the dinner rush was over. "You certainly know your way around a restaurant, the lady at the till told her."

"I've done my time in these joints, all the way from New York to Minneapolis."

"You looking for a job?"

"No, I just saw that you were short-handed and it came natural to help out. I needed something to do anyway. I'm only in town until my baby comes, then I'll be heading back home to our ranch by Reva."

"When is your baby due? By the looks of it pretty soon?"

"I'm not sure. This is my first, but I'm thinking the sooner the better so I can get back home before winter really sets in. I'm seeing Dr. Townsend this afternoon so I hope to know more then."

"Well good luck. Did you say your name was Anna?"

"Yes, Anna Tenold."

"You wouldn't be the folks with that herd of wild mustangs would you?"

"That's us," Anna smiled. "Well, I'm off to see the doctor."

Anna was the last patient of the day, and Dr. Townsend took his time, asking her all about the Larson family and how their little boy James was doing.

"He's growing like a thistle after a rain, and he's a whirlwind, just like his dad."

"I figured as much. Do you want a boy or a girl?"

"I don't care as long as it's healthy and happy."

"I don't think that you'll have long to wait, although I've been wrong many times. My guess is the middle of the week or even sooner."

Anna waited patiently and spent much of her time in the rocking chair, reading her way through most of the New Testament. She had made friends with many of the café workers by now, so she stopped there almost every day. She even offered to help with their baking, and on one especially busy day she made them two pies, which were gone by suppertime with the customers begging the cafe to get more of them. "They are delicious!" they exclaimed.

Dr. Townsend was wrong, but he was close. Anna started labor on Thursday morning. It wasn't fast or easy, and it took most of the day. But by nightfall Anna had a baby boy nursing her. She had already decided on his name, so she started calling him Obert when she first saw him.

Dr. Townsend promised to send a note with the mailman to Reva: *Iver, come get your wife and your son, Obert!*

Dr. Townsend offered a bed at his house until Anna had time to recover a bit, but she declined. "I'm ok, but thank you so much. I'm already paid up at the hotel for another two days and Iver should be here by then if he gets the message right away. I wouldn't want to be a bother to you and Minnie, I know how long and hard the two of you work. Did I ever thank you for everything you did for Reidun? She's a sister to me, and it meant a lot to all of us. If they ever give you doctors any time off, why don't you stop by Reva for a visit and I'll personally show you our mustang herd. If you can give us some notice I'll even bake a couple of pies."

"I would love to do that, Anna. Thanks for asking. I just might have to make a house call on you and Reidun some weekend and see how you and the babies are doing. And see the horse herd while I'm at it."

Iver was in Reva waiting for the mail when the mailman came in and delivered him his note. He was ecstatic. The mailman wasn't used to getting hugged. Iver jumped on his saddle horse and raced home, smiling that famous Iver smile. He pulled in and ran over to find Chris. "Hey, how's it feel to be a grampa!" he yelled.

"I'll be darned. I couldn't be prouder if it had been my own. Boy or girl? I suppose you'll be heading to Belle to get your family?"

"I'm off like a polecat up a tree to fetch my wife and my son, Obert. Anna already had the name picked out if it would be a boy. I hitched the team up this morning just in case the mailman had news. All I need is to unsaddle and throw my rifle in the wagon."

"You got grub and all those extra blankets for Anna and the baby loaded in the wagon? If not I'll get them loaded for you while you unsaddle your horse and get your head to working. You got water? Take it easy on the team, Iver. It's freezing cold out today."

"Ya, I noticed, my nose felt like it was froze when I got home from Reva. Can I borrow that horse hair coat of yours? Where's the big lap robe that's usually in the wagon?"

"It's with the blankets, Iver. Now spread one of them blankets or the robe or both over yourself and try to keep warm. Remember not to push the team."

"See ya in about three or four days, Chris. I can't wait to get back and show off my family!"

"I can't wait either, Iver. Just travel safe!"

It was very late when Iver arrived in Belle Fourche. He knew he should have waited until the next day to leave so he didn't have to travel so late and in the dark, but this just couldn't wait. Luckily he had a young and strong team of horses that took the long day in stride. Iver dropped the reins and tied them to the hitching post, then ran for the hotel. He knocked (pounded) on Anna's door, hoping that the hotel hadn't put her in another room. She came to the door, "Who's there?"

"Your frozen husband, Anna. Let me in please." She opened the door and Iver threw himself at her, picking her up and hugging her for all she was worth.

Anna shrieked. "I'm still awful sore, Iver. Take it easy on me. Besides, you're like hugging an iceberg."

"Sorry, Anna. I've missed you so much. Where's Obert Iver?"

"Right here in bed under the covers. He's a snuggler like his dad."

"Smart kid. Ain't he something? I'm so proud of you, Anna. I sure wish I could have been here to help."

"Not much you could have done, Iver, except maybe take pity on me as I moaned and groaned."

"You're even more beautiful than when I last saw you, Anna. Is there room for me in that bed tonight?"

"We'll make room."

"I'll bring in the robe and blankets so they can get warmed up, and the water bag is frozen solid so I'll bring it in too. Then I'll take that poor team to the livery stable and get them unhitched and fed. They sure earned their oats today. Be back as fast as it takes a Norwegian to eat his lefsa. Keep the bed warm!"

Iver was so overjoyed that he barely knew what he was doing. Anna just smiled at him, knowing how much he loved her. She felt better and safer already, just having him there. She couldn't wait to get her family back home to Reva. She couldn't wait to show her son to Chris, Odd, and Reidun.

An hour later Iver came bouncing in again and started undressing. "I'm absolutely frozen!" He jumped into bed. Anna had Obert in the middle.

"Iver, get those cold feet off of me. Snuggling will have to wait, at least until you thaw out. You think we'll be able to leave in the morning?"

"If the wind isn't blowing and the snow isn't drifting, I think we should if you and Obert are up to the long ride. We'll go round by Buffalo and see how you're feeling when we get there. We could find a hotel if you weren't up to the rest of the ride east to Reva or if it's getting late."

Anna wanted to know how the horses were, how Chris was, the cattle, the Larsons, even the chickens. They visited until Iver fell asleep exhausted. Anna was still asking questions when she noticed he wasn't listening. Little Obert was starting to wiggle. "Ok, you hungry little monster. Mom's right here."

Anna didn't get much sleep worrying about how the trip back would go, but she felt pretty well rested since she had a couple of days in the hotel before Iver arrived. Obert got her up again for some breakfast, and Anna noticed that a few sun rays were peeking out of the eastern horizon.

"It's daylight, Iver," Anna announced.

He could hardly open his eyes; he needed more sleep. "What's the weather doin'?"

"Not enough light to tell yet, but I don't think it's blowing."

"Let me get dressed and then I'll go check it out. Maybe someone in the hotel will have some idea of what we can expect. We'll wait till full daylight, and then decide whether to go or to stay another day. You feeling up to it, Anna?"

"Sure am."

There were only two people in the hotel lobby, and Iver overheard them talking about a storm moving in later in the week. He went over and asked them how they knew. "Just a hunch," the old timer told him. "We often get our first big one right before Christmas, and Christmas is just around the corner. You from Belle?"

"No. Reva. I'm trying to get my family back home."

"I'd light a fire if I were you, just in case, mister. My legs are acting up, sure sign of weather coming."

Iver took a cup of coffee that the hotel clerk gave him and the news back to Anna, who was nursing Obert.

"Wish I could help you feed him but I'm not equipped. Let me hold him up there so you can get a sip of coffee. They're talking the possibility of a storm coming in later this week. Wind isn't blowing yet. I think I'll go hitch up the team and get them fed so they're ready if we decide to leave. I paid the clerk for the room but told him we might be staying another day just in case we decide to or you don't feel up to leaving. What time does the general store open?"

"I'm not sure, but they get there early and might open for us before the regular time."

Iver was back in less than an hour. "I got the team hitched, and the store opened up for me so I was able to get us plenty of food, even got extra in case we get snowed in somewhere. You think you're ready for this, Anna? Its cold out, but I'll keep you and Obert bundled up under the blankets and robe so you should be snug as a bug. I'll load the water and keep it and the groceries under the blankets with you so they don't freeze. Think I'll put one blanket under you two and the rest on top of you. Just look at our little fella, Anna, all bundled up in that baby quilt Reidun gave us. You're a miracle worker, Anna darling. Are you sure that you're up to traveling?"

"For the fifth time, Iver, yes I am ready to go!"

It took until late afternoon for the Tenold family to reach Buffalo, so they stayed there overnight, leaving early the next morning for their home on the prairie. As it turned out they left Belle Fourche just in time. The storm hit the next afternoon, not long after the Tenold family arrived at the ranch. The old timer had been right.

Just before the storm started, Anna, Iver and Obert Iver had their reunion with Chris. "I know he isn't really my grandson, but it sure feels like it to me. Iver, you and Anna have made me so proud and so happy."

"I'm the same as your son, Chris. Anna's the same as your daughter. So that makes Obert your grandson. We're all one big family here on this ranch."

Chris already had the stove going, so their house was toasty warm. "I figured you'd be here tonight, and I wanted it to be warm for you and the baby, Anna."

They asked him in to share some of the food they had left from the trip for supper and he gladly said yes. "It'll give me some more time to admire my new grandson."

The wind had already kicked up. "Looks like that old timer mighta been right, Anna. Feels like a storm's coming our way."

"I'm so happy to be home," Anna reflected. "To be in our home with our son. This is *our* family. I feel so safe and secure here with you and Obert."

It snowed for several days until Christmas, when the sun came back out. Iver and Chris had been able to get to the stock every day except one, so they felt pretty good. They even stopped to chop a tree on their way back from the horses a couple of days before Christmas.

"It's not much, Anna, but we need a tree for our first Christmas as a family."

"Its perfect, Iver. I'll get the snow melted off the branches and see if I can find some makeshift decorations to hang on it. Maybe string some popcorn or something."

On Christmas day they gathered around the tree. Anna said a prayer of thanksgiving for all of them. Then they started a family tradition by singing happy birthday to Jesus and having some birthday cake that Anna had made in Jesus' honor. They all agreed that this was the best Christmas any of them had ever had. Anna snuck into the bedroom and fished under their bed for a package. "I had time do a little shopping while I was waiting for Obert to come into the world. They aren't much, but I've got presents for all the men in my life: my husband, my dad, and my son. I love you all so much."

The snow broke for a few days, and then started again on New Year's Day. They had over two feet when it finally quit and warmed up. "About time the January thaw arrived," Chris observed. "I hope it's done snowing for the year."

"Wouldn't that be something?" Anna smiled. "Say Iver, let's see how the team handles the bobsled you made. Why don't we all bundle up and take a ride through the horse pasture?"

Anna had been getting out a little more each day. She even did "wolf patrol" on the cow pasture. Rabbits and turkeys were thick this year, so the wolves had plenty to eat, but just the same she wanted to make sure that all of her animals were ok. Everything had frozen over, so she even helped Iver chop holes in the ice so the cattle could drink. They didn't chop ice for the horses. Iver explained that they get plenty of water out of the snow that they eat with every mouthful of grass they chew up. Horses didn't seem to need as much water as cows anyway.

The winter went slowly by. Obert kept growing, and Anna's men kept busy. It was already March. Anna and Reidun tried to see each other at least once a week when the weather permitted, comparing Esther and Obert and James. James was a year older so he had a huge edge in size. He was just starting to walk and had some teeth. Obert definitely had the chubbiest cheeks and was the hungriest. They all agreed that Esther was by far the prettiest. There was no contest in that regard. Of course the conversation changed when Iver and Odd joined in from how pretty Esther was to which boy was the strongest.

It was getting nice enough outside that spring plans were being made and new projects were starting. Odd was building a new windbreak for his calving pasture so that the newborn calves would have more shelter from the wind. Iver was adding on to their barn and wondering how to do the same to the house. He knew that three of them could fit, but what if they had more children?

Since the snow had melted in the corrals, both of the men had yearling horses in them, getting the colts ready for breaking in the fall. Iver had sold all but the last one of his yearling crop and was looking forward to foaling the mares. He timed it so that the cows were done calving about the time that the mares started foaling so that everything wouldn't happen at the same time. Earlier calves were better anyway as they were sold by the pound in the fall.

Both families felt the intense pressure yielded by all of the work that needed to be done. It was hard for the ladies to help as much as they wanted to, but sometimes they would take all three children to one of them to baby-sit so the other could assist with some project that their husband had going. They both dreamed of having enough money to hire someone to help their husbands get the work done. It was crazy in the spring. Calving, doctoring sick cattle, preparing the farm ground for planting, cleaning seed and planting it in the fields, feeding the cows, doing the chores, fixing the fences that had broken down from the winter snow, mending corrals, chopping more firewood, hunting for food…The list went on and on and each item on it added to the pressure.

Reidun cornered Iver one afternoon when he was at their place helping Odd with a sick cow. She told him that he should start planning to build a better home for his family. He explained that both he and Anna wanted to pay some bills and build their ranch up before spending money on a house. Reidun had to remind him that the bills were never all paid on a ranch and the work was never all finished. "You need to make this one of your priorities Iver. That one room home of yours just won't do."

March had come in like a lamb, but as the saying goes it went out like a lion. The sunny days disappeared and it started snowing again, almost every day for the first two weeks of April. It was a battle to keep the newborn calves alive in weather like this, and a few of them had frozen their ears. Both Iver and Odd had made special warming huts for the calves that became chilled to the point that they couldn't get up and nurse.

Iver was always tired but not tired enough that he didn't have time to play an "April fools day" joke on Anna. On April first he came running into the house and told Anna that the stallion and three mares had fell over an embankment and he desperately needed help. When she dropped the pan of bread she was holding and ran for her coat he yelled out "April Fools Day!" then confessed and apologized.

"That's not funny, Iver!" She picked up the pan and threw it at him. He ducked and backed out the door laughing. "I'll get even," Anna whispered under her breath, and then she smiled too.

April was typical, nice one day then naughty the next. After the week of snow they had a warm rain shower one day, so Iver came in from work early. "I think it's a good day to sit and watch it rain and enjoy my family." He put Obert on his lap, and Obert's fat little face lit up. Iver did the rich man's horse, poor man's horse, hunter's horse routine that he had learned from his father with Obert on his knee, bouncing Obert up and down the whole time.

"He's too little for that, Iver, you'll break his neck!"

"He likes it. Can I help with supper? Can we fry a deer steak? Any taters left in the root cellar? This is a million dollar rain, Anna, not a drop of it running off. The prairie is soaking it up like I soak up sunshine and those smiles of yours. I can almost see the grass growing and fattening up the cows. They'll be shedding their winter coats soon if this nice weather keeps up. Think I'll go check horses tomorrow if I get time. Maybe saddle up Blue for Obert and he can ride with me."

"Give him a few more years, Iver."

After checking the horses, Iver came back to the house. "Got news, Anna. We have a new foal in the pasture. Looks like his ears have been nearly froze off so he must've had a cold birthday, but other than that he looks fine. We'll name him Croppy."

"Guess that stallion isn't as smart as we thought, Iver."

"Must've been the mares' idea, Anna. You gals are always getting us guys into trouble," he laughed. "You want to ride over and see the new colt? I already asked Chris if he would watch Obert for an hour or two."

"I'd love to get out of this house for a while. I feel like a bird trapped in a tiny cage."

"Promise you won't fly away if I let you out?"

They put Obert in bed, and Chris came over to baby-sit. "How can I play with him if he's sleeping?"

"You can just be glad he is."

Chris commented that Obert did look like a little angel laying there sleeping and told Iver that he had probably looked that innocent once upon a time too. They all laughed and Iver and Anna went to check on the new foal while Chris enjoyed his time with his grandson. As soon as they left, he woke Obert up so he could hold him.

April turned into May, and their ranch turned into a gigantic garden of wild flowers and green spring grasses, soaking up the moisture from the recent rain and the spring snows. The cows were about finished calving with only a few stragglers left. Except for their early surprise there had been no more colts born. Either the stallion or the mares or both were back on schedule. Iver plowed up the wheat field and got it ready for planting but the flax would have to wait for another year. "Maybe I'll get that extra ground broke up this fall if we get some August rain. Then it'll be ready for next year," Iver apologized to Anna.

"Don't worry, dear. We'll get it done in due time, along with all those other things we dream of getting done."

It was early in May, just after dark, and they heard a knock on their door. "Who in the world would come calling this time of the day?" Iver asked Anna.

Iver went to the door and opened it. He looked beyond the man and saw wagons full of lumber and a crew of young men. "Are you lost, mister?" he asked.

"Is this Anna and Iver Tenolds house?"

"Yes. And you are…?" he asked the stranger.

Anna came around the corner. She looked like she had seen a ghost, let out a gasp, and fainted. Luckily Iver was able to catch her before she hit the floor. The two men eyed each other while they revived Anna. Rasmus knew that he had a lot of explaining to do. He had gone over his explanation several times in his mind but now he was in the spotlight. His mind raced back to the events that had started all of this.

16

Rasmus And Astrid

"*Rasmus?*" his wife Astrid asked as she often had. "Something seems to be on your mind. You just don't ever seem to be completely happy to me. I do wish you would let me know what you are thinking. Maybe I could help? You need to be taking more time with me and the kids, dear. All you do is work. Now that you have your own construction company and your own crew of builders, you should be able to take more time off."

Rasmus was still lost in thought. "Rasmus Johnson." Astrid physically turned his head and made him look at her. "If you don't start talking to me, I'm going to die of loneliness."

"What? I'm sorry Astrid. Did you say something to me?"

Conversations like this, if you could call them conversations, went on for a few months until Astrid blew up one day. "I'm leaving you, Rasmus. You're never here with me and the kids anyway."

"What do you mean, Astrid? I'm always here and I love you. What more do you want?"

"I want a husband who tells me what is on his mind. I want a husband who shares his thoughts and dreams with me. You're here with me physically, Rasmus, but I'd like to have all of you."

Rasmus looked at Astrid thoughtfully and almost tearfully. "You're right, Astrid. I've been holding something back from you since I picked you up at Ellis Island. It's been tearing at me all this time, and sometimes I feel like the weight of the world is on my shoulders. For better or for worse I think that I should tell you the story that I've been keeping from you. Sit with me. This will take some time."

Rasmus started at the beginning. "I was heartbroken when you called our engagement off. I couldn't understand how you could choose Norway over me. I had shared my dreams with you and had told you many times that America was to be a part of our future. I thought that you agreed with me."

"I did but the more I thought about it the more frightened I got at the thought of leaving my family and friends."

"I know, Astrid, and I even understand that. The thing is that I thought I would never see you again after I left Norway. I was certain of it. I was lonely and devastated. In my loneliness, I started visiting with a young lady on the ship. She shared my dreams of America and starting a new life. She was lonely too. I didn't mean to, and I don't think that she did either, but we gradually fell in love over the course of the voyage."

Rasmus went on. "Maybe it was the loneliness, maybe it was the fear of never finding anyone else. But we did fall in love and I asked her to marry me. We were supposed to be married on the day that I got the telegram from your mom and dad. If that telegram had been a day later, or if I had failed to go and get it, I would have been married to her. You would have been on a ship bound for America without anyone here to meet you. When I got that telegram, I didn't know what to think. I actually fainted. The girl that I…"

Astrid interrupted him, "What's her name?"

"Anna. Anna was out shopping for her wedding dress and had already made an appointment with a justice of the peace. I didn't know what to do, Astrid. I could hardly think. My mind was going crazy. I wanted to die! When I finally got up enough courage to face her, I went back to where we had planned to meet. She read me like a book and knew something was wrong immediately. It's hard to remember exactly what happened, since I was such a wreck, but I just stood there wordless and finally I gave her the telegram."

Rasmus had tears in his eyes as he went on telling Astrid the story. He told her that after Anna had read the telegram she started crying. Rasmus explained to Astrid that he had never told Anna about her or their engagement. He had meant to tell her, but it seemed like the right time never came up. He continued, "After Anna stopped crying she asked me about you. I finally found some words and told her our story. How we had known each other since we were children, how we grew up together and were best friends, how I loved your family, and how your dad treated me like his son. I told her how we went on walks together and watched the sunsets. I told her that we were engaged and that our wedding had been planned, but that you broke it off because you wouldn't go to America with me. I told her how I was heartbroken and didn't know what to do, but that I already had paid for our tickets on the ship so I just got on board and left by myself. I told her that you chose your family, your friends, and Norway over me."

Rasmus softly continued telling the story to Astrid. "Neither of us knew what to do or what to think. We both just sat there numb with grief and shock. Finally Anna suggested that we should go to our rooms separately and think this through to see if either of us could come up with a solution. Anna was so good at that. She was always helping folks and finding solutions to their problems for them. I saw it happen several times on the ship. Anyway, it was she who finally decided what do to."

"After many tears and much thought and deliberation Anna came to my room. She said she knew me well and that I would never forgive myself if I just walked away and left you there on Ellis Island looking for me. She told me that I had too much honor for that. I didn't even argue with her, Astrid. I let her make the decision. I think she loved me so much that she did it for me. And for you."

Astrid moved closer and put her arms around Rasmus. "Oh Rasmus, you should have told me. That poor girl, we should have tried to help her, Rasmus."

"I thought about it, but I didn't have the courage to see her again. I just left her standing there Astrid. Sometimes when I close my eyes all I can see is her standing there looking so alone and bewildered."

"Was she pretty?"

"I would be lying if I said no. Yes, she was pretty. And she was smart and compassionate. I don't think that I've ever known anyone who is so helpful to everyone around them."

"What did the two of you do during all of the time you spent together on the ship?"

"We weren't lovers if that is what you are asking. We just spent hour after hour together, mostly dreaming of America and how we would make our fortunes there and have a new life in the land of milk and honey. I made her so many promises, Astrid, so many broken promises. I think that all of those broken promises have weighed on me more than anything. I even promised her that I would build her a new house in America. We spent so many hours planning that house. I can just see it in my mind and I can see her smiling over it. There wasn't much else to do on the ship. The conditions in steerage were absolutely horrible. I was so relieved when the telegraph said that you had a second-class ticket. I doubt you could have survived steerage. Many didn't. They died trying to get to their dream, the same dream that all of us shared—America."

"Are you mad at me, Astrid? I feel so ashamed, not telling you about Anna. I didn't know how you would take it, and I didn't want you to feel bad about what happened. The only thing that I've ever wanted is to bring honor and honesty to you and your family. When I think about what your parents did for me, sending you here against your wishes just to defend your family honor, it makes me love them even more."

Rasmus thoughts went back to Norway and to Astrid's family. "What would they have thought if they had known that I was already engaged to someone else? Or if I hadn't been here to meet you? What will they think now? Oh Astrid, I have thought this over so many times in my mind, and the guilt has been weighing on me like a mountain of lead. Can you forgive me for not telling you sooner? I feel so badly. I know that I've been deceiving you all of this time."

"I think the question is do you still love me, Rasmus?"

"Of course I do, Astrid. Maybe now more than before, especially with our children in the picture. I know that I haven't been as attentive as I should be, and that you often find me lost in thought. It even makes it difficult for me to run the company sometimes. If it weren't for my love for you and my family, I wouldn't be working so hard to build the business and make your home—our home—nicer. I want my sons to have something to take over. I want the business to be big enough to support several families so that they all can be involved in it if they want to. I want us to be a happy family, Astrid, and believe me I have been trying to keep Anna and those promises that I made to her out of my mind. I try to seal it up like a tomb, but there is always a crack, and the picture of her standing there all alone seeps in. It's like trying to stop a river. What will I do?"

"I think I know what you have to do, Rasmus, and I think that you know too. You just haven't had the courage to tell me, or to admit it to yourself. What would you do if I weren't here? Think about it."

"I don't have to think about it, Astrid. I'd go and honor my promise to Anna. I would take my crew and go build her the house that I promised to build for her. I'm sure she is married and has her own family by now, but I'd go build that house anyway."

"Then do it, Rasmus! It's the only way that I'll ever have all of you again. Anna told you that if you didn't go meet me in Ellis Island that your honor would tear you apart and you'd be looking back the rest of your life. Now I'm telling you the same thing. Go and honor your promise to her. Then come back to me and your family and be the Rasmus that I used to know and love. I want all of you, Rasmus, and that means your honor too. I think that is what everyone knows and loves about you the most and why your business keeps growing. You are a man of your word and of honor, Rasmus Johnson. It's what makes you the person that you are."

Astrid and Rasmus had a family conference and told their children that their father would be gone for a few months. He had three homes under contract to build that spring and summer, so he arranged for another contractor to build two of them and lined up his foreman and two of his employees to build the other.

It was March already and Rasmus knew that he had to leave as soon as the winter broke. It would be tight, but if he left soon he might finish the house in time to return to New York before winter.

"How good are you at detective work, Astrid?"

"Why?"

"Because it's a big country and I have no idea where Anna is living. She might still be in New York, she might be in California, she could be anywhere!"

They started looking immediately, knowing that Rasmus had to leave right away if possible. Rasmus remembered the family that Anna had helped as they were leaving Ellis Island. "The family couldn't figure out what to do and Anna came up with a solution for them. I think that both the little girl and her mother went back to Norway. The father and the rest of the family were going to stay here in New York, at least until the mom and her daughter returned. If we can find them, and if they have kept in touch with Anna, we should be able to find her."

"What was their name?"

"I'm trying but for the life of me I can't remember. If I think long enough maybe it will come to me. Oh wait. There was also a lady by the name of Donna at the boarding house where Anna was staying. I don't know if she owned the place or was just working there as a manager or something. If she is still there, she may know where Anna is. They were good friends, and maybe even got to be better friends after I left. Anna may have stayed there a while longer. For all I know Anna might still be in the area. Wouldn't that be nice?"

The next week both Rasmus and Astrid set out to find where Anna was living. Rasmus still couldn't remember the name of the family. He thought that they were named after someone's farm, but he couldn't remember much more. They decided to look for the boarding house and see if it was still there. The next day they found it, but Donna no longer worked there. The owner told them that he thought she lived over on Boston Street, but he wasn't sure. "I think she found a better paying job. Or maybe she got married? I'm not sure. Sorry I can't be of more help."

They drove all of Boston Street the next day, stopping at every home and inquiring about a lady named Donna, probably around twenty-five years old. They found two Donna's, but neither of them had ever worked at a boarding house.

"Let's work on finding that other family," Astrid suggested. "You said it might have been a farm name?"

"Maybe?"

"Well, most of the Norwegian names that I know of having anything to do with a farm end in rud and start with the name of the farmer. Like Karlsrud, meaning that it was Karl's farm. Larsrud, Hansrud, Hersrud, Andersrud, and on and on. Does any of this ring a bell?"

"Let me think, Astrid. You may be on to something. Dang, I just can't come up with anything."

"DANG! That's it, Astrid! I think it was Dangerud!"

For the next few days they searched all the city and county records that they could find. They finally thought of Ellis Island and looked at those records. There they were! They had arrived the same day that Rasmus and Anna did, so it had to be them. "I'm so dumb, Astrid. I should have thought of looking here right away."

"No matter now, we found them. Now if we can find where they live. Nils Dangerud. Do you know what he did?"

Rasmus was sure that he had been a carpenter so they started the search by going to every building contractor that they knew. It was late in the afternoon when they finally found a trail. "Ya, he worked for me. Nice man, really a hard worker, but I think he liked home building better than what I do, which is large building construction. He may have struck out on his own. No, wait, I think he went to work for Hills Brothers Home Construction over on 5th street. They're more than likely closed for the day but you could try tomorrow."

The next morning Rasmus was waiting at Hills Brothers construction for someone to open up the business. Finally the owner showed up and unlocked the door. Rasmus followed him in. "I hate to bother you, but I'm looking for Nils Dangerud. I heard he might be working here."

"He sure is. He's starting his own home building business, but he comes over here in his slack time and helps me with finish trim. He said he'd stop by this morning if he could."

"Would you mind if I waited around a while to see if he does? It's sort of urgent."

"He isn't in trouble or something?"

Rasmus told him that Nils was just an old friend that had gone through Ellis Island with him. They had been on the same ship, and Nils might have some information that would help Rasmus find another friend.

"Well, another Norwegian. I thank God for you Norwegians every day. Most of my good carpenters are from Norway. Uff da, I'm even learning to speak some Norwegian, ya!"

Rasmus was just about to leave when Nils arrived. Nils recognized Rasmus right away. "You were on the same ship as my family! How are you doing? Why are you here"?

"I'm doing fine, thanks. I came here to find out if you remember Anna Ingevich? I'm looking for her."

"Do I remember her? She saved my family! If it hadn't been for Anna, I probably would have had to go back to Norway. Wasn't she your fiancée on the ship? You two were always together."

"We were engaged. By the way, I'm Rasmus. Can I call you Nils?"

"Of course you can. Why do you need to find Anna?"

Rasmus told Nils the story of how he had made Anna a promise back on the ship while they were engaged. Due to unforeseen circumstances, they had to part and break off the engagement. But Rasmus still intended to keep his promise to her. In order to do that he had to find her. "I'm praying that you know where she is."

"I do! She sent me a letter a few months ago. She asked how my wife Tove and our daughter Heidi were doing and if they had gotten back from Norway. She said that she had gotten married to a nice Norwegian man. They are living in South Dakota."

"South Dakota! I don't even know where that is." But Rasmus was excited.

"It's in the Midwest. I have friends there and we'd like to go visit them, along with Anna and her husband. I still owe Anna money, and I would love to repay her in person. Anna told us that she took the train from New York to Chicago to Minneapolis and then to Hettinger, North Dakota, where she got off and rode her horse to Reva, South Dakota."

"Rode her horse? That sounds like Anna all right! You've made my heart lighter today, Nils Dangerud. Can I get Anna's address from you?"

"Of course. All you need is Reva, South Dakota. Anna said that they live really close to that town, but that there isn't much there other than the postal station and a meeting place. What did you promise her anyway?"

"I promised that I would build her a beautiful house. Our world on the ship revolved around that house and our plans of living in it and making our dreams come true. It was one of the things that got us through living in steerage. We worked on floor plans for hours on end."

He told Nils that if it was the last thing he did it would be to honor his promise and that he wanted to leave right away. Then he asked Nils if he would do him another favor. "If you happen to write to her please don't mention this. Anna would try to have you talk me out of it, and even God himself couldn't do that."

Rasmus had already lined up three men to take with him. He gave Astrid and his family hugs and kisses, and they accompanied him to the train station, where his men were waiting. They all had their carpenter tools with them, which they loaded on the train from New York to Chicago. When they arrived in Chicago they got off and transferred to the train to Minneapolis.

In Minneapolis they went into town and bought the nails, cement, and rough lumber (pine and fir) and finish lumber (mostly oak) for Anna's home. The supplies were loaded on the freight train to Hettinger, North Dakota. Rasmus and his men rode the freight train the rest of the way so that they could help unload the materials as soon as the train reached Hettinger. When they got there they unloaded the supplies and inquired around town if anyone knew where Anna Ingevich lived. The blacksmith said that he had met her and he also knew the Larson family. He wasn't exactly sure where they lived but knew that it was close to Reva, so he drew Rasmus a map of how to get there.

Rasmus rented three wagons and used them to haul most of the lumber to Reva. From there they found out where Anna lived, and the three wagon loads of lumber pulled into Anna and Iver's yard a little after dark the next day. Rasmus went to the door and knocked.

17

Honoring Anna

Anna had fainted at the sight of Rasmus when she went to the door, just as Rasmus had fainted when he received the telegraph from Astrid's family. Rasmus had been going over what to tell Iver when he got there, but everything was happening too fast for him to even start. Anna opened her eyes to Iver's and Rasmus's relief. "What is this?" she gasped. "Rasmus, is this really you? What in the world are you doing here?"

The name Rasmus seemed familiar to Iver. Where had he heard it? Then it came back to him: the story of Anna being engaged on the ship. Was this really the man who had left her?

The two men moved Anna to a chair. She was now able to sit up and think clearly. Rasmus said to her, "Yes, it's me, Anna. Rasmus."

"This must be your husband, Iver."

"How did you know my name?" Iver suspiciously asked. "What are you doing here?"

"Please let me explain. I know your name because I have been trying to track down Anna. I found the Dangerud family, who told me all about your life here and how you were doing. Nils told me Anna was married to Iver Tenold, which is how I knew your name."

"Why were you tracking Anna down?" Iver was still upset at the thought of having Anna's former fiancée in their house. "What do you want with her?"

"I assure you that my intentions are entirely honorable and that I am not here to disrupt your family in any way. I am here for myself and my family only. I am here so that I can live the rest of my life in peace. That sounds selfish and it probably is, but a long while back, yet to me what seems like only yesterday, I made your wife a promise. I promised her that I would build her a house in America when we got there. You may know this Iver; we were engaged at one time. Life forced us to go our separate ways, and now I have a family in New York, and you and Anna have a family here. It may have all worked out for the best, who knows? But my life hasn't been complete."

He went on, thinking about each word. "Every day I think of the promise that I made your wife. I have to get that part of my life behind me if I am ever to be happy and to be a good husband to my wife, Astrid, and a good father to our children. I finally told Astrid about Anna and my promise to her, and she helped me come to this decision. She helped me every step of the way and is partially responsible for my being here. I have three wagons full of lumber in your yard and more lumber in Hettinger. If you and Anna will allow me to fulfill my promise, I will start building your house tomorrow."

Rasmus looked Iver in the eye. "I can completely understand if you don't want me here, Iver. Any man would feel that way. If you wish me to leave, I will unload the lumber, go back to Hettinger and get the rest of the lumber and bring it here, and then return with my men to New York. But I beg you to allow me to finish this. Let me build you and Anna a house. Please."

Rasmus could tell Iver was overwhelmed and was having a hard time putting all of this together. "I'll go back outside to my men while the two of you talk it over. We have bedrolls, and we have our supper with us. We will stay here in your yard overnight if it is ok with you, and I will return to your house tomorrow morning for your reply. Good night Iver." Rasmus thoughtfully looked at Anna. "Good night, Anna."

After Rasmus left, Anna spoke first. "I don't know what to say,

Iver. I had forgotten that promise a long time ago, and even if I had remembered it I would have dismissed it. How or why would I expect him to keep that promise when we didn't even get married?"

"I wanted to dislike him Anna, but I actually feel sort of sorry for him. How many men would have sacrificed so much and gone through all that he has just to honor a promise that was made so long ago, a promise that no one else on earth except you even knew of or would have cared about? He searched America for you and somehow found you, then came across the entire country just to keep his promise. How did he get that lumber here? Where did he find it? There isn't lumber anywhere around here that you can buy that I know of, and he certainly didn't cut it in the buttes. He said that he has three men with him to help. Who could afford that? Who would leave their business for a year just to honor a promise?"

Iver paused to think for a while, and then went on. "I sure don't know what to think either, Anna. The man in me wants to just tell him to leave. I admit that I'm already jealous; thinking of him here with you until the house is built. But I looked into his eyes, Anna. He truly is ridden with guilt for not having done what he considered to be the honorable thing. If we send him packing, like I'd like to, he'll probably feel like his honor has been taken away and he'll still have you and his promise to you on his conscience."

Iver had another thought. "Maybe it's the Lord looking after you, Anna. Heaven knows you need and deserve a real house."

After more deliberation he looked at Anna again. "One thing I know for sure, we need to let him know right away in the morning. The poor man deserves that much. I'm going to set my selfishness and my jealousy aside and leave this up to you. You know all my thoughts now, and you know his character. You have a way of cutting straight through to a man's soul, Anna."

Anna was up early. She had been praying about her answer all night. Everything Iver had said was true and she respected him even more after he gave her his blessing to do whatever she thought best. She knew that this couldn't have been easy for him. How could having an old fiancée around all summer and fall be acceptable? Most men would have just told Rasmus to get off their ranch. But Iver was just as honorable as Rasmus. Anna put a few extra loaves of bread in the oven and started some coffee and bacon.

Iver woke up to the smell of frying bacon and boiling coffee, his two favorites. He went to the kitchen to find Anna and see if she had made up her mind. "I think that I have," she said without giving it away. "Would you invite our company in for breakfast, Iver?"

Iver went to the wagons where the men were already up and packing their bedrolls. "We'd be happy to have you all come in for breakfast. You must be starving."

"I can smell the bacon and coffee from here," Rasmus smiled. "We would greatly appreciate it."

The five men all went in, and Iver introduced himself and Anna to Rasmus's crew. "Anna requires a blessing before eating the food, and then you can dig in." It was the best breakfast the men had had since leaving New York.

After eating, Iver took Rasmus's crew back outside and left Anna and Rasmus alone. "I think this is best left to the two of you," he gracefully said.

Anna started. "I'm still having a hard time believing that you're here, Rasmus. I've seen you in my dreams so many times, and I've even worked at keeping you out of them, but I never thought that I would ever see you in person again. At least not in this life. I've been praying about what you said all night, and Iver has been so patient and helpful with all of this."

"Seeing him made me feel better, Anna. You have found a great husband."

"Anyway," Anna went on, "I want you to know this, Rasmus. There is no way on earth that I expect you to keep that old promise that you made. You have a wife and family in New York and a business to tend to. I think that you should leave right now and consider that promise totally fulfilled. I honestly hadn't even remembered it until you mentioned it last night. I know you are a man of honor. I've always known and loved that about you. I want you to think this over carefully, Rasmus. I will always love you, but now I love Iver, and we have a family here. You have my blessing to just take your men and go back home, or if you prefer you can stay and build that house that we dreamt of in days long gone by. I'm leaving the choice entirely up to you and your conscience."

"Thank you Anna, you have once again made me a happy man. I only have two more questions for you," he looked into her eyes.

"Ok, what are they?"

"Where do you want us to build your house and do you want to keep the same floor plan that we drew up on the ship?"

Anna went out to find Iver. "I am going to let Rasmus build our house. Would you mind helping me decide where to put it? We had talked about building on that nice spot southwest of here so that it would be closer to the Reva/Buffalo/Bison trail. Is that still your choice? If it is we need to show Rasmus. He wants to start today if possible."

Rasmus and his men worked diligently on the house through the spring, summer, and fall. Iver and Odd had gradually become good friends with Rasmus and his workers and they helped whenever they could, with Iver working on the house at least a little almost every day. Odd and Reidun organized a neighborhood party over the 4th of July and over 20 neighbors were there working on the house all day. Some of them stayed on for several days. When the work started Rasmus had worried that he wouldn't get the house done before winter and would have to come back the following spring to finish it, but with all the extra help he was completely finished by Thanksgiving.

Their home on the prairie turned out as beautiful as Anna had imagined it in her dreams. There were three stories with hardwood flooring and crown molding throughout the house. The kitchen was ideal for someone who enjoyed baking as much as Anna did and it even had built-in flour and sugar bins. Rasmus had hand made oak and birch cabinets and oak pocket doors, along with an oak hutch and mirror in the wall between the kitchen and dining areas. He added a surprise screened in porch for Anna to put her rocking chair in and dream her dreams. The new home stood majestically on the eastern slope of the Slim Buttes close to the Reva trail in the center of what was to become Anna and Iver's ranch. Iver had planted a shelterbelt of various tree varieties around the building site, complete with the lilac bushes that Anna loved so much. From the upstairs window you could see Gap Creek and the mustangs. From the screened in porch Anna and Iver could watch beautiful prairie sunrises and sunsets. The soil around their house was rich and fertile and Anna had already laid claim to her garden spot. Where there once was only prairie grass now stood a true life dream come true and a testament to the honor and integrity of these incredible American immigrants.

Rasmus had fulfilled his promise and kept his word and all that was left was the good-byes. "I'll say good bye now, Rasmus," Iver offered his hand. "It truly has been a pleasure getting to know you, and I want you to know that you and your family are always welcome here. That guest bedroom upstairs is yours anytime you want. We'll have a reminder of your part in our lives every day that we live in this house. I have to admit that I didn't trust you at the start and had all kinds of crazy thoughts about you trying to steal Anna from me. Now that I have found out what kind of man you truly are I am ashamed of having had those thoughts. I am truly honored to have gotten to know you and to call you my friend."

Iver was at a loss for more words so he quickly added, "well, you have a lot of miles to travel and I better go check on that horse in the corral. Thanks again Rasmus."

Iver didn't want to see Anna hug Rasmus again, and he thoughtfully left them alone to say their good byes.

"I guess that this is it," Rasmus started. "For the second time in my life you've made me the happiest man in America, Anna. The first was when you said you'd marry me, and the second was when you allowed me to keep my promise to build you this house. Without doing this I would have been a miserable man all of my life with the thought of leaving you and the sight of you standing there all alone in New York haunting all of my days. Now I can think of you in your new house or riding through your horse herd. I can always dream of what might have been, Anna, but now I'll never have to wonder again about where you are and how you are doing."

"What can I say, Rasmus. You were my first love and you will always be in my heart. Now you will always be in my home too. I can only imagine how much your family must be missing you, and you them. Please send Astrid my love and tell her that there is nothing I'd like more than to meet her someday. May God bless you and your family, Rasmus Johnson." Tears were flowing, and Anna could say no more.

Rasmus got on the wagon, and she waved good bye to him and his men. She stood by her new home and watched Rasmus and the wagons until they blended into the prairie landscape and disappeared. Anna dried her tears and went to find Iver.

"Let's go and look at our house again, Iver. I agree with what you said to me while Rasmus was giving us the tour, we need to fill those bedrooms!"

THE END

Dedication

This book is dedicated to the immigrants that came to America and made it what it is today. Starting with the Pilgrims, America has been a place of sanctuary for people from around the globe that were looking for a place to call home. A place where they would be free to follow their dreams and where what they produced with their blood, sweat and tears belonged to them rather than to some King or dictator or government. Like Iver, Anna, and Rasmus they came here to become Americans and to share in the American dream. They were strong and proud, and America was built on their backs. They never once asked what America would give them but instead freely gave themselves to America.

It would be impossible to explain how arduous, harsh, and unyielding conditions often were for our early American immigrants, especially those first pioneers that settled in the Dakotas. They were on their own in an often hard and unforgiving environment. These poems are for those resilient souls that history has forgotten, but whose visceral memory is still touched by the morning sun and whispered on the prairie winds.

PRAIRIE WIND

Every time the prairie wind blows,
It blows for those souls that couldn't make it.
Every time the prairie wind blows,
It blows for those souls that couldn't take it.
And it just keeps blowing every day,
Keeps blowing their memories away.

Have you ever seen a shack?
With no shingles on its back?
That once was filled with laughter,
The prairie winds came after.
And those depressions in the ground-
Once had sod walls around,
On all the homestead acres,
The wind blows for their makers.
And it just keeps blowing every day,
Keeps blowing their memories away.

Douglas Hoff

WHEN I DIE

When I die please bury me,
Under yonder cottonwood tree.
Take my cow turn her loose right now,
Where the grass grows higher than your knee.
Take my saddle and saddle my horse,
Then ride him round the range for me.
Bring him home and give him some oats,
But please feed him under the cottonwood tree.
Please feed him there so that I might see.

When I die don't want nobody to cry,
Or say any sad words over me.
But would you say a prayer,
That the Lord would care,
For all of my critters for me?
Would you feed my dog and take care of him?
He's been a faithful friend you see.
And when the old dog dies please bury him,
Under yonder cottonwood tree.
Please place him there so that I might see.

Douglas Hoff

Fate?

Life is a puzzle to say the least. What would have happened if that telegram hadn't arrived or if it had arrived too late; or if it had just been ignored? To most of the world it wouldn't have been of consequence, but to me, over 130 years later, it still has repercussions. My wife, whose grandparents this story is about, wouldn't have been born. My children and grand children wouldn't exist and our entire family history would have been altered. Every decision in life that we make, no matter how small it may seem at the time, can alter history in many unseen ways. Life is indeed a mystery.

I would like to offer my sincere thanks to everyone that has helped me with this book. I pray that it will be a blessing to each person that reads it, that it will do justice to those it was written to honor, and that it will inspire our generation to the levels of honor and integrity that these immigrants had. ~doug hoff

Anna, Iver, and Obert Tenold

Iver Tenold and 2 of his brothers

Arthur (Molly's father), Iver, and Obert
Anna and Margie

Printed in the United States
By Bookmasters